Christopher Gadsden
and the American Revolution

Christopher Gadsden
and the American Revolution

E. Stanly Godbold, Jr.
Robert H. Woody

THE UNIVERSITY OF TENNESSEE PRESS /KNOXVILLE

Library of Congress Cataloging in Publication Data

Godbold, E. Stanly
 Christopher Gadsden and the American Revolution.

 Bibliography: p.
 Includes index.
 1. Gadsden, Christopher, 1724-1805. 2. South Carolina—Politics and
government—Revolution, 1775-1783. 3. United States—Politics and
government—Revolution—1775-1783. 4. Statesmen—United States—
Biography.
 I. Woody, Robert H. (Robert Hilliard), 1903-
 II. Title
 E302.6.G15G62   973.7'092'4 [B]   82-6915
 ISBN 0-87049-362-0   AACR2
 ISBN 0-87049-363-9 (pbk.)

to Cynthia and Louise

Contents

Illustrations

Preface

As a radical leader of the American Revolution, Christopher Gadsden was intimately involved in the major events of the eighteenth century. The sources for information about his personal life are limited, but his public writings, scattered business records, and the numerous references to him in the legislative journals and private correspondence of his age reveal the story of a colorful and significant man. His biography divides naturally into three parts. He was an ambitious youth before 1765, a revolutionary leader until the mid-1780s, and an elder statesman after the war.

Before 1765, the young Gadsden became a prominent merchant and factor, formed political and intellectual alliances with the merchants, planters, and artisans of Charleston, and used radical whig ideology to condemn royal policies in South Carolina. From 1765 through 1783, he became a familiar figure in the American Revolution, often speaking with the rhetoric of Patrick Henry and Samuel Adams. Gadsden was a leader of the Sons of Liberty, co-founder of the Continental Navy, and a delegate to the Stamp Act Congress and the first two sessions of the Continental Congress. He designed the rattlesnake flag with the logo "DONT TREAD ON ME" as an appropriate symbol of the Revolution. He was a brigadier general in the Continental Army and suffered a long imprisonment at the hands of the British. As an old man in poor health after the war, he commented freely upon the problems related to the writing of constitutions for the state and the nation, imbibed the federalist politics of John Adams and George Washington, and reflected upon the dramatic changes that had transpired during his lifetime. The story of Gadsden's life and thought illumines the culture that produced him and mirrors every significant episode in the transformation of the British North American colonies into a free nation.

In the long course of the preparation of this biography, almost half a century, manuscripts and documents have been shifted from one location to another, privately owned collections have been destroyed or misplaced, persons who were interviewed have died, and edited papers and new studies of the Revolution have appeared. The authors have made every effort to cite all information from its current or most accessible location regardless of where the research was done. If the name of an institution or individual who helped is inadvertently omitted from the acknowledgments, this error should not be construed as a lack of gratitude. At various times, one or the other of the authors received research grants from the Division of Graduate Studies in Valdosta State College, the Duke University Graduate School, the Office of Research and Graduate Studies in Mississippi State University, and the Social Science Research Council.

The staffs of the following libraries and institutions were very helpful: the Boston Public Library; the Charleston Library Society; the College of Charleston Library; the Frick Art Reference Library, New York City; the Gibbes Art Gallery, Charleston; the William R. Perkins Library, Duke University; the Historic Charleston Foundation; the Historical Society of Pennsylvania, Philadelphia; the Library of Congress; the Long Island Historical Society, New York; the New York Public Library; the Presbyterian College Library, Clinton, South Carolina; the National Register of Archives, Edinburgh, Scotland; the South Carolina Department of Archives and History, Columbia; the South Carolina Historical Society, Charleston; and the South Caroliniana Library, Columbia. Mattie U. Russell, Curator of Manuscripts in the William R. Perkins Library at Duke University, offered not only expert professional advice but also the warm encouragement of a friend. William E. Erwin, Jr., of the same department, was especially helpful in locating British sources.

Many other individuals gave their assistance. The descendants of Christopher Gadsden who made available to Robert Woody in the 1930s information about their ancestor include the following:

Miss Jeanne Gadsden and Deaconess Mary T. Gadsden, Charleston; Mr. Philip Gadsden, Philadelphia; Mr. and Mrs. George D. Shore, Jr., Sumter, South Carolina; and Mrs. Van Smith, Summerville, South Carolina. Pauline Maier supplied typescript copies of the Gadsden letters she found in the Dartmouth Papers; F. B. Stitt, Archivist of the Staffordshire County Record Office, England, sent copies of the originals; and the Right Honorable the Earl of Dartmouth granted permission to quote from his papers. Sir Ewan Macpherson-Grant, Ballindalloch Castle, Scotland, kindly granted permission to quote from the James Grant Papers.

Scholars who read an early draft of the manuscript and improved it considerably include Philander D. Chase, Kathleen Russell Haulbrook, Archie V. Huff, Jr., Richard M. McMurry, Glover Moore, George C. Rogers, Jr., and Harold S. Snellgrove. George Rogers generously shared information he had learned about Gadsden from his research in the James Grant Papers. Jack P. Greene and R. Don Higginbotham read a later draft and offered many useful suggestions. The enthusiasm and efficiency of Mavis Bryant, Katherine Holloway, and others on the staff of the University of Tennessee Press made enjoyable the job of seeing this manuscript through publication. All final judgments were made by the authors themselves, who assume responsibility for the deficiencies that remain.

The authors' wives, too, deserve special recognition. As a young bride in the 1930s, Louise Woody spent many hours in unairconditioned manuscript and archival repositories helping her husband copy information about Christopher Gadsden. After Godbold began work on the project in 1970, she dished out good food and good humor with the kind of lavishness that could inspire even the weariest scholar to persevere. Cynthia Godbold joined the team in 1979, just in time to apply her skills as an English teacher to the tedious work of polishing the manuscript and to offer fresh words of encouragement. Without their help this book probably would not have been written.

E.S.G
R.H.W

March 1982

Christopher Gadsden
and the American Revolution

CHAPTER ONE

Education of a Radical

When the Stamp Act crisis erupted in 1765, Christopher Gadsden was at the peak of his physical and intellectual powers. At forty-one years old he was healthy and vigorous. He was tall, with long arms, powerful hands, and a muscular body. His hairline had already receded, but his dark eyes were set in an oval face that seemed to radiate both strength and tenderness. From a portrait painted at about this time, he seems to gaze back at the viewer with shyness, confidence, and pride. He looks like a man who would have been equally at home in the company of philosophers, the councils of war, a gathering of clergymen, and the privacy of a family circle. And yet there is about his countenance a trace of the cockiness, contentiousness, and impetuosity that were also part of his nature.[1] But no portrait could reveal the Irish temper, the myriad strands of his personality, the classical education, the knowledge of British history, and the love of liberty and power that drove him to become a radical leader of the American Revolution.

The story of this American rebel begins about thirty miles north of London on the Gad River in Hertfordshire where two villages, Greater and Lesser Gaddesden, are located. The progenitor of the South Carolina family was one John de Gatesden, born in Hertfordshire in the thirteenth century and educated at Merton College in Oxford. He was the author of *Rosa Anglica* and was apparently the first English court physician, a position which caused him to be listed by Chaucer in the *Canterbury Tales*. Other Gadsdens owned land in Hertfordshire during the late Tudor period, but none seems to have risen to prominence.[2]

3

Details concerning the early career of Thomas Gadsden, Christopher's father, are exceedingly meager. The names of his parents, the date of his birth, the record of his education, and the way he got his start in the world are lost. Despite family tradition and the statements of older historians that Thomas was a lieutenant in the Royal Navy, the truth seems to be that he was in the merchant service. Sometime before 1718 he came to Charleston, South Carolina, and about 1722 he became the collector of customs at the port there.[3]

Thomas Gadsden's South Carolina was a young British colony not quite half a century old. Among the early settlers were wealthy planters from Barbados, some poor men and women, an occasional Scot or Irishman, Huguenots from France who were attracted by the colony's policy of religious toleration, indentured servants, and slaves. The fledgling city of Charleston was located on the strip of land between the Ashley and Cooper rivers. It was the seat of government and the economic and social capital of a colony whose unity of interests with the Crown increased in 1719 when a domestic insurrection against the lords proprietors transformed Carolina into a royal province. Bound to the motherland by ties of trade, Carolina's path to wealth lay through the rice plantations that flourished along the marshy Atlantic coast. The prosperity of the planters rested upon the work of enterprising merchants whose ships brought in supplies and exported rice and indigo. For an adventuresome Englishman like Thomas Gadsden, South Carolina was a land of economic opportunity.

Shortly after his arrival in Charleston, Thomas married a woman named Elizabeth. According to tradition, she was the daughter of an indentured servant.[4] In a political pamphlet written in 1797, her son Christopher stated that he was of Irish extraction, "by my mother's side, whose father was a native of Ireland, whom I am named after."[5] Nothing more is known about her.

Thomas and Elizabeth became the parents of Robert in 1718, and Thomas in 1720, and Elizabeth in 1722. All three died very young. On February 16, 1724, Elizabeth gave birth to her fourth child. Three weeks later he was christened in St. Philip's Anglican Church and was given the name of Christopher. His parents preferred to call him Kittie. Since he was the only one of their children to survive, perhaps they doted on him. But little Kittie's secure world was disrupted when in May 1727 his mother died. A little more than a year later, on April 11, 1728, his father was married to Collins Hall, a lady who came to him from England. She lived only two years after her marriage, once again leaving Kittie with no mother and no surviving brothers and sisters.[6] Two years later his father was married a third time; by then young Kittie was eight.

Christopher's second stepmother, Alice Mighells, was married to his father on July 25, 1732. She was the daughter of Anne and James Mighells of Stratford in Essex County, England. In the days of the later Stuarts, James Mighells entered the navy under the patronage of his uncle, Sir John Ashby; when James retired in 1722 to become comptroller of His Majesty's navy for the next twelve years, it was with the rank of vice admiral.[7] This marriage brought Christopher an occasional connection with naval affairs, which may have influenced his later life.

In colonial South Carolina a son was expected to emulate his father. For his first seven years Kittie lived at home, where Thomas Gadsden was probably his most important model. Kittie saw in his father a man who was religious, concerned with books and learning, conscientious about his work, ambitious to become a great landowner, a master of slaves, and a good family man who hoped to create his own dynasty in South Carolina. Thomas Gadsden also spent hours in social revelries. He was fascinated by the gaming table, where he often played for high stakes. And he kept his cellar stocked with many dozens of bottles of Madeira, claret, cherry brandy, Vidonia wine, ale, rum, and much more. Perhaps the child was sheltered from his father's drinking and gambling, or taught by his mother that such things were to be shunned. As Christopher grew to manhood, he rejected those two vices but absorbed and magnified his father's ideals and ambitions.

As collector of customs at Charleston, young Christopher's father was active in the performance of his duties. More than once he inserted a warning in the *South-Carolina Gazette* that smugglers and local merchants who carried on a clandestine and illegal trade with Spaniards and other foreigners must obey the law or risk prosecution.[8] His position did not carry the odious connotations that it was to have three decades later, and his steady acquisition of property suggested to his neighbors that he intended to be a permanent resident of the colony.

Shortly after his arrival, Thomas Gadsden began to purchase land which at the time of his death amounted to about 6,000 acres. He owned 97 acres in Berkeley County, 2,500 in Granville County, 2,200 in Craven County, 1,000 acres on the Waccamaw River, one lot in Georgetown, and another in Charleston.[9] Most of the many acres belonging to Kittie's father were too remote from Charleston to be under cultivation or immediately profitable, but he did operate two small plantations. The smaller was on Charleston Neck, up the Broad Path within a mile and a half of the city. It contained more than 100 acres of land, one good dwelling, and several outbuildings. The larger plantation, located 3 miles from Dorchester and about 10 miles from Charleston, contained 300 acres suitable for rice and corn. Apparently, this plantation is where the family lived. There were two barns, a small cypress dwelling, and houses for twenty or thirty slaves.[10]

On October 29, 1720, Thomas Gadsden bought 63 acres lying just north of Charleston and fronting on the Cooper River; in 1725 he lost it in a card game with Captain George Anson (later Lord Anson), commander of H. M. S. *Scarborough* and eventually commander of the royal fleet.[11] The story of the game and the payment worked its way into the lore of the city until it became something of a shadow under which Christopher grew up.

In the meantime, however, the young boy continued to enjoy the peaceful life of an only child. His father had a small library of about 125 volumes, in which Christopher probably learned to read and write. The books, which he later inherited, included such diverse items as the *Tatler* and the *Spectator*, an unbound volume of *The Beggar's Opera*, some Latin works, as well as French and English grammars and dictionaries. There were a number of works of a military and naval sort and others of a religious character. Even more important for his future leadership in the American Revolution, he later read Paul de Rapin-Thoyras's *History of England*. An exiled Huguenot, Rapin published his work in English between 1725 and 1731; his account of English history seemed to prove the theories of the antiestablishment whig writers.[12] His writings were very popular in the American colonies, and Christopher's early exposure to them probably contributed to the development of his radical thought.

The personal influence of Thomas Gadsden upon his son ended abruptly when Kittie was seven or eight. At about the same time Thomas Gadsden was married to Alice Mighells in 1732, he decided to send Christopher to England to live with relatives and attend grammar school. For a child of seven with no living siblings, and one who had already suffered the loss of two mothers, this change must have been unsettling. And after he had been removed from his father's house, the news that his stepmother had given birth to two sons, James and Thomas, may not have been entirely welcome.[13] Hence, young Christopher may have developed at an early age a sense of emotional independence.

The surviving miniature watercolor of Christopher, painted shortly after he reached England, might have been intended to comfort his parents in his absence. In the portrait there is a hint of directness and strength of purpose in the solemn-faced boy with the untrimmed and disheveled hair. The large nose, broad forehead, and well-formed chin are evident, although there is not much promise of the strength of body that later fitted him for a military career.

Little is known about Christopher during the eight years he spent in England. He resided with his father's relatives—the Gascoignes, Halls, and Gadsdens—near Bristol. He learned Greek, French, and the Latin with which he sprinkled his future political writings.[14]

In 1740, when Christopher was sixteen, he returned from England. Probably after a short visit in Charleston, he went to Philadelphia to begin a business apprenticeship. His father had arranged for him to receive his mercantile training under the tutelage of Thomas Lawrence. Lawrence was considered to be one of the best tutors in the colonies; he had widespread commercial interests, including the fur trade. In addition, he was active in civic affairs, serving as mayor of Philadelphia for five terms.[15] No doubt, Christopher learned something about politics as well as about trade from him.

Christopher's apprenticeship was interrupted in the summer of 1741 by the deaths of his parents. His stepmother died on July 3, 1741, and his father died the following August 6. Christopher

Watercolor of "Kittie" Gadsden. Artist unknown. Courtesy of George D. Shore, Jr.

was probably back in Charleston at the time of his father's death and attended the funeral at St. Philip's Church.[16]

When Thomas Gadsden's estate was settled, Christopher inherited a substantial fortune. He received the plantation near Dorchester, 1,000 acres on the Waccamaw River near Georgetown, the lots in Charleston and Georgetown, the furniture, the library, the vast stock of fine wines, and four slaves—Prince, Paine, Scipio, and Hannah. The Charleston lot was to be sold to maintain Christopher in his apprenticeship, and Richard Hill and John Guerard were to serve as executors of the estate until Christopher reached his majority. Christopher returned to Philadelphia to resume his training with Thomas Lawrence.

The remainder of Thomas Gadsden's property, which was considerably less valuable than what he had given to his eldest son, went to James and Thomas, who were only seven and four. The younger boys were sent to England to live with relatives until they grew up. The total value of the estate came to almost £5,000 sterling.[17]

In 1745 when Christopher reached his twenty-first birthday, he terminated his mercantile training and planned to go into business for himself. First, he sailed to England to visit relatives and on his return trip accidentally became involved in a war that delayed his plans. While a passenger on the British man-of-war *Aldborough* in the summer of 1745, his service in the Royal Navy began abruptly. In America, England was fighting King George's War and that twenty-gun ship was to be used in the defense of the colonies. The purser of the ship died in passage, and the captain appointed Christopher in his place. Christopher's service in the navy resulted from mere chance, but again he was following the example of his father, who as a young man had served in the merchant marine.

On Monday, July 28, 1746, while *Aldborough* was in Charleston Harbor, its purser was married to Miss Jane Godfrey. Her twenty-two-year-old husband called her Jenny. She was the daughter of the prominent and wealthy merchant Samuel Godfrey. The size of her dowry is unknown, but it was clear that young Christopher had married into a good family with a substantial fortune. Two weeks after his wedding in St. Philip's Church, the groom sailed with *Aldborough* for Cape Breton. From there, he wrote to his youthful bachelor friend "Harry" Laurens, then in London, "I am now out of your Class, for I was married a few days before I left Carolina to Miss Jenny Godfrey."[18]

Henry Laurens had been born in Charleston eight days after Christopher. They had grown up together. They had no doubt spent many hours playing in the city or on Christopher's plantation near Dorchester. Henry's father was a saddler who had attempted to provide Henry with the best education available in the province before sending him to England for his mercantile training. Henry was still in England at the outbreak of King George's War. In their early youth, according to David Ramsay, the historian of the Revolution and Laurens's son-in-law, Henry and Christopher "made a common cause to support and encourage each other in every virtuous pursuit, to shun every path to vice and folly, to leave company whenever it tended to licentiousness."[19] By making such a commitment to a virtuous life, Christopher deviated from the example of his father and unconsciously established himself as a critic of those who disagreed with his principles. That commitment, too, cemented a friendship with Laurens that later was to be tested severely by the controversies that raged in South Carolina during the two decades before the Revolution.

Whether Christopher's upright life caused him to be subjected to ridicule in the rough world of the British navy, he did not say. As a purser, or supply officer, he had a position of responsibility, but one that was looked down upon by sailors charged with more direct military duties. Nevertheless, Gadsden went where *Aldborough* went; he suffered the same threat of death in battle or in an Atlantic storm that the others suffered. During 1746 and 1747, the ship's voyages took him from Charleston to Fort Louisbourg, Boston, New York, Barbados, and Jamaica. *Aldborough* participated in the successful battle for the French Fort Louisbourg, convoyed vessels to New York, recaptured a large sloop loaded with mahogany lumber and *lignum vitae* that had fallen into the hands of the Spaniards, sought refuge in Boston Harbor to repair the main mast, which had been damaged in a storm, and occasionally prevented what Laurens called "the Insults of the Little Privateers which daily infest our Coast."[20]

At Barbados, Gadsden heard from Laurens that Jenny had

given birth to a daughter, her father's "own Stamp exactly." She was born on September 18, 1747, and was named Elizabeth, after her father's mother.[21] In the next spring Laurens wrote Gadsden that "we are in daily expectation of your arrival here." Jenny, too, hoped the letter would find him no longer in Jamaica, but on his way home. "I tell her," Laurens continued, "'tis better risquing a Little Paper & scribbling than disappoint you of a letter in case you are detain'd"; and, he added, "Mrs Gadsden & your Little one are both very well."[22]

Gadsden returned to Charleston in the spring of 1748 and saw his infant daughter for the first time. The war ended that year, and he resigned his position as purser. He had property and family which needed his attention, and he readily assumed his responsibilities. He did not drink alcoholic beverages, use tobacco, or gamble. A serious young man, Christopher concentrated upon earning a living.

That Gadsden had an aptitude for business had been apparent early. Three years before his apprenticeship ended, and while presumably he was still in Philadelphia, he had published his first advertisement as a merchant. He had started in a simple way, with relatively little risk, but for a lad of eighteen it was enough: "Just Imported from Philadelphia, and to be sold by *Christopher Gadsden* at his store on Shute's Wharff, good Flour, ship bread, soap and candles, also some of *Matlock's* best double Beer, at reasonable Rates for present Pay."[23] Christopher must have made periodic trips home to supervise his endeavor; probably he rented space on Shute's Wharf and hired a servant to take charge when he was away.

During and after King George's War, Christopher expanded his business. From aboard *Aldborough* in 1746, he wrote Laurens asking for information about the prices of commodities taken from enemy ships in case he had the chance to acquire some for resale in Charleston.[24] Within a year after the war ended, he advertised that he had imported from London an assortment of European goods to be sold at his store in Broad Street. By the following spring he had added silk, thread, and cotton stockings for men, women, and boys, as well as fustian frocks for men and boys, single and double mattresses, and refined sugar. As evidence of prosperity, he took a house in Elliott Street, one block south of Broad and about one block from the Cooper River, a fashionable section of town.[25]

Gadsden was on his way up. By 1756 he had registered three ships in Georgetown, the largest of which was *Darling*, a brigantine of forty tons.[26] With his Irish neighbor, James Gillespie, he was engaged in the boating business on the Pee Dee River, on the banks of which he had a plantation.[27] He owned at least two stores in Charleston, and one each in Cheraw, Ashley Ferry, and Georgetown. His wares included a variety of northern, European, and West Indian goods. He imported indigo seed, flour, kegs of milk and water "bisket," plain and striped "Duffils," pig tail tobacco, butter, violins, saddles, mahogany, sconce glasses, lead, linseed oil, china dishes, sugar candy, the best Scotch snuff, glass, stone bottles, and fireplace grates with brass fenders, shovels, and tongs. No sooner had the French and Indian War begun in 1754 than he stocked his shelves with military goods. There was an imposing array of powder, bar lead, shot and bullets, carbines, fowling pieces, as well as troopers' belts, buff broad cloth, gold hat lace, and portmanteau trunks.[28] His earliest imports were principally from Madeira, Philadelphia, and Jamaica; later he received goods from North Carolina and New York and exported to Bristol and London. The amount of duty paid tends to follow an ascending curve, reaching its highest point about 1757 and 1758 with a total of £1,000 current money.[29]

Gadsden was not one of the great importing merchants who acted as factors for British merchants. Judging from the type of goods he imported, as well as from the location of his various stores, one must conclude that he was a "country factor." He did not deal in slaves. He did not carry in stock the fine gold and silver laces from Flanders, the Dutch linens, the French cambric and chintz, or the silks from the East Indies as did so many prominent merchants of the time. Rather, his stock in trade was of the simple, everyday sort in common use which might be exchanged with the average planter. In return for his goods, Gadsden accepted current money or rice, indigo, and furs, which he sent abroad.

The scanty customs records indicate much less in the way of goods exported than imported. Some years later, before and after the Revolution, Gadsden was engaged in the wharf and factorage business, which put him more nearly in the relation of agent to the planters than a merchant. The interests of the country factor and of the planter were closely aligned. Neither had anything in common with the factor or agent of the British merchant who sought to sell in a dear market and to buy in a cheap one. The country factor was as anxious as the planter to see the country produce command a good price, and sometimes they were able for that purpose to withhold produce from the market.[30] This community of interests between the planter and the country factor may offer a clue to the alignment of planters and merchants on the eve of the Revolution.

About 1760 Gadsden determined to retire from the mercantile business, not because he was unsuccessful, but because he had become prosperous enough to aspire to become a planter. He began to dispose of his stock, first at Charleston and then at Georgetown and Cheraw. In the autumn of 1760 he sold many of his goods to William Godfrey, probably a relative of Jenny, for about £2,000 current money. He purchased from Godfrey three slaves—Warwick, Stono, and Primus—whom he probably intended to use on one of his plantations.[31] For a year or more after 1760, Gadsden printed notices in the *Gazette* asking all debtors to pay him by a certain date or face suit.[32] From 1758 through 1762 he brought numerous suits against his debtors, almost always securing a judgment or withdrawing the suit because the account was paid. The records do not indicate that Gadsden was ever countersued, an unusual phenomenon suggesting both Gadsden's honesty and very limited use of credit.[33]

Feeling the need for more money to support his family and to purchase land, Gadsden offered his business services to others on commission. He was a realtor on occasion, tendering for sale some 275 acres at Stono, good for rice, corn, and indigo; or the 97 acres on Charleston Neck, which may have belonged to his half-brother Thomas. He administered the estates of Benjamin Whitaker, a former chief justice of the province, and of William George Freeman, a London lawyer. For the latter he sold four "house wenches," some Negro men, a barn, and such household effects as a silver teakettle, a dozen silver-handled knives and forks, and a good chamber organ and harpsichord.[34]

He also served as collector for people outside the province. In 1753 he wrote his former business master in Philadelphia,

Thomas Lawrence, that he had collected £350 currency from one Bullard and would remit it as soon as he could get good bills of exchange. But Bullard was a hard customer. "I dun him very closely," wrote Gadsden, "& make no doubt of having about fifty pounds sterling more in a few weeks." Six months later Gadsden acknowledged Lawrence's invoice for seventeen barrels of flour and promised to keep after Bullard: "I make no manner of doubt of getting the money for you & I think you may rest satisfy'd that you'll at last recover this long winded Debt."[35]

A bit later he arranged accommodations for passengers on *Charming Martha* and secured freight for the snow *Industry*, sailing for Bristol with a cargo of indigo and deerskins.[36] After the outbreak of the French and Indian War, the commissioners of fortifications gave Gadsden orders for shingles to use in building barracks, which he probably obtained through his mercantile clients.[37] Once, as the executor of an estate, he offered for sale a library of books and manuscripts, including several hundred volumes in Hebrew, Greek, Latin, French, Italian, Dutch, and English.[38]

Gadsden used the money he earned from his miscellaneous business adventures, as well as that he received from the sale of his stores, to increase his landholdings. But he resold much of his new land at a profit. In July 1756 he purchased four lots in Georgetown for £2,500 current money and sold them in 1771 for three times as much. In 1757 he bought 1,300 acres on Thompson Creek and the Pee Dee River; he sold it in 1770 for £5,000 lawful money. For £370 he bought a small tract of 150 acres on the Pee Dee River, Craven County, on June 18, 1759; he sold it five years later for an unknown price.[39] He kept the land, about 1,000 acres, near Georgetown that he had inherited from his father, later added other acres to it, and by the end of the Revolution developed a thriving plantation there.

Gadsden's major investment was his purchase in April 1758 of the land that became Gadsdenboro. The cost was £6,000 current money. It consisted of 15 acres of high land and 29 of marshy land located in northeastern Charleston. The 15 acres was bordered on the west and south by a brick wall.[40] This area was bounded by Calhoun, Anson, and Laurens streets and extended down to the Cooper River. It included a considerable portion of that land which his father was reputed to have gambled away to Lord Anson. The possibilities it offered both as a subdivision and as a wharf site turned him away from the planting interest at about the time of the Stamp Act. Into the development of Gadsdenboro and the great wharf he later built adjoining it, Gadsden poured most of his energy and dreams. His drift away from becoming a planter, which was accelerated by the excitement leading to the Revolution, developed so subtly that, like the Revolution, it was upon him before he had time to realize fully what had happened.

Having centered his business in Charleston, Gadsden moved freely through the varied and often exciting life of the city. Nestled between the Ashley and Cooper rivers behind the shelter of an expansive harbor and within easy reach of the outlying plantations, this town of less than ten thousand, more than half of whom were black, enjoyed a cosmopolitan atmosphere that rested solidly upon its great wealth. The planters owned homes in the city as well as on their plantations; frequently they were also merchants. There were lawyers who had been educated in England; they, too, often enjoyed the distinction of being planters and merchants as well as lawyers. The physicians, who were usually not natives, were plentiful enough, but they lacked the knowledge to cope with malaria, smallpox, and the high death rate among women and children. Artisans and craftsmen abounded, and black house servants were always highly visible in the public places.

Beckoning to still wider horizons were the ocean-going vessels resting at anchor in the bay. Always at least a dozen, and frequently as many as one hundred, they included ships, brigantines, snows, schooners, sloops, and others, for Charleston was a crossroads of trade within the British Empire. This busy port, one of the most important in North America, funneled people, produce, and information into the waiting city and gave its people with their products and ideas easy access to the rest of the British world.

The town itself was carefully planned. King and Church streets ran from Charleston Neck and intersected Broad perpendicularly. Broad was an expansive avenue seventy feet wide, which extended to the bay. At the intersection of Broad and Church streets was a vacant lot called The Corner, only 1,200 feet from the bay. One block southwest of The Corner at the intersection of Broad and Meeting streets stood the State House, St. Michael's Church, the Court House, and Dillon's Tavern. Nearby in the compact city was one market where servants went to buy the vegetables and meats used to prepare the daily meals, and another where slave traders offered their wares for sale.[41]

The cultural life of Charleston was impressive for the time and place and was indicative of a society with wealth and leisure. There were schools and schoolteachers, the Library Society, and four newspapers. Charitable and social societies like the South Carolina Society, the Friendly Society, and the Winyah Indigo Society demonstrated that Charleston was far beyond the frontier stage. The St. Cecilia Society was organized in 1762; two theaters offered other forms of entertainment; and two race tracks provided a popular diversion. A half-dozen churches, including a synagogue for Jews and a meetinghouse for Quakers, offered opportunities to worship for Anglicans and dissenters alike, and revealed the fact that there was much religious diversity as well as harmony in Charleston.

All of the organizations that Gadsden joined were religious, educational, or charitable. By 1755 he was an active member of the Winyah Indigo Society, which had been organized in 1740 to teach beginners how to raise and process the indigo plant. The initiation fees and contributions were used to establish a free school at Georgetown.[42] On May 7, 1754, by a vote of four-fifths of the members, Gadsden was admitted to the South Carolina Society.[43] Its chief interests were to advance the members' knowledge of French, make charitable contributions to needy members, and maintain a free school. Before 1750, Gadsden joined the Charleston Library Society, the second public library in the colonies. In 1751 it had 163 members who paid a weekly fee of eighteen pence. Membership was a mark of social distinction, and except for one or two governors who rendered themselves particularly obnoxious, that official was always chosen president of the Library Society.[44] Sometime in the 1750s Gadsden also joined a small religious and literary society organized by Richard Clarke, the rector of St. Philip's. On Easter Monday 1755, Gadsden was installed as a member of the vestry of St. Philip's, the church whose building was completed in the year of his birth and with which he was to have an intimate association all his life.[45]

In the 1750s Gadsden changed his place of residence several times, trying to find a suitable home for his growing family and an acceptable address for a person of his means. The home in Elliott Street, although a good address, apparently proved unsatisfactory. In 1753 he complained that "for these two years past I have lived in a very inconvenient House which has been the Occasion of all my Family's & my own sickness." He added that he had recently "mov'd into a better & airier House since which I thank God I have had my Health exceeding well."[46]

This new house, the location of which cannot be fixed, did not become his permanent home. At some later date, probably still in the 1750s, he moved permanently to the northeastern part of the city and into a dwelling on the property he had purchased from Lord Anson and subsequently developed as the subdivision of Ansonborough, or Gadsdenboro. Formerly occupied by Lord Anson, this house was built of cypress. Although probably not one of the great mansions of the city, Gadsden's final residence had at least two stories, a basement, and a portico in front where he liked to sit in the summer.[47] It was across the street from the home of his good friend Henry Laurens.

Unfortunately, Gadsden's removal to an "airier House" did not prevent the death of his beloved Jenny in May 1755. She left Christopher with an eight-year-old daughter, Elizabeth, and an adored son, Christopher, junior, who was about four and one-half.[48] For six months the young father struggled to care for his small children, but he soon remarried.

On December 29, 1755, Christopher was married to Miss Mary Hasell. She was twenty-one, the daughter of the Reverend Thomas Hasell, formerly rector of St. Thomas's Parish, Berkeley County, and the niece of the wealthy Mrs. Gabriel Manigault.[49] The groom was thirty-one, handsomely proportioned, physically strong, avowedly virtuous, noticeably ambitious, and rich. In time, Christopher and Mary became the parents of four children. Thomas, born August 13, 1757, grew up to become a captain during the Revolution and lieutenant governor of the state from 1787 through 1789. Mary, baptized on September 17, 1759, later was married to Thomas Morris of Philadelphia, who went into business with her father and brother after the Revolution. Philip, baptized on October 11, 1761, was married to Catharine Edwards after the Revolution and became the father of the most famous

Gadsdens of the nineteenth century. Ann, baptized on October 1, 1763, later was married to merchant Andrew Lord; after his death in 1781, she was married to William Greenwood in 1796 and probably moved to England with him.[50]

The stability of Christopher Gadsden's family life, the expansion of his business enterprises, and his membership in leading charitable organizations suggested to his neighbors that he was a solid citizen who could be trusted with important political responsibilities. In October 1757 both he and Henry Laurens were elected by St. Philip's Parish to membership in the Commons House of Assembly. They took their seats on October 16. Gadsden was thirty-three years old and beginning a twenty-seven-year-long career that would place him in the center of dramatic political debates. Gadsden's election in 1757, however, was not related to any particular political viewpoint that he professed; he was chosen simply because his social and financial standing in the community identified him as a member of the relatively small pool of men who were eligible and competent to serve in the Assembly. In fact, in 1757 few people knew anything about Gadsden's thoughts on politics. The royal officials also looked upon him as reliable and trustworthy. Governor William Henry Lyttelton nominated him for membership on the Governor's Council, but since his name was third on a list of three proposed, he was not appointed.[51]

Although Gadsden himself did not know in 1757 what political stands he would soon take, the foundation for his imminent radicalism was already firmly established. It was determined by his reading and interpretation of British history and politics, the peculiar development of his native province, and the emergence of his distinctive individual personality.

Gadsden's education stemmed largely from his reading of the classics and the writings of the English whigs. The whigs, who traced their antiauthoritarian beliefs to the English Civil War and exploited the classics to support their theories, had developed their political ideas even further to justify the expulsion of King James II in 1688. Following the ideas of John Locke, they believed that the people had the right to revolt when their rulers violated an unwritten social contract and denied their natural rights of life, liberty, and property. Gadsden was intellectually at home with the whigs. He believed in a constitutional monarchy that restrained the ruler, and a representative legislature that did not fence out the middle class entirely but gave the preponderance of power to a wealthy, educated, propertied elite. He sometimes rose above his economic interests as a merchant to be an effective spokesman for the urban mechanics and upcountry farmers of early South Carolina, but he never became an advocate of universal manhood suffrage. His life as a student in England, experience in the Royal Navy, and mercantile training in Philadelphia, as well as his reading, had transformed him into a man of national vision in a largely provincial age.

Whatever ideas Gadsden had learned and exchanged in his travels within the British Empire were reinforced by the particular history of his native South Carolina. That colony had been born directly out of the victorious restoration of King Charles II to the British throne in 1660. The grateful monarch paid his advocates, including the eight lords proprietors of Carolina, with land in America. *The Fundamental Constitutions of Carolina*, written in 1669 by John Locke and Sir Anthony Ashley Cooper, was intended to create a model society. The details for the social and economic organization of that society were not practical and thus failed, but the antiauthoritarian spirit of liberty and the belief that a deliberately stratified society was proper flourished side by side in the new colony.

Partially the product of his time and place, Gadsden's radicalism sprang also from his distinctive personality. The sparse information about his childhood and youth inhibit a detailed analysis, but his public records and sayings project the image of a complex man. At the core of his existence was his intimate family life. He married young and was devoted to his wives, children, half-brothers, and even his in-laws. He was elated by their successes and severely grieved when he lost a member of his immediate circle. When the British imprisoned him during the Revolution, one of his major complaints was his separation from his wife and children. His drive to make money, win a respectable place in Charleston society, and to fight in the Revolution was motivated in part by his concern for the welfare of his immediate family and for that of his posterity.

Next to Gadsden's family, religion was the stabilizing influence in his life. A lifelong member of St. Philip's Anglican Church, his theology was puritanical but not narrow. He believed in the one omnipotent god of Christianity and a heaven to which he thought that he would someday go, but he was tolerant of those who disagreed with him and was always an advocate of religious freedom. He seemed to be fascinated by deism and unitarianism, although he never became an avowed devotee of either. In times of personal crisis he often found within his faith the strength to persevere.

The public image that Gadsden presented suggests a man of many and rapidly changing moods. He was mercurial, proud, ambitious, and egocentric. He cultivated his reputation for unselfish public service and absolute honesty. He was also compassionate and as quick to forgive as he was to become angry. When his enemies accused him of wrongdoing, he flew into a rage and published essays cataloging his virtues and excoriating his critics, but in the very same writings he was often self-effacing and diffident. His public defenses of his accomplishments, professions of humility, and courting of anonymity suggest that the inner conflict between disinterested service and ego is one that he never resolved. On the other hand, he readily assumed a stance of masterful command when addressing the middle and lower classes. His pride was tempered by a strong moral sense, a driving urge to do what he thought was right, even if it meant making major sacrifices. Often he was pious; rarely did he display a sense of humor. What saved him from being dull was a powerful intelligence, a flamboyant political style, and a colorful use of language.

When Gadsden burst forth in print with language that was reckless, fiery, and sometimes profane, his enemies called him a madman. To those who could not fathom a political existence apart from the British Empire, Gadsden's opinions no doubt did seem to be insane. But Gadsden himself was anything but insane. He had a remarkable ability to cope with victory and defeat in every area of his life, and there is no evidence that he suffered from even temporary mental disorders. His rise to great wealth, honestly acquired even in a revolutionary era, suggests that in managing his business affairs he was a man of reason and good sense. Gradually becoming convinced that the king, Parliament, and the ministry were pursuing policies that jeopardized established rights he understood to be his simply because he was a citizen of South Carolina and of the empire, Gadsden lashed out with reckless, passionate rhetoric that revealed his willingness to defy English authority.

CHAPTER TWO

First Defiance

The French and Indian War set the stage for Christopher Gadsden's first defiance of royal authority. He flailed out against the French, the Indians, several British officers, the Royal Council, two governors, and even his friend Henry Laurens. He fought to win and maintain the military victory over the French and Indians, and he fought even more vigorously to preserve in South Carolina the basic rights that he was convinced Englishmen had won in their Civil War and Glorious Revolution of the previous century. Gadsden himself was certain of his goals and of his methods, but those whom he attacked said he was crazy and dangerous. By the time the war ended, many people in both London and Charleston thought of him as a troublemaker. The events, both petty and great, that captured Gadsden's attention during the French and Indian War ultimately had a profound influence on him, shaping his politics.

Gadsden lived in a society as complex as he was. Fanning out from the smart, cultured city of Charleston was an untamed frontier inhabited by thousands of Indians and coveted by the ubiquitous French. White settlers, too, had moved into the backcountry, multiplying the opportunities for hostilities. The British had the awesome task of maintaining the security of the city, regulating the Indian trade, and defending their empire from domestic and foreign encroachments. In 1730 they had signed in London a treaty of friendship with the Cherokee, but a score of years later that treaty was being steadily eroded by the struggle between the French and British for empire in North America.[1] In 1746 Governor James Glen, a young Scot, promised the Indians a fort in their country to protect them from the French.[2] Not until 1753, however, when the French and Indian War was imminent, was he able to persuade the Commons to redeem his promise. In October of that year, Glen built Fort Prince George on the eastern side of the Keowee River, slightly above and opposite the village of Keowee, in upper South Carolina about 230 miles northwest of Charleston. Located at the foot of the mountains, the fort seemed to guard against the Cherokee themselves rather than protect them from the French.

The Cherokee were not satisfied; they wanted a fort built among the Overhill Towns, in what became southeastern Tennessee, where they were more exposed to the French. Fearful that the French would build a fort there if he did not, Glen agreed. The task of building the fort fell to Glen's thirty-four-year-old successor, William Henry Lyttelton. Exceedingly ambitious, Lyttelton was a short, slim man who intended to pursue policies in Carolina that would attract attention in London and soon win him a better appointment. Lyttelton himself led an expedition that reached the Overhill Towns in October 1756. With the help of 200 men and engineer John William Guerard De Brahm, he built Fort Loudoun, a strong and elaborate fort overlooking the Little Tennessee River, a short distance from the Tellico River, in what became Monroe County, Tennessee.

There were six different military organizations in the province. The Regulars, often Scotch Highlanders, were professional soldiers who were paid by the Crown. The Independents were a division of the Regulars, but they were raised in the province. The Provincials were recruited by the Commons House of Assembly for a definite term at a low salary. The Rangers were a division of the Provincials who patrolled the frontier on horseback. The militia consisted of all men between the ages of sixteen and sixty who might be required to serve at their own expense in case of a slave or Indian rebellion or foreign invasion. Occasionally there was a group of volunteers who served entirely at their own expense.[3]

As ambitious as Lyttelton, Gadsden saw an opportunity to render public service and to win glory for himself. He organized a colorful volunteer artillery company. In October 1757 the *South-Carolina Gazette* carried a notice inviting all those inclined to join

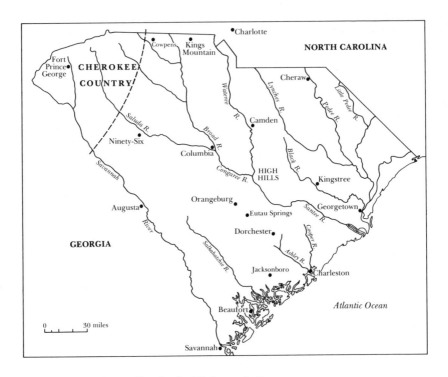

Map of South Carolina in the Eighteenth Century

such a company to leave their names with Elisha Poinsett at his tavern in Charleston. In December, January, and February, these men or their representatives met at Poinsett's Tavern to discuss the proper form of application to the authorities.[4] Gadsden's name did not appear in the brief newspaper accounts, but he was more influential than any other member in getting a bill to establish the company through the Commons, and he remained for many years the company's captain. Membership in the company became a mark of social distinction.

The Artillery Company made quite an impression. On November 10, 1758, the *Gazette* remarked that it far surpassed the militia in performance and appearance, the advantage of frequent exercise. The striking and expensive uniforms, which the members themselves furnished, consisted of "Blue Coatees turn'd up with Crimson, crimson Jackets & Gold laced Hats, with white Stockings." The group was so visible in the city that it easily won popular support.

But the legal status of this useful organization was uncertain. In November 1757, Gadsden, Laurens, and John Guerard presented to the Commons a bill asking for legal sanction. The bill passed easily, and on December 8 the Council agreed without amendment.[5] When the bill was presented to Governor Lyttelton for his signature, however, he decided that he himself already had the power to form the company and would not relinquish that power to the Commons.[6] Thus matters stood as long as Lyttelton remained governor. The whole question became an episode in a struggle for power between the executive and the legislature that was almost as old as the colony. Gadsden was now in the middle of that fight.

For the moment, however, Lyttelton and the Artillery Company turned their attention back to the Cherokee. In 1758 more than five hundred Cherokee warriors were armed by the governments of South Carolina and Virginia to help defend the Virginia frontier. Little Carpenter and his warriors, who had joined the English expedition against Fort Duquesne, deserted two days before reaching the fort. He and his group were disarmed, dismissed, and disgraced in Virginia. Little Carpenter was the only survivor among the seven chiefs who had gone to England in 1730 to sign the treaty of friendship. No matter how serious his desertion, Lyttelton still was dependent upon him to help maintain peace between the Cherokee and the English. Therefore, Lyttelton solemnly forgave him. But the governor's efforts at conciliation failed, because warriors from Settico near Fort Loudoun fell upon settlers in North Carolina and took more than twenty scalps. There were other atrocities committed by the Indians, but it was clear that the Cherokee were divided among themselves. The majority of those who lived in the Lower Towns were hostile, but the rest of the nation, except for two Upper Towns, appeared to remain loyal to the English.

Lyttelton's response to this volatile situation was rash. He immediately ordered a detachment of seventy provincial troops to Fort Loudoun while he prepared for a larger military display. He persuaded the Commons to appropriate pay for 1,500 men to be used against the Indians. The Commons, which resented this invasion by the governor of its prerogative to raise and pay Provincials, at first refused to appropriate an adequate amount of money but finally gave in because of the emergency. In the meantime, on October 17, 1759, a delegation from the Upper and Lower Cherokee arrived to negotiate with the governor. The stubborn Lyttelton, however, resolved to hold the entire Indian delegation hostage and to return them safely to their own country at the head of cavalry which he personally would lead.[7]

On October 26, 1759, the governor set forth on this mission accompanied by his staff officers, 1,500 troops, the Indian hostages, and Captain Christopher Gadsden with sixteen volunteers from the Artillery Company. This expedition was Gadsden's first experience in the field. Although the threat of death by disease was very real, Gadsden was to be denied the glory of participation in battle. During the difficult march of forty-five days, more than 200 of the soldiers deserted or became too ill to continue.[8] On December 9 the remaining troops reached Fort Prince George, where they became increasingly demoralized by an epidemic of measles and the fear of contracting the smallpox that was then raging among the Indians and whites in the backcountry. Faced with the likelihood that three-fourths of his men would desert, Lyttelton had to abandon his plan to fight. The smallpox plague and dissension among the Indians prevented their attacking Lyttelton. Both the governor and Little Carpenter were willing to negotiate.

Lyttelton informed Little Carpenter that he would release the Indian hostages only when an equal number of Indians were surrendered to the English for punishment. The two leaders then, in the treaty of December 26, 1759, reaffirmed the treaty of 1730. Lyttelton left the hostages at Fort Prince George until they could be redeemed by the surrender of the guilty Indians, and he returned to Charleston. His bloodless victory was entirely illusory, yet the impetuous governor was hailed as a conquering hero. He entered Charleston on January 8, 1760, and on February 14 the king gave him his promotion; he was appointed governor of Jamaica.[9]

Within this circle of glory rested Captain Gadsden and his volunteers. No sooner did they return to Charleston than they took up serious military study. Lord Jeffrey Amherst, the commanding general in America, sent Lieutenant John Mayne with a detachment of Regulars to Charleston specifically to train the Artillery Company.[10] Beginning in the last week of January 1760, Gadsden and his men turned out for their instructions at eight o'clock every Wednesday and Saturday morning. They were good students, for in April when Lieutenant Governor William Bull, Jr., took over the government from Lyttelton, Captain Gadsden's company performed so admirably in the review that Bull paid them "some very genteel Compliments." On the last Saturday in that month, the grateful company entertained the departing Lieutenant Mayne and his men at Poinsett's Tavern.[11]

While Charleston celebrated Governor Lyttelton's victory, the Cherokee wrecked his treaty and went on their bloodiest rampage of the century. They enticed the commander of Fort Prince George outside its walls and murdered him and two of his companions. When the men inside attempted to put the Cherokee hostages in chains, the Indians drew concealed knives and killed one of the soldiers and wounded another. Having no mercy, the soldiers massacred all the hostages. Thus began a bloody frontier war, extending from Abbeville to York, and scores of whites fell victim. When news of the massacres arrived in Charleston on February 2, Lyttelton appealed to the governors of Virginia and North Carolina and to General Amherst. Neither Virginia nor North Carolina gave significant help, but Amherst immediately dispatched Colonel Archibald Montgomery, who arrived on April 1, 1760, four days before Lyttelton left for his new appointment.

Before Montgomery's arrival, Lyttelton moved quickly to meet the emergency. He recommended that the Commons raise and pay troops to help the besieged frontier. The Commons resolved to raise, in addition to other troops, a new regiment of 1,000 men to relieve Fort Prince George and to punish the Cherokee, but it defeated a motion to ask Lyttelton to command this regiment personally. Many men in the Commons were displeased with the way the governor had raised and paid his troops for the 1759 campaign and were fearful that he was attempting to usurp the Assembly's power to raise and pay provincial troops. Six months later, the Commons had raised only 125 of the 1,000-man regiment and in effect was merely paying the people who lived in the backcountry to protect themselves.

Gadsden chafed under the Commons' inability to raise the new troops. Two years later he attempted to rationalize that failure by arguing that many members of the House had stayed away because of a smallpox epidemic in the town and that those who were present had not considered the issue thoroughly. If they had attempted to raise only 500 men, Gadsden argued, then that number would have been recruited promptly.[12] But Gadsden was mistaken, because there were very few able-bodied men in the backcountry who were not already in service or who had not fled in the face of the Indian menace.[13] Before the arrival on April 1, 1760, of 1,200 Regulars under the command of Colonel Archibald Montgomery, the backsettlers had to depend upon their hastily constructed stockades and whatever slight help the Rangers could give them.

In 1760 and 1761 there were two campaigns against the Indians in which Gadsden did not participate, but which later became very important to him. In April 1760, Colonel Archibald Montgomery led 1,650 heavily armed soldiers in the successful destruction of the Lower Towns and some of the Middle Towns, but he killed very few Indians. Shortly thereafter he returned to New York. In the meantime, however, the Cherokee besieged Fort Loudoun, forced the Englishmen inside to surrender, scalped 30 of them, watched 7 more drown while trying to escape, and took the remaining 120 as prisoners. In March 1761, Lieutenant Colonel James Grant, who had been with Montgomery as a subordinate, responded to General Amherst's orders to launch another attack against the Indians. He commanded almost 1,900 men, including 689 Provincials under Colonel Thomas Middleton and Lieutenant Colonel Henry Laurens. During most of June, Grant battled the Indians in their country and destroyed fifteen towns and 1,400 acres of crops in the Middle Settlements. But he killed very few Indians. After thirty days of fighting, Grant and his army fell back to Fort Prince George, exhausted. Here Colonel Middleton left the expedition in a huff because he thought that Grant had snubbed him by not seeking his advice about how best to conquer the enemy. Laurens took command of the Provincials, but the war had ended because the Indians were ready to discuss terms of peace.[14]

While the Montgomery and Grant expeditions took place in 1760 and 1761, Gadsden remained in Charleston, fuming because his Artillery Company had not yet won legal recognition. The company had become a pawn in the power struggle between the governor and the Commons. Gadsden and his men still wanted the legal recognition by the Commons that Lyttelton had denied them. Many of the artillerymen were themselves members of the Commons. With Lyttelton gone, recognition could be had. On June 25 the Commons passed a bill to establish and regulate the Artillery Company, on July 3 the Council concurred, and on July 31 Lieutenant Governor Bull agreed to it.[15] By then the war was almost over. Nevertheless, the company continued to flourish as a part of the city's military establishment. Gadsden was appointed captain, a position he retained until he was chosen as a delegate to the Continental Congress in 1774. A complete list of the members is not available, but the company grew to include seventy-two privates and several officers, including Thomas Heyward, Jr., and Edward Rutledge.[16] The majority of the members came from the elite group; they included planters, merchants, lawyers, and several of the wealthier mechanics of Charleston. All were rich enough to furnish their own supplies and uniforms.

Although Gadsden did not participate in the Montgomery and Grant expeditions, he soon became enmeshed in the details of those campaigns. Uninvited, he attended the peace conference between the Council and the Cherokee on September 15, 1761. The conference met at Ashley Ferry, about two miles outside the city, because a smallpox epidemic raged in Charleston. According to procedure, the Council was supposed to negotiate terms with the Indians and then submit the treaty to the Commons for approval. Grant and Laurens, the two principal commanders in the war, were present to advise the Council. Possibly Gadsden was there as an official representative of the Commons, but judging from his later behavior it is more reasonable to assume that he simply barged in uninvited.

The chances are that Gadsden was so angry that he jumped upon a horse at his nearby plantation and invaded the peace conference. His displeasure with the Council stemmed from an episode the previous August in which the Council had rejected a bill passed by the Commons for continuing the provincial regiment then under the command of Henry Laurens. Gadsden had immediately complained that a constitutional question was involved because "His Majesty's Council . . . [had] . . . usurped an Authority" that rightfully belonged to the Commons, namely the authority to raise and pay provincial troops.[17] Gadsden was already angry with Grant for not having decimated the Cherokee warriors when he had had the chance, and he became even more outraged when he now heard Grant recommend that the Council offer the Indians lenient terms. Then Gadsden turned upon Laurens for supporting Grant.

On that fateful day of September 15, 1761, at Ashley Ferry the friendship between Christopher Gadsden and Henry Laurens came to an end. The precise details of what transpired between the two men are not known, but two years later in a public letter Gadsden recalled "an affair of the nearest concern to me, which Col. *Laurens* had made appear very black indeed against me, at the ferry."[18] Two mutual friends, Gadsden continued, had inquired into the matter and produced Laurens's "acknowledgement from under his own hand that he had been wrong."[19] Laurens's written acknowledgment of his error, if it ever existed, is also lost. The alleged investigation by two neutral persons and Laurens's apology suggest the episode was so serious that it brought the two former friends to the very brink of a duel.

All that can be deduced from the surviving references to the controversy between Gadsden and Laurens at Ashley Ferry is that they disagreed vehemently upon proper treatment of the defeated Cherokee. Gadsden wanted the Indian leaders to be hanged in revenge and the most severe restrictions possible placed upon the Indians. Laurens thought that a permanent peace would be more likely if the Cherokee were not treated cruelly in defeat. He also knew that the royal and provincial troops were too exhausted and poorly supplied to continue the fight. Gadsden probably looked upon Laurens as something of a traitor for taking the side of Grant. Given Gadsden's temper, one can imagine that he used coarse language to inflict much verbal abuse upon Laurens, and perhaps Laurens retaliated. The episode not only ruined their friendship, but it showed Laurens to be a man of cool judgment and practical wisdom, whereas Gadsden was rashly theoretical and foolishly hotheaded.

The negotiations with the Cherokee dragged on until December 18, 1761, when Lieutenant Governor Bull and Little Carpenter and eight other chiefs signed a treaty in Charleston. The treaty represented a triumph for Laurens, Grant, the Council, and even the Cherokee themselves. It called for the Cherokee to surrender all their prisoners and Fort Loudoun, exclude the French from the Indian country, allow the English to build forts anywhere in their nation, execute any Indian who murdered an Englishman, reopen their trade as soon as all prisoners were released, and establish a line 40 miles east of Keowee as the boundary between the Indian country and that of the whites. This boundary was set by the Indians themselves and represented an increase in the size of their territory by 14 miles.[20]

On the very day the treaty was signed, Gadsden publicly grumbled that he was reminded of Sir John Falstaff "with the prisoner he took, who wou'd neither come along with him, nor let him come away himself."[21] Neither the Indians nor the whites gained much from the war; their relationship slipped back into the pattern it had followed since 1730.

Upon politics in Charleston, however, the war had a profound impact. It raised the question of whether royal placemen or elected members of the Commons could recruit, pay, and command provincial troops. The immediate cause of this constitutional crisis was the misunderstanding between Grant and Middleton. Middleton was a wealthy planter and merchant who had joined Grant's campaign in 1761. He accused Grant of purposely ignoring his advice and experience, of having no stomach to fight the Indians, and of being negligent of the real interests of South Carolina. Grant denied all charges, but after the two men returned to Charleston the personal animosity between them flared so violently that they finally met in a bloodless duel. Middleton had the support of the majority of the members of the Commons and of Gadsden, but Laurens, who had served as Middleton's second in command, bravely said that he thought Grant was correct.[22]

The Middleton-Grant affair evoked the first of Gadsden's many letters in the public press. His medium was Peter Timothy's *South-Carolina Gazette*, an organ that was consistently critical of royal authority. The thirty-seven-year-old captain's style was no more distinguished for its literary charm than he was for his military erudition. The qualities of compactness, unity, and coherence escaped the impetuous writer. In his anxiety to tell the whole truth, he succumbed to the spell of his own enthusiasm and piled line upon line. His energy and ardor and rashness knew few restraints. Vehemence of expression consistently put him in the public eye as the spokesman for a cause. But what delighted his friends provoked his enemies. He was not always right, but he always thought he was.

Denouncing Grant soundly, Gadsden's first letter appeared in the *Gazette* on December 18, 1761, the same day the treaty with the Cherokee was signed. He alleged that Grant had deceived the governor by not reporting to him an earlier conversation with Little Carpenter in which the Indian leader had been "insolent . . . in ye style of a Conqueror" and had demanded considerable gifts from the Carolinians before agreeing to a treaty. Gadsden blamed Grant for the failure of the Montgomery campaign in 1760, in which Grant had participated as a subordinate. Gadsden accused Grant of inflating the cost of the 1761 campaign, much to the advantage of some unnamed sutler whom Grant favored as the supplier of the troops. "What think you of £6 per Gallon for indifferent rum . . . & 12.5 per pound obligingly squeezed out of . . . poor fellows for brown sugar and butter . . . ?" Gadsden asked. By raising the issue of Grant's expenses, Gadsden was bidding for popular support in Charleston, whose citizens were already paying increased taxes to finance the Lyttelton campaign.[23] As for Colonel Grant himself, Gadsden continued, his character, if known in London as in Charleston, "wou'd serve, like other bugaboos, to keep naughty & perverse children quiet." Interspersed with the tirade against Grant were hardy words of praise for Middleton. Gadsden thought Middleton's provincial regiment, raised and paid by the Commons House of Assembly, was an honor to the province. Abhorring Grant's refusal to consult Middleton, Gadsden argued that Middleton had "blown ye trumpet, and like a good Watchman & warned ye People; and whosoever had heard ye sound of ye trumpet, and taketh not warning, if ye sword come & take him away, his blood shall be on his own head."

This first letter, signed "PHILOPATRIOS," which means "lover of homeland" (Gadsden cleverly did not say whether he meant by homeland South Carolina or England), was followed by a second, printed in May 1762 and more specifically directed against Grant and in defense of the provincial Rangers.[24] By reference to four letters Grant had written during the campaign of 1760, Gadsden endeavored to prove three propositions: that Colonel Grant had the principal direction of Montgomery's ill-fated campaign of 1760; that he lost two fine opportunities during that campaign to relieve Fort Loudoun and to conquer the Cherokee; and that the Rangers "did not deserve the cruel treatment they met with from him." Grant was such an incompetent officer that he had refused to learn from experience; his conduct glaringly demonstrated that "his whole dependence was in the known cowardice of the Indians." Grant "was sent to us the first time, and did worse than nothing: He was sent to us again, a second time, and did twice as much," Gadsden wrote.

Gadsden's charges were pointed, public, and reflective of the greater portion of public sentiment, but they were not entirely just. Certainly Montgomery's campaign was a failure, but it would be difficult to prove that Grant was responsible. And Grant's campaign was a success because there were no further open breaks with the Cherokee before the Revolution. That a man of Henry Laurens's balance and judgment should support Grant is sufficient indication that Grant was not incompetent. Gadsden was defending a provincial officer and provincial soldiers against, as he thought, the haughty imperiousness and mismanagement of a royal officer who refused to seek advice from the Provincials.

After James Grant had left Charleston, his friends kept him informed of Gadsden's outbursts. "The turbulent spirit of Gadsden pursued you still further," one of them wrote, "and in less than two months usher'd itself forth in *a second Letter to the People of Carolina*, which, notwithstanding of his utmost labour, had little more consequences than that of Reflecting Infamy and Ridicule upon its Author. I have Reason to think that *the Performance* has been sent to you from Carolina, and therefore will take leave of Mr. Gadsden as a dirty Subject, unworthy of your notice."[25]

Henry Laurens, too, thought Gadsden was an unsavory subject but did not immediately take leave of him. In a long, unpublished essay that he circulated privately, a defensive Laurens said he felt compelled to answer Philopatrios's "dirty invectives."[26] He accused Gadsden of being shortsighted. He defended Grant and mildly chided Middleton, supporting his arguments with copies of letters written by both colonels during the campaign. Gadsden's demand to kill more warriors was not only inhumane, but entirely unnecessary to win the war. As a participant in the campaign, Laurens could speak with greater authority than Gadsden. Laurens deplored "this unhappy time when all respect for the Authority of Government . . . seems to be at an end." He hoped Philopatrios would confess his error and drop the matter.

But Gadsden was not repentant. After a heated exchange of public letters in February that nearly caused Laurens to publish his essay,[27] on March 12, 1763, in the *South-Carolina Gazette* Gadsden dismissed Laurens's allegations against his character as "mere talk and say-so." Rejecting an offer to read Laurens's unpublished writings, he hoped to force Laurens to publish them and thus win an excuse to vindicate himself publicly. But Laurens did not take the bait, and Gadsden concluded by warning him to beware of false friends who favored the prerogative of the Crown over the authority of the Commons House of Assembly.

Gadsden had transformed the feud between himself and Laurens into a major constitutional question. That question was whether the Crown, as represented by the royal governor and Council, or the Commons House of Assembly had the greater authority to govern the province. In dealing with the problem of commissioning Gadsden's Artillery Company and the need to raise provincial troops hurriedly to fight the Cherokee, Lyttelton had taken the view that the will of the Crown superseded that of the Commons. Grant and Laurens supported him, whereas Middleton and Gadsden had argued the opposite. In 1762 the struggle for power between the governor and the Commons crystalized over a second, more volatile issue: the right of the Commons to control its own elections. Again, Gadsden was at the center of the crisis, and the royal governor whose fate it was to bear the brunt of his fury was Thomas Boone.

Boone, the first royal governor to come to South Carolina since Lyttelton had departed in April 1760, arrived in Charleston three days before Christmas 1761. As a former resident of the colony and a descendant of the prominent and influential Colleton family, he was greeted with the fanfare of military display, salutes, and flying colors. After the reading of his commission at the Council chamber, he proceeded to Granville's Bastion, where the commission was again read and where Christopher Gadsden's Artillery Company fired a salute.[28] In less than a year, however, he collided with Gadsden and the Commons in a way that ultimately brought about his recall.

In February 1762 Boone informed the Commons that he had reviewed the election act passed in 1721 and found it so loose, general, and nonbinding on the churchwardens that a new law was absolutely necessary.[29] Boone did not explain his reasons for undertaking an examination of the election act, but they probably rested in the controversy between the Commons and Governor Lyttelton over control of the provincial troops. Perhaps Boone hoped to draw a new election law that would insure a membership in the Commons that would be more agreeable with the royal instructions. Unfortunately for him, the Commons viewed the election act of 1721 as inviolable. That law was a revision and extension of the act of 1716, which the proprietors had refused to accept and which had been one of the principal causes of their overthrow in 1719. It had established the parish as the unit of representation and churchwardens as election officials. They were required to take an oath before a justice of the peace and then to execute the election writs that had been issued by the governor and Council.[30]

It was Boone's great misfortune that his first chance to test the law grew out of circumstances involved in the election of Christopher Gadsden. Charles Lowndes declined the seat in the Commons to which he had been elected by St. Paul's Parish, Colleton County, and in a special election on June 22 and 23, 1762, Christopher Gadsden was chosen by 76 votes out of 94 cast.[31] When the Commons reconvened on September 9, the clerk reported that the election return from St. Paul's Parish was blank. The two wardens who had conducted the election were called before the Assembly and presented the writ of election so that they might make the proper return thereon. This action was taken, and then by the narrow vote of 14 to 13 the Commons decided to ask the wardens whether they had been sworn by a magistrate of the county before they had executed the election writ. Before this question was put, however, the wardens were asked to withdraw, whereupon the Commons voted not to pose this question. Gadsden was called in and given the qualifying oath as a member of the Commons. Since the churchwardens had not been properly sworn, the letter of the law had been violated, but the spirit had not. It was a minor infraction which the Commons had overlooked in the past, and certainly there could be no doubt that Gadsden was the overwhelming choice of St. Paul's Parish. Accompanied by two witnesses, he was sent to the governor to receive the state oath.

Governor Boone, whose curiosity had been aroused by the delay in the proceedings of the Commons, decided to examine the journal. He summoned the Commons immediately to the Council chamber to hear the reasons why he could not administer the state oath to Gadsden. If he could have enforced his will, he would have ended the right of the Assembly to control the election of its own members. Boone announced that in the case of Gadsden the election act had been violated and that he would publicly show his disapproval by dissolving the Assembly and calling for new elections.[32] Perhaps Boone was inexperienced and had not realized the importance that the Commons attached to the elections of its members. Apparently he was accused of seeking revenge against Gadsden, a known troublemaker, for Boone later denied that he had "the least Objection to Mr. Gadsden" personally.[33] Despite Boone's disclaimer, Gadsden's public outbursts against former Governor Lyttelton and Lieutenant Colonel Grant had identified him to the royal officials as a potentially dangerous man who should be watched and perhaps fenced from power.

In the new elections, 37 of the 48 dismissed assemblymen, including Gadsden, were returned. Gadsden received a higher percentage of the votes from St. Paul's than he had in the previous election. The state oaths were administered to all members on October 25, 1762, and the governor thought the affair had blown over.[34] After a brief meeting on the next day, he prorogued the Assembly for a month. When the Commons reconvened on November 22, the governor made a formal speech and suggested some items of business for the Assembly to consider. The Commons made a formal and courteous reply but calmly ignored his suggestions.

The Commons then appointed a committee on privileges and elections to decide whether or not Boone had violated the election act by refusing to commission Gadsden after he had been elected the previous June. As an intended insult to Governor Boone, Gadsden was appointed to the committee. The Commons named John Rutledge chairman. A twenty-three-year-old London-trained lawyer, Rutledge was a member of one of the most powerful families in Charleston; he was committed to the political philosophy that a legislature of planters and their allies under royal supervision should dominate the colony. Fully prepared to appeal over the governor's head if necessary, the Commons also appointed Gadsden to a committee of correspondence with its agent in Great Britain.

On December 4 the Commons sent a copy of the report of the committee on elections and privileges to the governor with the observation that his dissolution of the previous Assembly had deprived the House of its fundamental privilege to determine the election of its own members, a right guaranteed by the "ancient constitution of our mother country."[35] The governor replied on December 7, denying that it was an inherent right and privilege of the House to determine the elections of its own members, "because that house might determine an election in opposition to law." He concluded that he thought he was right; if the House thought otherwise, let it refer its "complaints to the royal ear."[36]

The Assembly was neither ready to give up the point nor appeal to the king. On behalf of the Commons, Gadsden pre-

pared a reply to the governor's speech. The majority in the
Commons apparently looked to Gadsden alone to defend his
election. Gadsden rose brilliantly to the occasion. His report to
the governor drew heavily upon the writings of English whigs
who had supported the restoration of Charles II in 1660 and the
expulsion of James II in 1688. His appeal was to the sanctity of the
ancient British constitution, not to revolution or independence.
It showed that he was a careful student of the best writing of the
Enlightenment. A decade and more later, the same ideas re-
sounded in the pamphleteers of the American Revolution,
seeped into the thinking of the colonists' elite, were translated
into an emotional struggle for freedom in the minds of the
middle and lower classes, and were a positive example of what
John Adams meant when he said that the Revolution was in the
hearts and minds of the people. The report pointed out that the
Parliament of Great Britain, "since the happy revolution [of
1689]," had been entirely free "to determine their own elections;
and, as his majesty's other governors have had the modesty to
decline asserting such a right, so we hope, that Your Excellency
will not, for the future, attempt any such dangerous innova-
tion."[37]

The governor gave not an inch, and on December 16 the
Commons voted 24 to 6 not to enter into any further business with
him. Among the minority votes were those of William Wragg and
probably Henry Laurens. Laurens was probably the richest merchant in South Carolina at the time. Wragg was a wealthy planter
and a sensible man who had been educated at Oxford and was a
member of the English bar. In 1750, when he was about thirty-
five, he had inherited more than 7,000 acres on the Ashley River
where he lived in splendor. Both Wragg and Laurens usually
defended the Crown's prerogative, but in this case they believed
that the Commons was correct on constitutional grounds.
Nevertheless, they cast their negative votes because they thought
that halting the business of government was too drastic a solution.[38]

The dispute could not be settled in South Carolina. Governor
Boone stepped up his appeals to the Lords of Trade, and the
Commons instructed the committee of correspondence with
Great Britain, consisting of four councilors and eighteen assem-

blymen, to send to their agent in London a full account of the argument to be printed and circulated among prominent Englishmen. Loyal and conscientious in his dealings with his colonial employers, agent Charles Garth labored under the handicap of being a first cousin to Governor Boone, who had helped him obtain his appointment.[39] Yet he was responsible to the Commons, not to the governor, and inclined to minimize personal considerations in the performance of his official duties. Gadsden, Laurens, and Wragg were members of the committee that instructed Garth.

Before the report could be prepared and sent to London, the dispute moved with a vengeance from the halls of government into the public press. Peter Timothy's *South-Carolina Gazette* became the voice of the Gadsden faction, and Robert Wells's *South-Carolina Weekly Gazette* published the opinions of Wragg and Laurens. On December 11, 1762, Gadsden, using a pseudonym, placed an advertisement in the *South-Carolina Gazette* that satirized the governor in terms that were extreme and unfair. The piece announced the forthcoming publication of a treatise allegedly written by Boone, which would prove that the "rights and privileges of the people of this province" are "*permissive*, not *inherent*," a doctrine allied with the "deeply erudite positions of the *divine right of Kings, passive obedience, and non-resistance.*" An appendix to the treatise would prove that "the foundation of the present El[ectio]n of an M[embe]r of A[ssembl]y is in a *particular* oath of the Ch[urch] W[arde]n, and not in the choice of the freemen of the pa[ri]sh." The signature to the advertisement, "*Auditor Tantum*" (Only a Hearer), was Gadsden's way of accusing Governor Boone of reacting to hearsay rather than fact. The use of Latin phrases, the style, and the gross overstatement of Boone's position were clearly the work of Gadsden. Two months later he publicly confessed to its authorship.

Arguing for the other side, William Wragg explained in an open letter to his constituents why he opposed the resolution to do no business with the governor.[40] He thought its passage would create economic chaos for the colony. Bounties to encourage immigrants might be curtailed and financial support might be withdrawn from Fort Prince George, "thereby abandoning the back-settlers to the rapine or drunken frolicks of the Indians."

The public credit would suffer, and South Carolina might be deprived of her share in a parliamentary grant to the southern colonies. He pointed out that the final settlement of the dispute would have to be made in England and that it was very likely the Crown would support Governor Boone.

In response, on February 5, 1763, Gadsden published a letter of some 12,000 words in the *South-Carolina Gazette*. He argued that Wragg had not given a fair picture of the economic situation in South Carolina. Sufficient money was already on hand to pay bounties for immigrants, and it was very unlikely that the colony would get any additional funds from Parliament. Gadsden showed also that the Commons House had already passed a resolution authorizing the governor to pay the expense of transporting provisions to Fort Prince George.

Wragg's speculation that the king would take the side of the governor irritated Gadsden most and inspired a brilliant discussion of the natural rights of Englishmen. Gadsden effectually denied the British theory of virtual representation and anticipated the arguments that Americans were soon to use against Great Britain. Despite his turgid prose, his letter became one of the earliest and most important defenses of the rights of the colonists. "Thank God!" he exclaimed, "we have as good a king upon the throne as ever graced it; who has . . . tenderest regard for the liberties and privileges of his subjects, and has . . . shown, his inclination . . . to reign solely *in* the hearts of a *free* people. . . ." Should it have ever been thought that the laws of England were reserved to persons residing in England only, Gadsden wrote, then "the sons of Britain would have been thinly, very thinly, scattered on this side of the Atlantic ocean."

None would deny that the right of being freely represented in Parliament was "the most essential and inherent right of the British subjects residing in Great-Britain," Gadsden continued. Since British subjects living in America were not permitted to send representatives to Parliament, it was their natural right to be represented in their own assemblies. This right was guaranteed by the charter that had established the colony, by the provincial law of 1712 which declared that all the statutes in England relative to the rights and liberties of British subjects should be endorsed in the province, and by the laws and customs of Parliament. Since

Parliament had the right to determine the election of its own members, the colonial assemblies also had the same right, Gadsden argued. "What?" he asked, "a son not have a right to imitate his good parent, when nature tells him it ought to be his chief pride, as it most certainly is his chief duty!"

Rehearsing again the origins of the dispute over the proper return on the election writ and over the churchwardens' having taken the oath, Gadsden pointed out that in the past writs had frequently been presented to the clerk of the Council without any return at all and that the clerk often had lent his assistance in making them out after they had been brought to his office. Even if it could be proved that the electors had broken the law, the "innocent member" who had been elected was not the one to be punished. The election law clearly stated that in such a case he should retain his seat while the investigation was being conducted. Furthermore, the churchwardens from Prince William's Parish had not been sworn either, but perhaps "the gentlemen returned in that writ were greater favourites with his excellency's own officer than Mr. Gadsden was, is, or desires to be."

Gadsden reminded his constituents that there had been many complaints against American assemblies, the "grand cause" of which was "unexperienced Governors . . . dizzied with a little power." He urged the colonies to appoint a common agent to speak for them before Parliament. If they presented a unified front, then all royal governors in America "would perhaps be a little more cautious, how they first causelessly trampled on the people's liberties." Gadsden was certain that if the colonies took such action, then "we might hear, *now and then*, of an instance of a governor being severely and publickly censured."

Although he was calling for the censure of Governor Boone, Gadsden wished for Parliament and the Lords of Trade to understand that he intended no disloyalty to the British government. The majority of Americans, he said, were "as quiet and loyal subjects as any his majesty has, utter abhorrence of absolute monarchy, and no friends to republicanism." To the English mind, a republic suggested a government in which all power came from the people and none from royal authority.[41] Gadsden was trying to make the point that it was Governor Boone, not himself, who was disloyal to the British government. The American settlers were asking for nothing that had not already been given them under the British constitution—a parliamentary monarchy that protected the inalienable rights of the governed. When they came to America, free Britons were not "such fools, like Esau of old, to sell their birth-right for a mess of pottage," Gadsden concluded.

This passionate letter elicited a flurry of responses. Writing anonymously in the *South-Carolina Weekly Gazette*, former Chief Justice William Simpson and Henry Laurens raised more personal animosities than constitutional questions.[42] Simpson, who had been clerk of the Council at the time Gadsden's election was contested, chided the *South-Carolina Gazette* for having published Gadsden's "long and unintelligible" and "incoherent chime of inconclusive arguments." He charged Gadsden with being motivated by "a mean passion for popularity." Laurens, displeased with being called "an artful flatterer of specious talents," raised anew the debate over the Cherokee wars and leveled specific criticisms at Gadsden's Philopatrios letters. In private he concluded that "one poor rash headlong Gentleman who has been too long a ring leader of people engaged in popular quarrels . . . is not a fit person to judge of Public affairs."[43]

In the *South-Carolina Gazette* of March 26, 1763, one "By-Stander" wrote in defense of Gadsden. He said Gadsden had arisen with "a spirit of love and zeal" and with "great pains" had stated the matter "with candour, reason and good arguments." It appeared to him "somewhat extraordinary" that a man who attempted to vindicate the public "should have so many persons to peck at him, as if he was a strange bird among a new flock of turkies." He was rebutted by "Man in the Moon," who in turn was refuted by "By-Stander's Standby." In the summer "Well Wisher to the Country" praised the Commons House for boldly and strenuously asserting its rights but urged that it resume business to provide for inoculations against a smallpox epidemic and for the sake of public creditors.[44]

As the newspaper battle raged in South Carolina, news of the controversy reached London. In February 1763 the Commons had sent the full account of the disturbance, including transcripts of the Journal of the Commons House of Assembly and Gadsden's letter of February 5 to Charles Garth, with orders to have it printed. William Wragg and Henry Laurens had refused to sign the report. Garth desired to alienate neither the governor nor the Commons but as the official representative of the Assembly in London was bound to do its bidding. He had the report published as a pamphlet entitled *A Full State of the Dispute Betwixt the Governor and the House of Assembly* and circulated it privately to the other colonial agents in England.[45] In July 1764, Garth submitted the pamphlet officially to the Lords of Trade. They declined to take either side and ignored the question of whether the governor had violated the Assembly's right to control the election of its members. In March they informed Boone that he had dissolved the Assembly without sufficient reason.[46]

Disappointed and defeated, Boone notified the board that he would return to England before the end of May. In June, possibly before Boone's letter arrived, he was recalled. On May 11, 1764, he departed from the colony without ceremony, leaving Lieutenant Governor William Bull, Jr., to restore harmonious relations with the Assembly. The Board of Trade reported that Boone had "taken up the matter in dispute with more zeal than prudence." It also reprimanded the Commons for having "allowed themselves to be so far provoked as to forget their Duty to His Majesty & to their Constituents."[47]

One issue remained to be settled. For two and one-half years, while the controversy raged, the Assembly had refused to pay Governor Boone's salary.[48] The governor had drawn £1,000 sterling per year from the imperial authorities, but he was also entitled to £500 sterling per year from the colony. The tax bill prepared by the Commons House in May 1764 was rejected by Lieutenant Governor Bull and the Council because it did not provide the appropriation for Boone's salary. To consider this problem, the Commons appointed a committee, from which Gadsden reported that the rejection of the bill gave a great shock to the public credit and that the Assembly could not enter into any expense until the public credit was placed on the proper basis by the passage of a tax bill.[49] On the same day that Gadsden made his report, Bull prorogued the Assembly until September 18. Laurens again placed much of the blame for the deadlock between the Council and the Commons on Gadsden. The situation, he wrote, "created much animosity amongst People who made a

Cloak of Patriotism merely to hide self-love & ambitious views."[50]

Laurens's allegations against Gadsden's character were serious and not entirely without truth. Gadsden's fights with Grant and with Boone occurred during the years his personal finances were in a state of flux. He was almost forty, at a stage in his life when he felt an urgency to make his fortune if he were ever to make it, and he was responsible for a large and increasing family. Because he was getting rid of his stores in the interest of becoming a planter, he did not make any enormous profits from selling war supplies. The fact that he served as an agent to sell goods for others suggests that he felt a need for more money. Gadsden's public criticisms of royal officials had also fenced him away from positions of power that could be achieved only with royal approval. In fact, Gadsden's only hope for political power now rested with his popularity among the natives of the province; he had no recourse except to attack the royal placemen if he himself were ever to have his way in the future. On the other hand, Gadsden was probably jealous of his former friend Henry Laurens. Laurens lived across the street with his family, was established as a wealthy merchant, and had not yet alienated himself from royal favor. Whether or not Gadsden consciously used a cloak of patriotism to hide his jealousy and ambition cannot be proved, but the uncertain status of his financial and political careers at the time make it a question worth pondering.

Regardless of Gadsden's personal motives, however, the point at issue in the debate over payment of Boone's salary was the authority of the Council to amend money bills. Since 1725 the Commons House had gradually limited the money powers of the Council; by 1755 it had barred the Council from as much as a comment on money bills. The Council and governors, however, attempted to rely upon the pre-1725 equality of the two branches and especially upon the explicit thirty-fifth instruction given to Governor Francis Nicholson in 1719. That instruction said that assemblies which took upon themselves the sole responsibility to frame money bills were violating His Majesty's prerogative and must share with the Council the power of framing, amending, or altering those bills.[51] In the case of Boone's salary, however, the Council realized that the question would ultimately have to be decided in London and passed the supply bill without any provision for him.

In the long interval before an imperial decision could be communicated to the colony, the issue, which had been skirted in the Assembly, was hotly debated in the public press. On December 3, 1764, after reading "two very extraordinary anonymous letters" in Wells's *Weekly Gazette*, Gadsden undertook to clarify the mind of the anonymous writer and of the public on the meaning of the thirty-fifth instruction and the privileges of the Assembly. With his usual gusto, exaggeration, and muddled style, he placed a long letter in the supplement to the *South-Carolina Gazette*. He tried to prove that the Assembly had never adopted that part of the instruction relating to the money powers of the Council because it had not been included in the election act of 1721. The eleventh clause of the election act, providing that the powers and privileges of the Assembly should be in accord with the king's thirty-fifth instruction, related only to members individually and not to the Commons House, he argued. This explanation was strained because the clause seemed to relate both to individual members and to the Commons.[52] Before 1725 the Assembly had winked at "the council's sometimes amending Tax-bills," but never after that date.

From that somewhat biased interpretation of the royal instructions, Gadsden proceeded to another defense of the rights of colonials as Englishmen. When the proprietors had surrendered to the Crown in 1719, the people had in no way deprived themselves of "any of those valuable privileges we have an inherent right to as Englishmen, and are confirmed to us by charter." The people were not the slaves of the proprietors, and the transfer applied to the soil only. "Thank God, we have not yet politically cut our own throats," Gadsden continued. "An haughty, arbitrary governor our assemblies have shewn themselves a pretty good match for," he wrote.

To this communication the anonymous correspondent replied in Wells's *Weekly Gazette*,[53] and shortly thereafter, on December 24, 1764, Gadsden again addressed Peter Timothy and reviewed the meaning of the election act, the thirty-fifth instruction, and money bills. Gadsden reiterated his belief that the people's rights had been "established since the happy revolution." He hoped that resistance to the Crown would not be necessary, but he implied that he was prepared to resist if the cause of right demanded it.

As in the case of the election controversy, the issue between the

Portrait of Christopher Gadsden in 1766. Jeremiah Theus, artist. Courtesy of George D. Shore, Jr.

Assembly and the Council could not be settled locally by mutual agreement. In November 1765 Thomas Boone presented a memorial to the Lords of the Treasury, asking that he be paid his back salary of £1,250 sterling out of the South Carolina quit-rents.[54] The Treasury referred the memorial to the Board of Trade, which in turn recommended an instruction to the Assembly to make good the salary, since the "mere matter of privilege" did not appear to be a "just reason" for withholding a governor's allowance.[55] When the new governor, Lord Charles Greville Montagu, arrived on June 12, 1766, he brought the instruction to recommend to the Assembly that it make good the salary.[56] Charles Garth, now a member of Parliament and still the colony's agent, wrote from London that Boone's lobbying for repeal of the Stamp Act made him worthy of receiving his back pay.[57] The Assembly concurred, and Boone was paid.

The long debate over the election of Christopher Gadsden to the Commons House of Assembly and the payment of the royal governor's salary revealed an inherent weakness of the British constitution. There was no written imperial constitution and no colonial constitution beyond the governor's instructions and whatever precedents and English common law might be successfully applied. The judiciary, consisting of a chief justice appointed by the king and never a native of the province, and two assistants who were natives and were chosen by the Assembly, had virtually no authority in constitutional questions. Appeals could be made to the governor and the Council. By the time of Gadsden's contested election, the Council, twelve men who usually were recommended by the governor and appointed by the king through the Board of Trade without limit of term, had so thoroughly declined in power that it served as little more than an occasional irritant to the demands of the Commons. The judiciary, the Council, and the governor were the embodiment of the royal prerogative in the colony, but it was only the governor who had any real power. With a new and ambitious young king on the throne in 1760 and a procession of his often contradictory advisers for the next two decades, the matter of interpreting an unwritten constitution and applying royal decisions equitably to all parts of the empire was almost certain to foment internal political chaos.

For almost two years while his controversy with Governor Boone lingered, Gadsden was embroiled in another debate; he was attempting to persuade the Library Society to expand its holdings of the classics. At the society's quarterly meeting on January 10, 1764, at Dillon's Tavern, he moved that the society prepare a list of the best editions of the classics, including all the ancient Greek and Latin authors through the fourth century, leading ecclesiastical writers, and the most prominent philologists and their critics. Gadsden chaired the committee which drew up the list. In April the society appropriated £70 sterling to buy the books, but in July that appropriation was withdrawn as "Irregular, Precipitate and contrary to the Charter." Very few of the classics already in the library were being taken out, and many members of the society thought that the collection they already owned could be expanded inexpensively.

Gadsden became so angry that he stayed away from the meeting on January 8, 1765. But he sent a letter by his friend Peter Timothy in which he stated his intention to resign. The secretary did not record the letter, nor apparently has it survived, but after it was read a lively debate ensued, and the society voted to invite Gadsden to appear before it in person.

At the next meeting, April 3, 1765, the members gathered in sufficient numbers to suggest that they anticipated a high time. The president, Lieutenant Governor William Bull; the other officers; and thirty-four more members constituted the largest attendance in the history of the society. Gadsden appeared and offered to remain a member if the society would pass his resolution of January 1764 requiring that £70 sterling be appropriated annually for the purchase of the classics. The society debated his offer, entertained a motion in his favor, and then voted against it. This decision was not total defeat, however, for the society did agree to refer the matter back to a committee and discuss it again at the next meeting. By the time it met in July 1765, the excitement surrounding the Stamp Act had already begun and Gadsden enjoyed greater favor than he had in January 1764. The July meeting reduced the sum to £30 annually, and in October, when Gadsden was representing South Carolina at the Stamp Act Congress in New York, it ordered the revised list of the classics to be sent to the bookseller. This partial victory was enough for Gadsden; he did not resign.[58]

Gadsden was not simply being stubborn; he was genuinely interested in the contents of the classics. Many leaders of the American Revolution embellished their writings, as did Gadsden, with Latin quotations from the classics, but Gadsden, like Thomas Jefferson and James Otis and others, was a thorough scholar of the ancient texts. He owned Greek, Latin, and Hebrew grammars and spent many hours studying. From the works of Tacitus, Plutarch, Sallust, and Cicero, he learned that incipient corruption brought about the crumbling of the Roman Republic in the second century. In the writings of Homer, Plato, Herodotus, Aristotle, and Epictetus, he rummaged through the autopsies of dead republics and learned something about the valor of men who perennially yearned to be free. Gadsden concluded, as John Adams later stated, that Britain was to America "what Caesar was to Rome."[59] Underlying Gadsden's argument with the Library Society was his urgent desire to disseminate knowledge that would help the local population comprehend the growing dangers of contemporary British rule.

During the French and Indian War, Christopher Gadsden defied royal authority on three issues: the governor's interference with the House's prerogative to raise and pay provincial troops, the House's right to determine the election of its own members, and the Council's debate with the Commons over jurisdiction relative to money bills. On each of these questions, the Commons seemed to win, but the basic problem of whether the Commons or the officials appointed by the king had greater authority remained unsolved. That solution required a higher level of statesmanship than was forthcoming from either London or Charleston. Since neither the Crown nor the Commons offered strong leadership, the unsettled political atmosphere invited ambitious men in Charleston to seek their own goals and increased the likelihood that inept politicians in London would stumble into great errors. Although Christopher Gadsden remained loyal to the king, his very presence in Charleston contributed to the social and political instability of the city. If a royal officer such as James Grant could be rebuffed and a royal governor such as Thomas Boone virtually expelled, the door was open for an emerging revolutionary to defy Parliament itself.

CHAPTER THREE

Liberty, and No Stamps

The Stamp Act crisis was the great event in Christopher Gadsden's life. He was swelled with pride because he had participated in it. "No man in America strove more (*and more successfully*) first to bring about a Congress in 1765, and then to support it *ever* afterwards than myself," he exulted thirteen years later.[1] For the remainder of his life, he believed that the Stamp Act Congress marked the genesis of the independence movement in America. Sometimes he lost his struggle to appear humble and let slip an expression of extreme joy at the memory of his presence at the creation of the new nation. "Massachusetts sounded the trumpet, but to Carolina is it owing that it was attended to," he boasted. "Had it not been for South Carolina, no congress would then have happened. She was all alive, and felt at every pore."[2]

In the heat of enthusiasm, Gadsden did not credit sufficiently the complex events in London and the corresponding responses in the middle and northern colonies that brought about the Stamp Act Congress. Yet, his boast was not altogether an exaggeration. Since South Carolina was the only southern province that sent delegates, and since Gadsden himself was the most vociferous advocate of liberty in that assembly, the Stamp Act Congress would have been less successful without the colony's delegates. But Gadsden's work would have been in vain if the Stamp Act had not touched almost every segment of the population and been added to other recent imperial decisions that had offended the American colonists.

The ferocity with which the Stamp Act storm broke over South Carolina created the illusion of a new crisis, but in truth it was a continuation of the colony's struggle for political and economic autonomy. That fight went back at least to the debate between Governor William Henry Lyttelton and the Commons over financing his campaign against the Cherokee and to Gadsden's election controversy. When George Grenville accepted the appointment as the king's first minister in April 1763, he set about balancing the British budget without regard for the possible ramifications of the disturbances in South Carolina that surrounded Gadsden's dispute with Governor Boone.

The American legislation that Parliament enacted under Grenville's leadership in 1764 was not intended to be punitive or obnoxious, nor did it elicit an immediate public outcry in South Carolina. The American Duties Act of 1764, which placed a tax of three pence per gallon on imported foreign molasses and instituted the machinery to collect it, also placed new duties on indigo that were intended to assist South Carolina.[3] The Currency Act of the same year, aimed principally at Virginia, prohibited the colonies south of New England from printing any more paper money, but it did not ban the use of money they had already printed. Since South Carolina had a paper currency reserve of more than £100,000, there was no immediate public protest. After the stamp crisis subsided, however, the dwindling supply of currency became a major source of irritation to the province.[4]

Early in 1764, Gadsden and other members of the Commons attempted to block the passage of the Stamp Act.[5] Gadsden served with Rawlins Lowndes, Charles Pinckney, and John Rutledge on a committee that sent the province's agent Charles Garth, who was also a member of Parliament, the arguments he was supposed to use against the proposed law. First, the stamp duty would be inconsistent with the inherent right of every British subject to be taxed only by his own consent. Second, any tax imposed by England that impoverished the colonies would also impoverish British merchants with whom they traded. Third, South Carolina was still in debt as a result of the Indian wars, and the danger of future Indian attacks made it absolutely essential that the province not be so crippled by taxation that it would be unable to raise the necessary supplies for its defense. In conclusion, the committee appealed to Parliament's sympathy; it was difficult to believe, they wrote, that Parliament, "instead of alleviating, parent-like, the many hardships and difficulties peculiar to her sons settled in this hot and unhealthy climate," would endeavor "to reduce us almost to despair, by . . . laying an internal tax upon the province."

Garth followed his instructions, but the arguments of his Carolina constituents did not sway Parliament or George Grenville. The law required that all legal documents, newspapers, and playing cards should be printed on stamped paper or have stamps affixed. The Stamp Act easily passed both houses of Parliament, received the royal assent on March 22, and was to take effect on November 1, 1765.[6]

The North American colonies responded with a fury that Grenville had not anticipated. On June 8, 1765, the Massachusetts House of Representatives, under the guidance of James Otis, issued a circular letter to the legislatures of all the colonies inviting them to meet in New York City the following October to implore Parliament to rescind the law. New Hampshire declined the invitation, and the governors of Virginia, North Carolina, and Georgia refused to convene their assemblies in order to prevent them from choosing delegates.

Meeting in mid-July in a highly charged atmosphere, Gadsden and the other members of the South Carolina Commons House of Assembly debated the Massachusetts letter amidst scenes of high drama that are barely suggested in the sparse record of the event. One unnamed member audaciously proclaimed that the diversity of the colonies rendered the idea of a congress preposterous, but the majority thought otherwise. The specific arguments of individual members were not recorded, but one can assume that Gadsden was on his feet many times vigorously defending the positions taken by Patrick Henry and James Otis. A sympathetic contemporary said that Gadsden was unimpressive as an orator but that his "honest zeal, ardor, and energy" influenced the Assembly to respond positively to the call for a congress.[7] If Gadsden followed the pattern of conduct he had established in his fight with Laurens at the end of the Indian wars, his manners must have been rude and his language pungent. He undoubtedly offended some members, but the majority shared his viewpoint.

The journal of the House recorded simply that Speaker Peter

Manigault handed the Massachusetts letter to a committee of ten chaired by Gadsden. On July 26 Gadsden reported that the proposal by Massachusetts was sound and recommended that South Carolina choose delegates. On August 2 the Commons voted to pay the expenses of three men who would attend, and six days later, Gadsden, Thomas Lynch, and John Rutledge were named. The Commons adopted and ordered printed resolutions against the Stamp Act, the American Duties Act, and the Currency Act. It did not give its delegates the authority to sign any documents that might be drawn in New York but instructed them to report the proceedings back to the Commons.[8]

On September 1, 1765, Gadsden and his colleagues boarded the brigantine *Carolina-Packet* bound for New York. Gadsden thought of himself as the spokesman for Charlestonians whose business enterprises, like his own, might be wrecked by the new mercantile laws. And he had a secret following among the middle-class artisans of the city who had already adopted him as their spokesman and hero. The opportunity to represent his colony allowed Gadsden to mingle his idealism with practical politics, to nourish his human frailties by blending a chance to serve with a desire for wealth and public acclaim. Concealed beneath his robust and benign appearance was a fiery temper that could explode if he did not have his way.

Thomas Lynch and John Rutledge were more temperate. Lynch, about thirty-eight, was a third-generation planter in South Carolina. He was an ardent champion of resistance to encroachments by the Crown, but he was moderate and judicious in his speech. At twenty-six, John Rutledge was the youngest member of the Congress. Trained for the legal profession in England, he had an understanding of the British constitution and would be quickly recognized as a valuable member of the gathering. There was no disagreement among the three South Carolinians. They passed several days together on board *Carolina-Packet* before a high tide lifted her over the bar on Wednesday, September 4. Eleven days later they reached New York. When the news of their safe journey arrived back in Charleston, Gadsden's Artillery Company fired three volleys of small weapons to celebrate.[9]

On October 7, all twenty-seven delegates from nine colonies

met at New York City Hall. Gadsden and James Otis were the most outspoken critics of the British Parliament there. Otis was one year younger than Gadsden, a graduate of Harvard, very knowledgeable in the classics and British common law, moody and unpredictable. Richard Henry Lee, Patrick Henry, Samuel Adams, and Isaac Sears, other extremists with whom Gadsden's name would eventually be associated, were not present at the Stamp Act Congress. The most important friend Gadsden acquired at the Congress was not a radical, but a man who was the epitome of learning and reason. He was William Samuel Johnson of Connecticut. A conservative lawyer, the thirty-eight-year-old Johnson had been trained for the clergy at Yale and had been awarded honorary degrees by Harvard and Oxford. He said that he would not support the Crown against the people, nor the people against the Crown. Other delegates included John Dickinson of Pennsylvania, and Thomas McKean and Caesar Rodney of Delaware. On the whole the body was more conservative than the public clamors suggested.[10]

Johnson's moderating influence upon Gadsden was countered somewhat by a pamphlet that Edward Tilghman of Maryland gave to the South Carolinian. A large landowner, Tilghman himself was scarcely an extremist, but he distributed an inflammatory pamphlet that had been published in Virginia. Gadsden was so impressed by it that he later had it circulated in South Carolina. Which pamphlet it was is not known, but it was probably Daniel Dulany's *Considerations on the Propriety of Imposing Taxes.*[11] Dulany argued that the colonists were not virtually represented in Parliament, as some English writers claimed, and therefore could not be taxed by that body. The controversy quickly became one over the nature of representation.

The first fruit of the Congress's long and tedious sessions was a Declaration of Rights and Grievances. Choosing their words very carefully, the writers affirmed their allegiance to the Crown and subordination to the British Parliament. But they reminded the king and Parliament that all of His Majesty's "Natural born Subjects," whether in England or in the colonies, had the "undoubted Right of *Englishmen*" to be taxed only by their own representatives. They therefore thought it their filial duty to address George III and to make applications to both houses of Parliament to procure repeal.[12]

If Gadsden could have had his way, the Congress would have stopped with the Declaration of Rights and Grievances and a petition to the king. He begged the other delegates not to offer petitions to the Lords and Commons, because, remembering his election controversy, he thought that the colonial assemblies were equal to Parliament and therefore not bound to petition it. He concluded, as had Dulany and others, that since the colonists were not represented in Parliament the laws of nature and the British constitution denied Parliament the right to impose upon them an internal tax to raise a revenue.

Gadsden was willing to acquiesce to the power of Parliament to regulate trade, but he adamantly refused to support the first, rejected draft of the Declaration, which specifically stated that the laws of Parliament were obligatory upon the colonies. He reluctantly accepted the use of the ambiguous phrase "due Subordination" to describe the relationship of the colonies to Parliament. To have accepted the first draft, he said, would have won him no thanks from the South Carolina Commons House of Assembly. Thomas Lynch and John Rutledge agreed with him.

The majority of other delegates, however, were willing to recognize the authority of Parliament. Robert R. Livingston of New York and William Samuel Johnson of Connecticut believed that their colonial charters were adequate protection against unconstitutional acts of Parliament. Gadsden responded that they were naive if they thought the king would grant exemptions claimed under the charters, and, furthermore, an appeal to the charters for protection would turn the colonies against each other. Since the charters were different, he said, all of the colonies should "stand upon the broad and common ground of those natural and inherent rights . . . of Englishmen."[13] He thought it would be blasphemy "to think a Good Being would create human nature to make it unhappy, and countenance its being deprived of those natural rights without which our existence would not be tolerable." Suggesting an acceptance of the deism that characterized some American thinkers of the time, he concluded, "Our cause may, therefore, be justly called the cause of God also."[14]

During the debates in New York, Gadsden revealed an intriguing new turn in his politics. The intransigence that had characterized his provincial fights with Lieutenant Colonel Grant and Governor Boone was gone. He had become a more practical politician and was willing to make compromises. The same arguments he had used in South Carolina and his forthright style remained, but he replaced the verbal abuse of royal officials in his own province with more moderate tactics. In New York he understood that he would need the help of other colonial leaders to achieve his goal, and he attempted to use his powers of persuasion with them. But more important, his willingness to compromise on points that he could not win is the first significant indication that he placed continental interests above provincial ones, a characteristic that became increasingly noticeable as the other events leading to the Revolution unfolded. Perhaps his education in England, travel with the Royal Navy, mercantile training in Philadelphia, and life in the cosmopolitan port city of Charleston all contributed to his broad perspective.

For the sake of unity, Gadsden agreed to compromise at the Stamp Act Congress. In the final vote he won one point and lost the other. The documents drawn up in New York clearly placed natural rights above charter rights, but the majority insisted upon sending petitions to the Commons and Lords as well as to the king. Gadsden thought the presentation of a united resistance was more important than the number and wording of the petitions sent to London. Any province that attempted to act separately should be branded "with ever lasting infamy," he wrote. "There ought to be no New England man, no New Yorker, *etc.* known on the Continent, but all of us Americans."[15]

The South Carolina representatives were eager to report to the Commons House of Assembly in Charleston as soon as possible. When a messenger informed them that their Assembly would convene on October 28, they conferred and decided that Gadsden should rush home as soon as possible after the Stamp Act Congress adjourned on October 25. On October 27, he left New York in a small, crowded schooner, but the cautious captain "stretched too far to the Eastward" to avoid Cape Hatteras, and Gadsden did not reach Charleston until November 13, long after the Assembly had adjourned. Forty-eight hours later, Lynch and Rutledge arrived after a short passage from Philadelphia.[16] They waited until the Commons reconvened near the end of the month to make their report.

In the interim before the Commons met, Gadsden learned

about the events that had transpired in Charleston during his absence. At the very time he was searching for constitutional redress in New York, the local Sons of Liberty were rioting in his hometown. They were drawn from the artisans or "mechanics" of the colony, the craftsmen who comprised perhaps 20 percent of the city's population. They were a small middle class, talented and prosperous, but not wealthy. Among them were shipwrights and coopers, makers of candles and leather goods, silversmiths and cabinetmakers, house painters and portrait painters, and occasionally printers such as Peter Timothy. While some were aided by British mercantile laws, others found themselves in competition with their counterparts in the mother country. The shortage of currency hurt them far more than it did the merchants and planters. Even slavery sometimes worked to their disadvantage. Most of them trained slaves as their assistants and frequently sold them after their value had appreciated, only to discover that the new owners placed the skilled slaves in competition with their former masters.[17]

The mechanics paid sufficient taxes to vote, but they did not have the wealth or support necessary to be elected to the Assembly. Some believed that their role in society was not commensurate with their skills or proportionate to the amount of taxes they paid. They were the unpredictable element, the people least likely to fear change. No one of their own group emerged as a leader, but the writings of Christopher Gadsden in Peter Timothy's *Gazette* often seemed to express their feelings. They adopted Gadsden as their spokesman.

The secrecy with which the Sons of Liberty evolved obscures its origin. Writing in 1822, the son of one of the members said that Gadsden had met with them in 1764.[18] That date is probably correct. The Currency Act of 1764 would have had a profound impact upon the mechanics and artisans long before it would have touched the merchants and planters. The chances are that Gadsden met with them in 1764 to discuss the adverse effects of the stricture on the currency and to plan what could be done. Gadsden and the mechanics were already members of the Fellowship Society, which had been organized in 1762 to provide help for the poor. Many of the members of the Fellowship Society joined the Sons of Liberty. Several of the mechanics were also members of Gadsden's Artillery Company. The Fellowship Society and the Artillery Company were the parent groups from which the Liberty Boys sprang.[19] Although Gadsden himself was in New York when most of the rioting occurred in Charleston, the Sons of Liberty were demanding the political changes about which Gadsden had instructed them before he left for the Stamp Act Congress.

The impetuous Gadsden and the restless mechanics made an explosive combination. The example of the northern provinces, which earlier and even more vigorously resorted to such violent actions as the virtual destruction of Governor Thomas Hutchinson's house in Boston, had a definite if delayed effect in Charleston. Although Gadsden was away from Charleston from September 4 through November 13, his mechanics were as eager to use tar and feathers as he was to use pen and ink. In November, Bull wrote that before the reports came from New England, "the People of this Province . . . seemed generally disposed to pay a due obedience." By the "artifices of some busy spirits," he added, "the minds of men here were so universally poisoned with the principles which were imbibed & propagated from Boston and Rhode Island" that "the People . . . resolved to seize & destroy the Stamp Papers."[20]

Late on Friday evening, October 8, *Planter's Adventure*, reported to be carrying a stamp officer and stamps or stamped paper, dropped anchor under the guns of Fort Johnson. The next morning the first rays of the sun illuminated a 20-foot-high gallows that had been erected in front of Dillon's Tavern. Hanging from the gallows was an effigy of a stamp distributor. On the effigy's right was the figure of the devil, and on the left, a boot with a head dressed in a blue bonnet upon it. A label that read "Liberty and no Stamp-Act" was attached to the front of the gallows. To the rear was the warning: "Whoever shall dare attempt to pull down these effigies, had better been born with a mill-stone about his neck and cast into the Sea."[21] In the evening the protestors, taking down the exhibit, hauled it in a wagon drawn by eight or ten horses and followed by a procession estimated at 2,000 people. They continued to the green where the effigies were committed to the flames, as the day ended with the muffled bells of St. Michael's giving a touch of solemnity to the proceedings.

The spirit of Gadsden carried the day. William Bull thought that "these very numerous assemblies of the People" were "animated by some considerable man who stood behind the curtain."[22] But Henry Laurens soon had occasion to be more specific. The Liberty Boys heard a rumor that the stamps had been removed from Fort Johnson to Laurens's house. When Laurens would not grant them entrance to his home, they searched his outhouses and cellar where they found no stamps but consumed his supply of fine wines and liquors. Laurens described how one of the mobsters, taking hold of his shoulders, "said they love me and everybody would love me if I did not hold with one Govr. Grant. This provoked me not a little as it exhibited to me the cloven foot of a certain malicious villain acting behind the curtain."[23] The mobster's reference to James Grant, around whom the first Gadsden-Laurens quarrel had centered, caused Laurens to think that Gadsden was the man who "could be reached only by suspicion." Laurens's aversion for the Stamp Act was matched by his dislike for rich men who "too often make Use of the poorer Sort for Purposes of their own." He deplored the "dark Steps" of those "*zealous, untrained* Sons of Liberty, who had honoured me with that irregular Visit."[24]

Christopher Gadsden was hurrying home from New York, too late to witness the demonstrations of the Liberty Boys. As for the protests that had occurred in his absence, however, he had no complaint. He wrote his friend William Samuel Johnson and agent Charles Garth that "the friends of liberty" in Charleston were "as sensible as our brethren to the Northward." The "true sons of liberty among us" had not done "the least mischief," he said. South Carolina had more "cunning, Jacobitical, Butean rascals" than did her sister colonies, but he hoped that those "wretched miscreants" would be frustrated. "Nothing will save us but acting together," he concluded.[25]

In the elections held during his absence, Gadsden had been chosen to represent St. Paul's Parish in the Commons House of Assembly. When the Assembly convened on November 26, he presented a report on the proceedings of the Stamp Act Congress, including the minutes, the Declaration of Rights and Grievances, and the addresses to the king, Lords, and Commons. The Commons House, with the exception of William Wragg, agreed to the whole and ordered their speaker to sign the petitions. The next day those documents were enclosed in a letter to Garth from the Committee of Correspondence and put on board *Charming Charlotte* bound for England. The House then passed resolutions thanking its representatives to the Stamp Act Congress and approving their conduct in New York.[26]

In South Carolina, as in New York, Gadsden plunged into the struggle to unite the forces of resistance. He was the most active man in the Commons House of Assembly.[27] With Charles Pinckney, John Rutledge, James Parsons, and Thomas Wright, he wrote resolutions condemning the acts of Parliament that materially affected the liberties and properties of British subjects in America.[28] On December 16 Gadsden wrote a letter from the Committee of Correspondence to Charles Garth urging him to work with the other colonial agents to bring about the repeal of the Stamp Act. He emphasized the importance of maintaining the independence of the provincial legislatures, the necessity for colonial unity, the ill consequences that Great Britain herself would suffer from the Stamp Act, and the continuing loyalty of the colonies if the mother country would treat them in a constitutional manner. South Carolina was asking for nothing more than rights "belonging not virtually but actually & efficaciously to us," he said.[29] Gadsden wished to counter the British doctrine of virtual representation, the idea that every member of Parliament represented every citizen of the empire. In their private discussions at the Stamp Act Congress, the representatives had agreed that they were not asking for the privilege to send voting members to Parliament, but for the repeal of the Stamp Act.[30]

While the controversy lasted, all business and legal transactions that required the use of stamps came to a halt. The courts were idled, newspaper presses fell silent, and dozens of ships, many with valuable cargoes, accumulated in the harbor. Gadsden suspended his own mercantile business until the crisis passed. In March 1766, Peter Randolph, surveyor general of customs for the Southern District, finally granted permission for ships to sail without stamped paper. Scottish merchants apparently attempted to circumvent the slowdown in Charleston and circulated rumors in England that the Carolinians would soon succumb to the stamp law. Gadsden liked those merchants no more than he liked the Scottish general during the Cherokee wars. He judged the Scots to be opportunists, eager to amass fortunes to be spent in England and indifferent to the welfare of the province, and he warned a private correspondent in England that their reports should not be accepted as representative of sentiment in South Carolina. The Grenville ministry "must have thought us Americans all a parcel of Apes and very tame Apes, too," he wrote, "or they never would have ventured on such a hateful, baneful expedient."[31]

To prove to the mother country that her subjects in America were not a parcel of tame apes, Gadsden worked for a complete boycott of British goods. Nonimportation agreements had already been signed in New York, Boston, and Philadelphia. Although the sentiment in favor of nonimportation ran high in South Carolina, the Stamp Act was repealed before any formal agreement could be made. In the meantime Gadsden turned to the public press to sustain the voluntary boycott already in progress. At the head of his column in the *South-Carolina Gazette and Country Journal* on February 11, 1766, he emblazoned the phrase "AUT MORS AUT LIBERTAS" — Liberty or Death. Gadsden was writing almost ten years before Patrick Henry's use of the same phrase echoed throughout the colonies. Gadsden used the nom de plume "Homespun Free-man," implying that if the colonists wished to enjoy the rights of free men they should dress in blue homespun rather than imported black cloth.[32] In South Carolina "the Family of the Homespun's and that of the Freeman's" had intermarried to "drive their Monsters before them," he bragged. "Help our industrious Family, my dear Friends, for God's Sake; by wearing Homespun as much as possible."

Homespun Free-man was especially infuriated with Georgia for not joining the resistance. Since he himself had sent copies of the proceedings of the Stamp Act Congress to Georgia, Gadsden looked upon Georgia's "Apostasy" as a personal affront. Despite some activity by the Sons of Liberty, Georgia was the only colony where the stamps were actually sold. Gadsden roundly condemned the Georgians for obeying the law simply because the "pensioned Government" there told them to do so. "Poor G[eor]gi]a, G[eorgi]a, How have you out cunninged yourselves." Gadsden thought that the cunning of English placemen was more dangerous to the liberties of British subjects in America than military force could ever be. Georgia was the prime example, a "broken Reed . . . deluded and bullied" out of the rights and privileges of Englishmen. "Like Esau of old," she had sold her birthright. Only cowards, sissies, and English placemen would submit to the Stamp Act, he continued. Posterity would curse them. "Let us not . . . bow the Knee to Baal, and tamely submit to a Yoke that our brave uneffeminated Fathers never wore," he pleaded.[33]

Henry Laurens thought that Gadsden had gone insane. He wrote Gadsden's former adversary James Grant: "Your old friend Philo I think is now ten times mad[d]er than ever he was. I'm sure he thinks himself nothing less at this time than Brutus or Cassius."[34]

Despite the hundreds of words Gadsden had published on February 11, he still had more to say. On February 18 and March 4, 1766, he placed identical advertisements in the *Country Journal* for a pamphlet on the history of Carolina. The author, Homespun Free-man, would prove that if Carolinians would· "now behave with only *half*" the "Spirit and *Constancy*" of their ancestors, they would leave their own children free. The pamphlet would also prove how the loss of civil liberty would soon lead to the loss of religious liberty. The "*unfeeling* Rich" could move away, but "the Middling and poor People" would be left to be "the ASSES to bear the Burdens not of one, but a thousand Masters."

The crisis abated, apparently causing Homespun Free-man to abandon his plan to write the pamphlet, but the readers of the *Country Journal* in the spring of 1766 learned that Gadsden had not finished his say. On February 25 he urged planters and merchants to deal with no one who used "those *worse* than pestilential, those *Liberty-destroying Stamps.*" All of "*unstampt* America" had declared "the Stamp-Act UNCONSTITUTIONAL, and the Stamps a BADGE of Slavery." Those who wished to obey the law should be compared to "unbroke Asses, upon whose Backs it is extremely difficult to lay the *first* Sack, but *that one fixed*, a *second* may be put on with less Difficulty, a *third* with still less; and so on till you be completely the very tame silly Drudges that Ministry designed to make you." Resistance to such encroaching power of the ministry "ought to be dearer to us than Life itself." Again on April 1 the aroused patriot urged his fellow subjects not to accept any compromise "as a *temporary Expedient*." He feared that any submission to taxation for revenue would give the king's ministry an opening sufficient "to drain us of all our Specie, and to entail . . . hungry Time-serving Place-Men upon us, as . . . *Ministerial* Spies." Then South Carolina would become like Georgia, "*that milldewed Ear blasting its wholesome Brother.*"

To increase pressure for repeal of the Stamp Act, Gadsden wrote to private correspondents in England. These letters, only two of which survive, were more temperate than his outbursts in the Charleston press. It would be impossible to alienate South Carolina's affection for her "*dear* Mother Country," he said in one of them. "We have therefore generally flattered ourselves that . . . your Bowels would again Yearn over us as Brethren and Nature compel you to . . . repeal the dreadful Sentence." Gadsden did not want his correspondent to think that he wanted the law repealed only for his own financial gain; he would sacrifice his entire estate "on the Altar of Liberty & in the Cause of my Country" if necessary. He said that the majority of the people in Charleston agreed with him; those who did not were royal officials, the "pensioned part" of the population.[35]

Henry Laurens was not a pensioned member of the population, but neither did he agree with Gadsden. Although Laurens disliked the Stamp Act, he disapproved of the rioting. In 1766 he apparently preferred to obey the law rather than suffer the confusion that resulted from the closing of the courts and the port. He thought that the rioters were innately irrational and often drunk. He complained that his neighbor Gadsden and "the Secretary of the Post Office," presumably Peter Timothy, did "not slacken in their opposition to the . . . Stamps." Sometimes, too, these vigilant gentlemen were "a little humm'd too, as the phraze is," by certain deceptive notices calling for meetings to be held at Bacchus Tavern. On one such "artfully made" occasion, Laurens said that Gadsden made a fool of himself: "my neighbor who attended & plumply took the Chair—as if of right it did to him belong—was exceedingly Chagrin'd to find that nobody knew what they were conven'd for; . . . he grew very crabbed which it seems made other folks laugh & me too when I heard it." Laurens suggested that the publication of a copy of the Stamp Act, which could not be found in Charleston, would help "to set those poor people right" on the "merits of the cause."[36]

The unavailability of a copy of the Stamp Act led the Commons

House to launch a belated attempt to deny its legality by questioning its very authenticity. On January 22, 1766, nearly four months after the Stamp Act Congress and the local riots, the Commons sent a message to Lieutenant Governor Bull inquiring if he had received the Stamp Act from the secretary of state, the Lords of Trade, or in any other authentic manner. In reply to this message, delivered by Gadsden and Thomas Bee, Bull explained that he had received the act from Attorney General Egerton Leigh, who had arrived in June; he had also received it from Governor Thomas Boone, and he had no reason to doubt its authenticity. In response, Gadsden, reporting for a committee of the Commons, said that they did not think the manner in which it was received was authentic. As for Governor Boone, they were sure Bull would join them in thinking that "whilst he is out of the province he hath nothing to do with a government." On the twenty-eighth, Bull replied that he had consulted with the Council, was certain the act was authentic, and could not suspend its execution, but would use every measure to prevent any distress to the province.[37]

Since Bull would not retreat on that front, the resistance attempted to reopen the courts without using the stamps. They had been closed since November 13 because no stamps were available, and the chief justice refused to do business without them. Gadsden joined almost one hundred other Charleston merchants whose businesses were being ruined because they could not sue for debts, in a petition asking that the courts be reopened. Chief Justice Charles Shinner, an unpopular placeman, refused. Despite a valiant effort to overrule him, the Commons still lost because Bull and the Council backed the chief justice.[38]

The decision of Bull and the Council made Gadsden very bitter. He said that the Council was just a body "of Placemen and men of known arbitrary principles and very slender abilities." Toward Bull, Gadsden was more charitable. He thought the lieutenant governor was polite, a gentleman, and well loved in South Carolina. As an executive officer, however, Bull was "the weakest and most unsteady man I ever knew, so very obliging that he never obliged."[39] Despite Gadsden's complaint, Bull was under legal obligation to the Crown and refused to yield to those who would disobey the law.

But the Commons was as stubborn as the lieutenant governor.

Believing that the cause of liberty was at stake, it attempted to keep the issue alive by printing and distributing the resolutions and addresses of the Stamp Act Congress.

To more than half of the population of Charleston, however, the term "liberty" meant something very different from the constitutional rights of Englishmen. "It was feared there would be some trouble with the negroes," one diarist noted in December 1765.[40] In January 1766 some black men paraded through the streets of Charleston crying "Liberty! Liberty!" According to Henry Laurens, they were only mimicking "their betters." The frightened whites organized armed patrols to ride day and night for two weeks to prevent an insurrection. The episode ended, Laurens continued, with "the banishment of one fellow, not because he was guilty of instigating an insurrection but because some of his judges said that in the general course of his life he had been 'a sad Dog'—and perhaps it was necessary to save appearances."[41]

Gadsden was troubled by the contradiction between the existence of slavery and his belief in the natural rights of man. In the spring of 1766, after the fear of a slave insurrection and after a prohibitive duty on new slave importations had taken effect, he commented privately on the subject. He thought that South Carolina was weakened by her large slave population. "Slavery begets slavery," he said. He feared "whatever might have been the consequences" if the prohibitive law of 1764 had been delayed "a few years longer, when we had drunk deeper of the Circean draught and the measure of our iniquities were filled up."[42] But he did not offer to manumit his own slaves, nor did he advocate ending the "peculiar institution." In fact, he later increased his own holdings until he became one of the largest slaveowners in the state after the Revolution. Never again, insofar as the surviving evidence suggests, did he equate slaveownership with evil. Within the frame of his society and economic class, men could be virtuous, as he thought he was, and own slaves too. His remark in 1766 seems to have been prompted less by a guilty conscience than his concern that the influx of slaves would deflate their value and increase the chances of a rebellion. No insurrection occurred in 1766, but the fear of one lasted as long as the institution itself.

A more direct threat came from the white settlers in the backcountry. Coming from Ireland, France, and Germany and trek-king southward from Pennsylvania, they were filling the backcountry from Ninety-Six and the Congarees to the Broad and Saluda rivers. With their axes and their livestock, they roamed the forests, unlettered, unkempt, unbaptized, and un-afraid. Between them and the inhabitants of Charleston, there was a distance that could not be measured in miles. Without clergy, churches, courts, sheriffs, jails, or schools, the fron-tiersmen were without the benefits of civilization, and what they lacked, they greatly desired. They were provincials without the benefits of citizenship. Yet they were taxed at the same rate as the rich slaveowners of the metropolis. They helped support the comfortable clergymen of the city, although they themselves were without preachers to marry them; they journeyed at great ex-pense and inconvenience to Charleston for the most petty legal matters, and they were given no protection from the rogues and villains who moved freely among them. They were without repre-sentation in the Assembly; they were denied the vote of free men, for the polling places were at a great distance and sometimes when they journeyed there, they found the election over because they had been told the wrong day by "mistake."[43]

These people's spokesman was Charles Woodmason, who had first appeared in South Carolina in 1752. After struggling for ten years to become a merchant and planter, he had gone bankrupt. But he made friends among the royal placemen in Charleston and got an appointment as justice of the peace, a position in which he earned notoriety for being a moral reformer who closed down Mary McDowell's "receptacle for lewd women," or brothel, in Pinckney Street. Ambitious for a higher office, he applied for a job as stamp distributor in 1765 before he knew anything about the popular reaction to the Stamp Act. But Woodmason was refused that job and soon fell into popular disfavor because he had applied for it and because he remained friendly with the royal judges. He then decided to become a missionary to the backcountry and went to England late in 1765 to take holy orders. Returning to South Carolina in June 1766, he began his work in St. Mark's Parish.[44]

Woodmason thought that the Liberty Boys and their Gadsden, "the Scriblerus of the Libertines," were great hypocrites. "While these provincials were roaring out against the Stamp Act & Impositions of Britain on America, they were rioting in Luxury and Extravagance—Balls—Concerts—Assemblies—Private Dances—Cards—Dice—Turtle Feasts—Above all—A Playhouse—was supported & carried on."[45] Money which was being so sinfully wasted, Woodmason thought, should be used to bring civilization to the backcountry. The backsettlers had no use for the Sons of Liberty. "Their Throats bellow one thing—But their Hands would execute the reverse. . . . These are the Sons of Liberty!—On Paper, and in Print—But we will never believe them such," Woodmason said.[46]

Despite Woodmason's complaint, Gadsden and others in Charleston were sympathetic with the plight of the backcountry. In February 1766 Gadsden served on a committee of the Assembly to bring in a bill to establish circuit courts for the remote parts of the province, and about the middle of March, he reported a bill to establish courts in Granville and Craven counties and at the Congarees.[47] These bills and other legislation were swamped by the Stamp Act crisis, as Woodmason commented. "Ev'ry thing lay suspended till the Repeal of the Stamp Act—for they seem'd resolv'd to starve themselves, to starve their Mother Country."[48]

The excitement surrounding the repeal of the Stamp Act early in May temporarily drowned the complaints from the backcountry. British merchants who were anxious to collect debts and sell goods to the nonimporting Americans began to petition Parliament for relief. When the Rockingham ministry came in, William Pitt, whose support Rockingham needed, arose from his sickbed to rejoice that America had resisted. The power to tax was not part of the legislative power, he said, and a "distinction between legislation and taxation" was "necessary to liberty."[49] Shortly, Caleb Lloyd, the erstwhile distributor of stamps in South Carolina, was informed that the ministry "had the strongest Inclination to give all the Redress in their power. . . ."[50]

When Gadsden heard that the Stamp Act had been repealed, he almost fainted.[51] To bring about that repeal he had left no stone unturned. He had labored in the Stamp Act Congress and the South Carolina Commons House of Assembly, encouraged the riots in the streets, exhorted mechanics, merchants, and planters to boycott British goods, and addressed letters to acquaintances in England who might help. For ten months he had worked himself into such a frenzy that the sudden news of victory almost left him in a state of shock. Whether he joined the celebrants who once again took to the streets is unknown, but surely no one could have been more excited than he. Henry Laurens dryly remarked that the victors were "insolent enough."[52]

Gadsden and his colleagues who had attended the Stamp Act Congress were the heroes of the hour. The city named Gadsden, Rutledge, and Lynch streets in their honor. The Commons requested them to sit for their portraits, which were to be drawn at full length and preserved in the assembly room.[53] The Commons also shifted some of the glory to the friends of liberty in London; it appropriated £1,000 sterling to erect a marble statue of William Pitt in Charleston. On June 6 Gadsden was appointed to a committee to prepare an address thanking the king, but not Parliament, for repealing the hated law; on June 20, for the committee, Gadsden praised the king for his "great goodness" in "graciously relieving" the people of the Stamp Act.[54]

The rejoicing spilled over into the celebrations that greeted the arrival of twenty-four-year-old Lord Charles Greville Montagu, the royal governor, and his bride. They arrived on June 11, amid the salutes of cannon, the ringing of bells, and the display of colors. Accompanied by Captain Gadsden and his Artillery Company, Lord Charles paraded to the State House, where he was joined by other distinguished persons who escorted him to Dillon's Tavern for the afternoon. Two weeks later, Montagu had "the pleasure of informing" the Lords Commissioners "that all riots and Tumults are at present subsided here."[55]

Yet all was not well. Gadsden and the Sons of Liberty were not so dizzied by the celebrations that they overlooked the ominous Declaratory Act. Passed by Parliament for "better securing the dependency of his Majesty's dominions," it provided "that all resolutions, votes, orders, and proceedings in any of the said colonies or plantations whereby the power and authority of the Parliament . . . to make laws is denied or drawn in question, are and are hereby declared to be utterly null and void." Nothing could be more specific. A few carefully chosen phrases could fix the supremacy of the king and Parliament to a degree never anticipated before the Stamp Act. Soon the determined Gadsden met with William Johnson; Tunis Tebout, Johnson's partner in the blacksmith business; Daniel Cannon, a carpenter and the oldest and most influential mechanic in Charleston; Edward Weyman, upholsterer; and some twenty-one other painters, coachmakers, saddlers, and wheelwrights. They gathered under a live oak tree in Isaac Mazyck's pasture in Hampstead on Charleston Neck, then a suburb not far north of Ansonborough. These men constituted the nucleus of the Sons of Liberty; their meeting place was known thereafter as the Liberty Tree.[56]

Describing that meeting under the Liberty Tree more than forty years later, George Flagg, a painter who was there, said Gadsden "harangued them at considerable length, on the folly of relaxing their opposition and vigilance, or of indulging the fallacious hope that Great Britain would relinquish her designs or pretensions." Gadsden warned the somber group that it would be absurd to rejoice "at an act that still asserted and maintained the absolute dominion of Great Britain." They should be prepared for "a struggle to break the fetters whenever again imposed on them." His speech "was received with silent and profound attention; and, with linked hands, the whole party pledged themselves to resist."[57]

Gadsden wanted liberty, home rule, and self-government in all internal matters, but not independence. Perhaps the memories of those who said years later that he spoke out once for independence in 1763 and again in 1764 were correct.[58] Perhaps Gadsden did in a moment of passion declare for separation, but that moment passed quickly. Never during the Stamp Act crisis did he draw a distinction between natural rights and the rights of Englishmen. He was fighting for the "natural rights of Englishmen" and for the reconciliation of all Englishmen under the British constitution. Shortly after he returned from the Stamp Act Congress, he wrote William Johnson and Charles Garth that he hoped God would "send the desired success, and establish harmony once more between us and our Mother Country."[59] Like the Sons of Liberty in all the colonies, Gadsden and his followers in Charleston were battling for liberty everywhere in the empire, not just in their home provinces. "God grant that our stand may be of service to the cause of liberty in England," he wrote.[60]

Resting beneath Gadsden's idealistic whig politics was the

economic reality of his life as a merchant in Charleston. The real fear of economic chaos formed an easy buttress for the shouted constitutional principle. If the new British mercantile laws went unchallenged, Gadsden and hundreds more like him feared they might slip into a depression. The only plan of resistance that worked was nonimportation. While imposing distress in the mother country, it favored provincial mechanics by promoting domestic manufacturing and enabling merchants such as Gadsden to sell their surplus stock.[61]

Gadsden's own business enterprises were changing. He was selling his stores, attempting to purchase enough land to become a great planter, beginning to develop his real estate in Ansonborough, and earning extra money by acting as an agent for anyone who needed his services. He is certain to have been anxious about his own financial security, for in 1766 he did not know what the principal sources of his income in the future would be.

In South Carolina, widespread economic anxiety meshed with the reformers' demands for liberty to unleash a popular force. The merchants and planters wanted economic sovereignty, the mechanics wanted seats in the Assembly and security of their livelihood, the people in the backcountry wanted the privileges of citizenship, and the slaves simply wanted freedom. In his urgency to have the Stamp Act repealed, Gadsden played to all groups except the slaves and thus helped to initiate a revolution that he never envisioned, a revolution that continued far beyond his lifetime.

In 1766, however, Gadsden was content to have won a hearing in South Carolina and farther. He was now known throughout the colonies and even in London. Upon his return to Boston from the Stamp Act Congress, James Otis told Samuel Adams about the spirited South Carolinian. Although Gadsden was still a stranger to him, Adams felt a certain kinship with the man whom historians would eventually label "the Sam Adams of the South." Writing to Gadsden for the first time in December 1766, Adams praised him for his service in the Stamp Act Congress and his commitment to colonial unity. Samuel Adams, too, foresaw troubles to come and hoped that Gadsden would not allow the cordial spirit that the Stamp Act crisis had generated among the colonies to subside. He warned Gadsden to remember the "lurking Serpent," which "not noticed by the unwary Passenger" was ready to dart "its fatal Venom."[62] If Samuel Adams had known Christopher Gadsden well, he would also have known that Gadsden needed no such warning.

CHAPTER FOUR

Gentlemen in Homespun

The nonimportation crisis, which reached its climax in 1769, coincided with traumatic events in Christopher Gadsden's personal life and a new turn in his struggle for financial security. The deaths of his eldest son and of his wife, the building of a very large wharf adjacent to his property in Ansonborough, and the passage of the Townshend Acts in London brought out the best and the worst traits in his character. For comfort and strength he fell back upon his religion, his family, his friends, and the hope of losing himself in frenzied activities. He searched anew among the classics to support his belief that the colonists should boycott items upon which the British ministry had imposed an unconstitutional tax. His temper, his rashness, and his readiness to attack his enemies in the press flared to the same feverish pitch that it had during the stamp crisis, but surely much of his public emotionalism sprang from the frustrations of his private fate.

Christopher Gadsden, junior, died on August 20, 1766. His father was so grief-stricken that all the turmoil over the Stamp Act crisis became temporarily unimportant. Even Henry Laurens, who thought the boy's death was caused by the heat, was touched by the tragedy. "My Neighbor Gadsden has met with a very affecting stroke indeed in the death of a fine Lad his eldest Son last night," he wrote.[1] Laurens's son Jacky, who grew up to be Colonel John Laurens, was one of young Christopher's playmates. Perhaps Jacky and Christopher, junior, shared the same boyhood closeness that their fathers had known, but they would never have to test their youthful brotherhood in the arena of adult politics.

Gadsden was left with his wife Mary and their four children, Ann, Philip, Mary, and Thomas, ranging in age from three to nine. Gadsden's eldest daughter, Elizabeth, age nineteen, was now the only surviving child of his first marriage. In 1767 she married Andrew Rutledge, a younger brother of John Rutledge, who had been one of Gadsden's fellow representatives in the Stamp Act Congress. Andrew was a successful merchant, but apparently he had no strong political convictions. He died in less than five years after his marriage, and his childless widow was married to Thomas Ferguson on August 4, 1774.[2] Another merchant, Ferguson became one of Gadsden's most solid friends. The marriages of Elizabeth brought Gadsden into closer contact with the merchant's point of view. But whatever pleasure he took from his new in-laws and whatever hope he had for the future of his younger children were small consolations for the loss of his namesake.

To divert his mind from the death of his son, Gadsden began to build a great wharf on the Cooper River adjacent to his landholdings in Ansonborough.[3] The construction itself became the high drama of a determined man's struggle with the elements as he battled to forget his troubles and to achieve wealth and public esteem. He attacked the problem of building with the same boundless energy with which he had fought the Stamp Act, and ultimately he achieved the same success. Early in 1767 he advertised for 500 pine logs 16 to 18 feet long and from 10 to 12 inches thick. The following year he wanted 150 "very straight Pine Spars for Piles," and two years later he needed 3,000 pine logs 8 inches through at the thickest end and 15 to 20 feet long, freshly cut and with the bark stripped off. The next year he ordered 300 cords of green pine wood, five or six "Schooner Loads" of clean dead shells, and again, a few months later, 4,000 bushels of shells. In the midsummer of 1771, he advertised for ten good Negro spadesmen to work for three months. The first major test of the fitness of the structure came in the summer of 1770 when a violent wind and rainstorm that did considerable damage to the city did not harm the wharf.[4]

While the wharf was still under construction, Gadsden advertised for business. In the fall of 1767, he announced that he had framed a wharf at the north end of town which had every convenience, including space for two vessels to be loaded or unloaded at the same time. Business was good enough to prompt him to expand his operation. Planters, but not merchants, could store their rice for one week without charge, provided it was sold from his wharf with Gadsden acting as factor or agent. In the summer of 1772, however, he relinquished the factorage business at his wharf for one year only to Messrs. Gibbes and Hart while he concentrated on enlarging the structure itself. In March 1773 he advertised for 10,000 bushels of clean, dry shells, and before the end of September, he thanked God that his wharf had been extended to 840 feet, which he believed to be the largest and most convenient in North America. He could store 10,000 barrels of rice, and unless the weather was extremely bad, a vessel could be dispatched from any part of the wharf within an hour.[5] According to family tradition, the cost of construction was $20,000. On March 7, 1774, the *South-Carolina Gazette* reported that the *"stupendous work"* was "nearly completed" and was "reckoned the most extensive of the kind ever undertaken by any one man in America."

Dotted with so many wharves that it looked like a floating market, the Cooper River was the principal thoroughfare for bringing country produce to market and the perfect place for a country factor to build a wharf. Gadsden intended to serve the rice and indigo planters by keeping "stores" or warehouses on his wharf for the storage of their produce. To attract them he had to offer better facilities than the other wharfowners. Because he was their factor, his economic concerns became entwined with theirs; he was dependent upon the local population for trade and goodwill.

Building his wharf influenced Gadsden's political career in a way that he had not foreseen. It enabled him to combine his well-known leadership of the mechanics with his increased association with merchants and planters. Gadsden became the catalyst who could bring together the diverse minds of the mechanics, the merchants, and the planters to negotiate a nonimportation agreement after the passage of the Townshend Duties in 1767. But that would take time and require the support of the rank and file and the help of other leaders.

Wharf ownership, too, brought Gadsden into competition with

the great Scottish merchants whom he and many of his contemporaries already hated. As the favorite representatives of English and Scottish mercantile houses, their economic interests conflicted with those of the country factors, small merchants, and planters. Nor were the Scots likely to be sympathetic with the provincials' resistance to new British mercantile laws. They did not want to be paid in colonial currency and thus tended to prosper even more after the Currency Act of 1764.

One Scot, Captain Roderick McIntosh, journeyed from Savannah to Charleston with a devious plan: "That reptile in Charles Town, Gadsden, has insulted my country, and I will put him to death." When asked what Gadsden had done, he answered, "Why, on being asked how he meant to fill up his wharf in Charles Town, he replied, with imported Scotchmen, who were fit for nothing better."[6] The irate young man's friend persuaded him to return to Savannah, and whether Gadsden ever heard of the threat is unknown, but Gadsden is not likely to have been intimidated. Gadsden called the Scots "that detestable *Stuart* race! a race of pedants, pensioners and tyrants."[7] The failure of the Scots to agree with Gadsden's whiggish interpretation of the British constitution, not their attempt to monopolize trade, seems to have been what irritated him most, for the Scots did not control as much of the trade in South Carolina as they did in Virginia.

Despite the wealth they were accumulating under the trade laws of the empire, Gadsden and other South Carolina merchants increasingly found reasons to despise the royal placemen who were sent to Charleston to enforce the law. The man they hated more than any other was Sir Egerton Leigh, who had managed to become appointed both attorney general and judge of the Vice-Admiralty Court. Before the Stamp Act, Leigh's life in Charleston had been beyond reproach. He had come over with his father in 1753, eventually married the niece of Henry Laurens, acquired extensive property, become close friends with Laurens, and been elected to the Commons House of Assembly. During the Stamp Act crisis, however, Leigh had favored obeying the stamp law, thus wrecking his reputation. The offices of attorney general and judge of the Vice-Admiralty Court, which he held in 1767, were supposed to serve as checks upon each other, but when the same person held both positions they could not possibly check each other. When Leigh realized that the Commons and the British ministry were going to force him to resign the judgeship, he asked the Commons to raise his salary as attorney general. If the Commons did not grant his request, he threatened to secure the defeat in England of a circuit court bill that the Commons had just passed.

Since Gadsden had sponsored the circuit court bill to help the people in the backcountry, he was infuriated by Leigh's request. Gadsden arose in the Commons and violently accused the attorney general of having acquired his offices through immoral conduct in England and gross misbehavior in Charleston. Gadsden also alleged that Egerton Leigh's father, Peter Leigh, who had been chief justice of South Carolina from 1753 through 1760, had been as wicked as his son. After Gadsden's speech, the House easily defeated the motion to increase the attorney general's salary. The shaken Egerton Leigh went to the home of his friend Laurens the next day, March 31, "and in much Agitation of Body and Mind, complained of the malicious Aspersions thrown out against him, as well as upon the Memory of his Father." "I truly pitied him," Laurens wrote, "he wept—I endeavoured to console him, by saying that Mr. G— — was a Man of warm Passions—his Reflexions had met no Marks of Approbation, and I was persuaded that he himself was sorry for what he had said."[8]

Gadsden was not sorry, and within less than a year Laurens himself had a major dispute with Leigh. Three vessels which Laurens owned or in which he was a partner were seized by the customs officials. The cases were brought before Judge Leigh, who was torn between his friendship for Laurens and his obligation to defend the customs officials. While purposely leaving loopholes that allowed Laurens's lawyers to win acquittal, Leigh also appeared to compromise his own integrity. The case was not a simple confrontation between an honest provincial merchant and a corrupt placeman; both Laurens and Leigh were probably honorable men who had stumbled into a web of British law that was hopelessly tangled by two of Leigh's subordinates. The episode ended the friendship between Laurens and Leigh and touched off a pamphlet war in which Laurens not only attacked Leigh himself, but the whole system of vice-admiralty courts, customs officers, and imperial administration. The British ministry forced Leigh to resign as judge of the Vice-Admiralty Court in September 1768, but there was no royal official wise enough to repair the damage.[9]

The British ministry and many members of Parliament were not unmindful of the disturbances in America. In January 1767, when Chancellor of the Exchequer Charles Townshend revived an old idea to impose customs duties upon certain items sold in the colonies, he met with powerful opposition in Parliament. Townshend hoped to relieve the burden on the British taxpayer by forcing the provincials themselves to pay a greater share of the cost of their government; he also wanted to reestablish the principle that Parliament could tax the colonies. He proposed a customs tax on glass, lead, painter's colors, paper, and tea. Some members of Parliament remembered too vividly the disturbances after the Stamp Act, some wanted to consult with the British East India Company before placing a tax on tea, others questioned using the revenue to pay part of the salaries of royal officials, and still more simply wanted Townshend to fail for political reasons. Not until June did the American revenue bill receive a successful third reading and the royal assent. While the bill was being discussed in Parliament, Charles Garth had informed the South Carolina Commons of its progress. Not a single one of the provinces attempted to block its passage.[10]

The opposition to the Townshend Acts that gradually evolved in South Carolina was caused directly by the suffering that stemmed from the Currency Act of 1764. The prohibition against printing paper money gradually began to deprive all the colonies of an adequate amount of currency and to endanger the economic prosperity that had existed in South Carolina for two decades. In 1769 the Commons House again began to print money illegally to replace the notes in its permanent fund of £106,500 that were lost or worn out, creating a desperate shortage of cash. The mechanics suffered first from the shortage, but by 1769 the merchants and planters were also in dire straits.

When South Carolina's act allowing the currency to be reprinted was presented to the Privy Council in November 1770, the Crown disallowed it. The Commons did not withdraw from circulation the reprinted currency; in fact, it printed more the following year. But the angry colonials were now ready to enter an association against the Townshend Acts. Charleston began a systematic boycott of the taxed items not only to prove a constitutional point but also to lessen the demand for paper currency in the province and stop the drain of coin to England.[11]

Boston protested the Townshend Acts first, followed by New York and Philadelphia, but Charleston moved slowly down a long path to nonimportation. On July 10, 1768, the Commons debated circular letters it had received from Massachusetts and Virginia. These letters, the stronger of which originated in Virginia, expressed an opinion in favor of resistance, called for an exchange of views, and invited the other colonies to join the demand for redress. Peter Manigault, speaker of the Assembly, wrote Massachusetts and Virginia that South Carolina had already instructed her colonial agent to join with the other agents to obtain repeal of the acts. In the meantime, Lord Hillsborough, secretary of state for the colonies, ordered Massachusetts to rescind her circular letter and instructed every royal governor to warn his assembly against seditious communications that tended to inflame the people. By a vote of 92 to 17, the outraged Massachusetts legislature rejected Hillsborough's command.

In Charleston, Christopher Gadsden, Peter Timothy, and the mechanics swung into action. Preparing for the election of a new Commons House of Assembly on October 5, they joined with a number of small merchants to organize the first political party in South Carolina. In what amounted to a nominating convention, they selected as candidates from St. Philip's Parish, Gadsden, Thomas Smith, Sr., and Hopkins Price; for St. Michael's they chose Thomas Savage and Thomas "(Broad Street)" Smith. Thomas Smith, Sr., was a small merchant and a member of the Library Society; Hopkins Price was a tanner and cobbler who later became a small merchant. The candidates from St. Michael's were both successful merchants. The names of Henry Laurens and Charles Pinckney were proposed, but they did not get enough votes to be nominated. Pinckney was a lawyer and wealthy planter who had not supported the opposition to the Stamp Act.

In the election, Gadsden was chosen, apparently with no opposition from either side. Thomas Savage also won, but the Smiths and Price were defeated. Both Laurens and Pinckney, who had been rejected by the mechanics, won in the election. Although

Laurens, according to his biographer, wrote "almost like a Gadsden or an Adams" in opposition to the Townshend Acts, he had no use for the mechanics' party caucus. It was "a grand barbecue . . . given by a very grand simpleton," he said.[12] The mechanics held their "grand barbecue" in Dillon's Tavern on Saturday, October 1, 1768. After agreeing upon their candidates, they "partook of a decent Entertainment" and then journeyed to the Liberty Tree where they elected Gadsden as their "president." Returning to town at eight o'clock in the evening, the revelers drew up before Lieutenant Governor Bull's door where their "president" gave a toast to the ninety-two members of the Massachusetts legislature who had voted not to rescind their circular letter. Gadsden's toast was followed by three loud huzzas. When they reached Robert Dillon's Tavern, they again halted, and their leader gave another toast: "May the ensuing Members of Assembly be unanimous, and never RESCIND from the Resolutions of the MASSACHUSETTS NINE-TWO." Three huzzas were again given, and the whole company repaired to the Long-Room where they ordered forty-five candles to be placed on the table with forty-five bowls of punch, forty-five bottles of wine, and ninety-two glasses. Some of their toasts were to the notorious John Wilkes, allegedly an English friend of liberty, who in the *The North Briton, Number 45* had defied the king.[13]

When the newly elected Commons met in an atmosphere of sobriety on November 16, only twenty-six of the fifty-five members were present. Perhaps some of the members simply did not arrive in time for the meeting, but others probably avoided the session deliberately because their constituencies were not strongholds of nonimportation sentiment. The men present soon became famous as "the unanimous twenty-six." They included Gadsden, Thomas Savage, Henry Laurens, and Charles Pinckney. Benjamin Dart, Barnard Elliott, Thomas Lynch, Peter Manigault, and John Rutledge were also present. All were estimable men, usually rational, with comfortable fortunes. There were no hotheads among them. Gadsden himself believed that "the prevailing Opinion of thinking men in this Province" was to wait and hear what the new British Parliament would do.[14]

But Governor Charles Montagu, an inexperienced youth in poor health, overplayed his hand. He had just returned from a visit to Boston where he had consulted with Governor Thomas Hutchinson. Addressing the Commons, Montagu warned it to treat with contempt any seditious communication that it might receive from the other provinces. After Montagu left the chamber, Speaker Peter Manigault again read the letters from Massachusetts and Virginia. The Commons then appointed Gadsden, Laurens, Pinckney, Rutledge, and others to a committee which assured Montagu that "no paper or letter appearing to have the smallest tendency to sedition . . . has ever been laid before us."[15]

The House then locked its doors, voted approval of the Massachusetts and Virginia letters, framed an address to the king asking him to intercede with Parliament to bring about the repeal of the Townshend Acts, and sent a letter to Garth asking him to join the other colonial agents in a petition for repeal. Gadsden, Lynch, and Rutledge, the former delegates to the Stamp Act Congress, were the principal authors of these letters. The Commons ordered that the documents be printed, sent to Massachusetts and Virginia, and made public in South Carolina. When Montagu heard what they had done, he angrily dissolved the Assembly.[16]

Montagu reluctantly issued writs for the election of a new Assembly, but by a series of prorogations and an adjournment, it did not come into session until June 26, 1769. The "unanimous twenty-six" were again elected. Gadsden was appointed to a committee on grievances, which reviewed in detail the period from the time the Assembly was adjourned on February 12, 1768, to the present, enumerated the prorogations, and found them contrary to the meaning of the election act of 1721 and a dangerous precedent.[17] The Commons also refused Montagu's request that it provide barracks and "necessaries" for British soldiers who had been stationed in the city since the winter of 1768. Without winning any concessions from the Assembly, the ill Montagu sailed home to England for a long visit.[18] Scarcely had he sailed before the Assembly took up matters that were certain to widen the gap between the Crown and the colony. But the Assembly never proposed a nonimportation agreement.

Although Gadsden was very active in the assemblies of 1768 and 1769, most of his time was spent managing his property, expanding his wharf, and caring for his family. He was a dutiful husband and father. If he lacked a sense of humor and a willingness to compromise, perhaps he more than compensated with an unswerving loyalty to the persons whom he held dear. One can imagine that he found time to take little Thomas and Philip down to his wharf or on a boat ride to his plantation near Georgetown. Perhaps on occasion he took them into his library and helped them unravel the mysteries of Greek and Hebrew script. He did not neglect their religious training, for he went with the family to St. Philip's Church. Since he did not gamble, he probably did not waste any of his very limited leisure time at the horse races. Nor is it likely he went with his wife Mary to the romantic comedies that were often staged in a local theater. As a prominent citizen of Charleston, he must have circulated through many private homes where he enjoyed the pleasures of good food and good company and a temporary refuge from the burdens of business and politics. He was well acquainted with the fullness of life.

Less than three years after the death of Christopher, junior, however, Gadsden's private world was again shattered when his wife Mary died on January 17, 1769, "after a long and severe indisposition." What thoughts passed through his mind when he buried "one of the best of wives and most excellent of women" can only be imagined.[19] Mary was the mother of his four youngest children, and she had been his companion for almost fourteen years. Christopher himself was only forty-four when she died; Mary was almost ten years younger than he. Gadsden could take some comfort in the fact that his married daughter, Elizabeth, would help him care for the younger children, now ranging in age from eight to twelve. There were also house servants who could cook and clean and female relatives who could help ease the trauma of losing a mother. Gadsden himself was to remain a widower for eight years.

Outsiders did not comment upon Gadsden's grief, but newspaper editors from Charleston to Boston took note of Mary Gadsden's funeral. The bereaved husband stood beside the open grave dressed in blue homespun rather than the traditional imported black cloth. Gadsden's dramatic appearance was the first public indication of a nonimportation crisis in South Carolina. Peter Timothy's *South-Carolina Gazette* hailed "the patriotic example lately set by *Christopher Gadsden, Esq.,*" and the *Boston News-Letter* reported that the whole expense of her funeral "of the manufacture of England, did not amount to more than 3£10s, our currency."[20] The custom of wearing black mourning garments was so important in Charleston society that only a serious crisis could have driven leading citizens to abandon it.

A nonconsumption agreement appeared in the same issue of the *South-Carolina Gazette*, dated February 2, 1769, that carried the description of Mary Gadsden's funeral. The agreement urged Charlestonians to manufacture their own goods or purchase them from other American colonies and to discontinue entirely the use of mourning apparel. Exactly a month later the same newspaper reported that many people in the province were wearing homespun. On June 1, "A Planter" urged his fellow planters to wear their old clothes, patronize only American manufacturers, and thus compel the merchants to come into a nonimportation agreement by refusing to trade with them. Two weeks later, June 15, 1769, the *Gazette* reported that "Societies of Gentlemen" had agreed "to purchase no kind of British goods that could be manufactured in America and to clothe themselves in homespun as soon as it could be got."

Charleston's enthusiasm for nonimportation was not immediately shared by the backcountry. In 1767, Charles Woodmason, who had endorsed the formation of an extralegal group of vigilantes called Regulators, claimed that the country was full of "Whores and Bastards" and rogues who stole cattle, murdered farmers, chased whole families naked from their homes, and threatened the "Chastity of many beauteous Maidens."[21] Woodmason feared that the nonimportation debates would interfere with the passage of Gadsden's circuit court bill, which would establish circuit courts in the backcountry and help stop the rapines and pillages there. Despite Woodmason's apprehension, the circuit court bill was passed in July 1769, but it was not enforced until 1772. The three representatives of the backcountry who were seated in the Assembly in 1768 never really had the opportunity to participate in the political process because that body was so frequently prorogued.

Using the name "SYLVANUS," Woodmason published a public complaint in the *South-Carolina Gazette and Country Journal* on

March 28, 1769. He wondered if it were not paradoxical that the "Interior Inhabitants should pay Duties and Taxes" to a government in which they were not represented when that very government was protesting similar treatment at the hands of Great Britain. The "Men who bounce, and make such noise about Liberty! Liberty! Freedom! Property! Rights! Privileges! and what not" were at the same time keeping "half their fellow Subjects in a State of Slavery," Woodmason said. These "very Scribblers, and Assembly Orators" did not care "who may starve so they can but eat—Who sink, so they swim—Who labour, and are heavy laden, so they can keep their Equipages."

Gadsden answered Woodmason immediately. Using the name "AMERICUS BRITANNUS," in the same newspaper on April 4 he urged patience. The South Carolina Assembly was working for unity with her sister colonies, he said, and the possible violations of the voting rights of backcountry men in one parish did not mean that the Assembly condoned such violations or that a general lack of equitable representation prevailed in South Carolina. He hoped that the people in the backcountry could not be persuaded to turn against those who lived in the lowcountry. All South Carolinians, indeed all British Americans, must stand together, he argued, or they can be "rivited in a Slavery beyond Redemption."

In an unpublished reply to Gadsden, Woodmason sneered that "Have Patience! has for many Years been the Prescription of our Political Quacks." The backsettlers had rather "throw themselves under Protection of the British Parliament" than be "Subjects of a Junto in Charleston," he threatened.[22]

The tension between the backcountry and the lowcountry complicated the Revolution in South Carolina and later played a significant role in the state's politics, but during the nonimportation crisis the backsettlers seemed more inclined to follow Gadsden than Woodmason. Gadsden was attentive to their needs and eager to win their support.

Although Gadsden courted the backsettlers, he understood that the success of nonimportation would rest primarily upon agreements among planters and merchants. In a public letter printed in the *South-Carolina Gazette* on June 22, 1769, he addressed the planters, mechanics, and freeholders, and indirectly attacked the Scottish merchants. Signing himself "PRO GREGE ET REGE" (For the People and the King), Gadsden warned his fellow citizens that unconstitutional measures had been revived since the repeal of the Stamp Act, revenues were raised without the consent of those taxed, and the colonists were deprived of their "best inheritance, a trial by jury and the law of the land." South Carolina should join other colonies in a general resolution not to consume British manufactures. "Only be ROUZED from your sleep," he exhorted; "dare to SEE the *truth*, to SUPPORT the *truth*, and the God of truth will make you FREE."

England should take caution, Gadsden continued, lest she "drive her colonies to some desperate act." If the colonies were "disposed to be independent," then not even thirty of the mother country's best regiments could maintain control of the continent, he warned. He argued that in both King George's War and the French and Indian War the Americans had proved their military might against France, and he implied that they might prove it again against the parent country. The mother country should remember that the principal tie between herself and her colonies was the bond of trade, and she should understand also that in mercantile matters there were several other European nations who were better customers for the products of the colonies.

Gadsden then proposed a six-part nonimportation agreement. First, he suggested that the colonists give preference to buying items made in South Carolina or elsewhere in North America. Second, Americans should buy as few British goods as possible, and third, they should wear no mourning apparel and give no mourning gifts. Fourth, when buying British goods they should purchase only the cheapest items and only when absolutely necessary. Fifth, men should observe the strictest economy when buying articles for their wives, daughters, and younger children and when buying furniture that had not been manufactured in America. Sixth, all citizens should be particularly sparing in the use of tea, paper, glass, and painter's colors as long as the duties thereon remained.

On July 13, 1769, Timothy's newspaper published a reply to Gadsden. The author, who used the name "PRO LIBERTATE ET LEGE" (For Liberty and Law), made fun of Gadsden's peculiar style and urged him to "lay aside his warm disposition, and let prudence direct that share of sense he has." He warned against those who would show disloyalty to the king or raise the standard of liberty for selfish reasons. He criticized Gadsden sharply for disparaging the "importers of European goods," pointing out that Gadsden and members of his family had been or were importers and that the leading gentlemen of the colony had begun to make their fortunes in the mercantile way. And the writer laughed at Gadsden's reference to the ladies. "At least wear out your old silk gowns, purchase no new ones 'till this heavy storm is past . . . Great God! What strange ideas must have crept into the brain of our enthusiastic addresser!"

The opinions of a few people like PRO LIBERTATE were less damaging to the nonimportation movement than the disagreements among the planters, merchants, and mechanics. Before any nonimportation agreement could be reached, they would have to decide which items they could reasonably live without. In June and July they met separately to discuss the crisis. Finally, on July 22, all three groups came together under the Liberty Tree. Christopher Gadsden was present. He read aloud the agreement which all now said they were ready to sign. Then he reread it paragraph by paragraph for discussion. The gathering agreed to establish a General Committee of thirty-nine, composed of equal numbers of planters, merchants, and mechanics. The General Committee was charged with doing whatever might be necessary to enforce the new association.

Gadsden asked to be excused from service on the General Committee. He also asked to be listed as a merchant rather than as a planter; he probably wanted to set an example for the Scottish merchants who were not likely to sign. Gadsden did consent to serve with eight other persons, including three printers, who would circulate the subscription lists for signatures. Before the next issue of Timothy's paper went to press, 268 men had signed the agreement.[23]

The agreement called for the encouragement of American manufactures; no increases in prices; extreme economy; a ban on mourning goods; the nonimportation of slaves from Africa after January 1, 1770, and from the West Indies after October 1, 1769; no trade with transient persons after November 1, 1769; and no purchases from any resident who refused to sign the agreement within one month. Any subscriber who did not strictly adhere to this agreement "ought to be treated with the utmost contempt." The signers pledged not to break the association until all the objectionable acts of Parliament had been repealed.[24]

Gadsden's closest associates during the nonimportation debates were John Rutledge, Thomas Lynch, and John Mackenzie. Gadsden, Rutledge, and Lynch seemed to have developed common bonds during their service in the Stamp Act Congress that continued to hold. Gadsden was a merchant, Mackenzie and Lynch were wealthy planters, and Rutledge was a lawyer. These four provided the leadership for the rank and file; it was upon them that the opponents of nonimportation aimed their fire. Lieutenant Governor Bull thought that Gadsden, Lynch, and Mackenzie were the "tribunes of the people." He said that Lynch was "a man of sense" but "very obstinate in urging to extremity any opinion." Bull called Gadsden "a violent enthusiast in the cause," who viewed "every object of British moderation and measures with suspicious and jaundiced eye."[25]

Bull's analysis of Gadsden and his fellows was kept private, but William Henry Drayton soon dragged Gadsden and his friends into one of the most colorful and important newspaper battles of the revolutionary era. Born at Drayton Hall on the Ashley River, William Henry was educated at Westminster and Oxford. His fondness for play took precedence over academic interests, and he was not awarded a degree. He returned to South Carolina in 1764, married an heiress, and gambled so recklessly on the horse races that he was often in financial distress. He was eighteen years younger than Gadsden and had first taken his seat in the Assembly in November 1765, representing St. Andrew's Parish, on the very day that body heard Gadsden's report on the Stamp Act Congress.[26]

In the ensuing newspaper debate, the basic arguments of Gadsden and his protagonists drew upon the teachings of the classics, the Bible, the *Book of Common Prayer*, William Blackstone's *Commentaries on the Laws of England*, and the whig interpreters of the British commonwealth and Glorious Revolution. Gadsden put forth anew the same ideas he had used during his election controversy and the Stamp Act crisis and went one step more to explain how those ideas were relevant to the current dispute. The gist of his debate was that British citizens living in America could be taxed only by their own representatives; they were not represented in Parliament and therefore should not yield to the ministry's tax laws. To boycott British goods would hurt Great Britain more than the colonies; rather than creating economic chaos in America, the boycott would lead to the opening of avenues of trade outside the empire and to increased prosperity. If Great Britain did not withdraw her objectionable laws, Gadsden concluded, then the colonies should decide whether or not they wanted to be independent.

Gadsden's antagonists drew upon the same sources to argue that the boycott itself was illegal, unconstitutional, and as tyrannical as Gadsden was accusing the ministry of being. It would wreck the colony's credit and cause severe economic hardships for the very people whom Gadsden wished to help, they contended.

Both the protagonists and the antagonists generously interspersed their thousands of words of exhausting political debate with vigorous attacks upon the character and motivations of their opponents. Charges of ignorance, stupidity, selfishness, lying and lunacy were hurled with about equal force in both directions. The disputants were men who had wealth and power, or who desired it, but they were also men of integrity who were neither criminal nor crazy. In truth, the merchants, planters, lawyers, and mechanics who participated in the debate were virtuous men whose slanderous accusations against each other sprang from the heat of argument rather than documented facts. But their words provided much entertainment, as well as information, for the citizens of Charleston who scurried for their weekly newspapers in that summer and fall of 1769.

Signing himself "FREE-MAN," William Henry Drayton published his first pungent attack upon Gadsden in the *South-Carolina Gazette* on August 3, 1769. Drayton charged that the association was illegal, especially in its attempt to punish those who did not sign. This form of intimidation was like "the popish method of gaining converts to their religion by fire and faggot." Drayton said that Gadsden was a phony friend of liberty whose patriotism sprang from desire for "lucrative posts," implying perhaps a judgeship for himself in the backcountry. Drayton supported the authority of those who were in power in Great Britain and argued vigorously against Gadsden's interpretation of British history. Cromwell, "the *patriot* of *his day*," Drayton alleged, had actually enslaved his fellow subjects while pretending to give them greater liberties. The patriots who had risen from time to time in British history were opportunists and traitors, and Christopher Gadsden was no exception. Gadsden should be placed in the local facility for the insane, Drayton wrote, "and there maintained, at least during the ensuing change and full of the moon, at the public expense."[27]

"What pity it is," Gadsden responded in the next issue of the *Gazette*, that "the mamma of that pretty child . . . FREE-MAN . . . had not now and then whipt *it* for lying." Gadsden was incensed by Drayton's charge that he was only seeking lucrative appointments. "Fie upon that naughty person, fie upon him," Gadsden screamed. "Master Billy" was not only a liar but an obstacle to the passage of the circuit court bill, which Gadsden himself was sponsoring to help the people in the backcountry.[28]

Drayton lashed back at Gadsden, "the Hen-Hussy Kitty." Drayton thought that the "hussy must certainly have had a good time" sprinkling his "production" with false quotations and equally false understandings of British history. If Gadsden were a thinking, reasonable man, Drayton contended, "he would not have been seen, in the course of a few years, to assume the various unconnected characters of shopkeeper, soldier, farmer, statesman, founder, scribler, and buffoon—a mere pretender to wit." Drayton hoped that his "sanguinary friend Kitt" would come to his senses and follow the constitutional example set by Virginia. In that province, the nonimporters had met in Raleigh's Tavern and voted not to impose sanctions against those who refused to join the association.[29]

Young John Mackenzie then leaped to Gadsden's defense. A wealthy planter, he had been educated in England, owned two large private libraries in South Carolina, and was as knowledgeable of British history and law as anyone in Charleston. In his letter to Peter Timothy, he appealed to English constitutional principles from the Magna Charta on. His arguments were typical of those that had characterized the English whigs for centuries. Presenting a long list of grievances, he complained of a Vice-Admiralty Court that was as oppressive to the innocent as to the guilty, a military force that terrified citizens into servile submission, assemblies dissolved, juries superseded, and men dragged from their native country to be tried for treason. Machiavelli himself could not have "invented a plan on a broader bottom, for the total eradication of every trade of liberty." In a second "Letter to the People," Mackenzie called upon the colonials to "bring their haughty parent to a generous way of acting, if not of thinking, without having recourse to measures the least violent."[30]

The arguments of Mackenzie and Gadsden made sense to those people who were suffering under the Currency and Townshend Acts. Public opinion was running strongly in favor of the association. John Gordon, a merchant who imported goods that were used in the Indian trade, wrote James Grant prematurely on August 1, 1769, that "Mr. Gadsden, some years ago, fell on a plan of hatching poultry by an intensified heat but he recon'd on more chickens than came through the shell."[31] If the "chickens" were intended to refer to signers of the association, the intense heat that Gadsden had been applying since 1765 was getting results. Other than Crown officials, only twenty-one persons had failed to sign. One pro-association correspondent reported that only three or four of the nonsigners were planters with substantial property; the rest were "little Scotch shopkeepers of little consequence."[32] The General Committee had determined early in September to close the subscription lists on the seventh, and accordingly a list of the twenty-one nonsubscribers was published in handbills. William Henry Drayton, John Gordon, and William Wragg were on the list.

William Wragg, the wealthy planter who had been at odds with Gadsden at the time of his election controversy, determined to vindicate himself and on September 21, 1769, addressed a letter to Peter Timothy. The association itself was tyrannical and incommensurate with the tradition of British justice, he said. The subscribers were not only violating the liberties of nonsubscribers but also destroying customs that were beneficial to society. The use of mourning clothes was a custom long established and sometimes gave rise to serious reflection; he would, however, "heartily join in abolishing the . . . use of the bowl and tankard at funerals." Wragg hoped "that men of suspicious tempers, and pretending to a greater degree of shrewdness than their neighbors," meaning Gadsden and his friends, were not "groping in a labyrinth of errors."[33]

In the same issue of the *Gazette*, the angry Drayton announced that he had not been mortified at seeing his name in the handbill; rather, he considered it a public testimony to his resolution and integrity. He was not angry with the printers of the handbills, he said, but with "that harlequin medley committee" that had directed their publication and trampled upon "the sacred liberty of a citizen." He thought that men who could "'boast of having received a liberal education'" should make use of it and not consult "with men who never were in a way to study, or to advise upon any points, but rules how to cut up a beast in the market to the best advantage, to cobble an old shoe in the neatest manner, or to build a necessary house."[34]

John Mackenzie, who was a member of the General Committee, quickly answered Drayton. He argued that the association had been drawn up by intelligent, honest, conscientious men. Members of the association were not arbitrary and unjust; they had broken no law and they had as much right to enter the association as Drayton had to steer clear of it. The mechanics, whom Drayton had attacked without cause, had merely signed to protect their property.[35]

The mechanics were so infuriated by Drayton's insinuations that they were not fit to participate in the affairs of politics that they also entered the newspaper battle. They wondered if Drayton could claim any merit for having inherited a fortune. And they doubted that if he had to earn his bread with either his hands or his head he would be qualified to do so. They promised Drayton, as Drayton had Gadsden, a room in the asylum where he would be barred the use of pen, ink, and paper, lest he should aggravate his disorder. Their letter, signed "MECHANICKS of the Committee," seems to have hit Drayton in a sensitive spot; it was the only one that he did not reprint in *The Letters of Freeman, Etc.*[36]

Drayton ignored the mechanics and attacked their prompters, Gadsden and Mackenzie. Stunned by the sheer power of the opposition to him, Drayton now attempted to turn the ideas of John Locke, their favorite philosopher, against them. Arguing that the General Committee had displaced the Commons as the legislature of the province, Drayton said that the committee should be rejected because it did not serve the common good of the citizens. The philosophy of John Locke, the example of the Roman Empire, and the message of Christianity would all support his argument, he claimed. "Oh! my countrymen! suffer not an arbitrary power to get footing in this state: *Rome* . . . was enslaved by almost imperceptible degrees." Drayton begged the nonimporters to heed Locke's warning against unconstitutional assemblies, and to "*Do unto others, as you would they should do unto you.*"[37]

In the next two issues of the *Gazette*, Gadsden attempted to bury Drayton under a deluge of almost 12,000 furious words. In the context of the history of the British constitution, Gadsden reviewed the actions that Parliament had taken against the colonies and the petitions and protests that the Americans had sent to London. He discussed the natural and constitutional rights of all citizens of the empire, answered the arguments of the non-subscribers to the association, and explained why the merchants, planters, mechanics, and farmers in the backcountry all should stand solidly in favor of nonimportation.

Answering William Wragg's letters, Gadsden accused Wragg of being "constantly and uniformly" opposed to every measure that would "support the most essential rights and liberties of the people." For Wragg to insist upon the use of mourning apparel was to force the dead to enslave the living, he said. Wragg had no regard for the thousands of people in the province who had never worn mourning clothes; in fact, Wragg seemed to have nothing but contempt for the middle and lower classes. Gadsden did, however, agree with Wragg that a reduction in the number of "dram-shops" might be in order.

Gadsden then took up the case of "Mr. *G*.," John Gordon, a merchant involved in importing items used in the Indian trade. Gordon had signed several nonimportation agreements that the merchants agreed upon among themselves before the general meeting of merchants, planters, and mechanics under the Liberty Tree on July 22. He had, however, refused to sign the final agreement and thus found his name published in the list of nonsubscribers. Gordon had argued that if he gave up the Indian trade for only a season he would not be able to resume it. Gadsden said that Gordon would suffer no greater hardships than the other merchants who had signed; all of the signers would actually suffer less distress than their "oppressors" in Great Britain, and whatever hardship they did suffer was a small price for the recovery of their essential rights as British subjects. Gadsden hoped that Gordon would reconsider and "unite with us, in this common cause."

Attempting to unite all economic groups in the protest, Gadsden offered a perceptive analysis of the social structure of the province. He believed that South Carolina was divided into groups of planters, farmers, merchants, and mechanics. He attempted to prove that these four groups were interdependent and all entitled to the same privileges of British subjects. Without advocating social or political equality, he demanded that all persons in the province be given equal treatment under the law. He displayed such deep sympathy for the middle and lower classes, who were largely farmers and mechanics, that he inadvertently explained why they were so willing to follow his leadership. When the British constitution was upheld, middle- and lower-class peoples in the province enjoyed a better standard of living than did their counterparts in other parts of the world, he said. But when the British constitution was defied by the British ministry, the poor in South Carolina were the first to suffer. "When oppression stalks abroad, . . . tyranny . . . falls upon the honest laborious farmer, mechanic, and day labourer."

Gadsden defined a farmer as a backsettler who owned no slaves. He thought it was a happy circumstance "that the farmers, in our backsettlements, are become so numerous," because they would provide the province with a white population that outnumbered its slaves. The farmers had settled on small tracts of land which they would eventually subdivide among their children. Since their farms were so small, it was unlikely they would ever become slaveowners. Gadsden was slyly taking advantage of the constant fear of a slave insurrection among the planters to pressure them into cooperation with the farmers. Gadsden continued to explain that the farmers were "the most intrinsically useful people we have." In the future, the farmers would be more plentiful than the rich planters and their potentially rebellious slaves, and then the planters would "anxiously wish for much greater assistance, from the man in low circumstances."

Gadsden dealt harshly, but cautiously, with the planters. Since Wragg was a wealthy planter, Gadsden perhaps feared that other planters would be attracted to his point of view. Planters who could easily afford the rigors of nonimportation should set an example of frugality for the farmers, he said. The teachings of Christianity and the bonds of humanity demanded that the rich help their poor neighbors. The good of one group was also the good of the other. Gadsden implied that if the planters set themselves against the farmers in a class struggle, then the planters would be likely to lose much of their wealth and influence and the entire province would fail to recover its liberties.

Gadsden offered few new comments about the merchants and mechanics because those groups had already shown great enthusiasm for the association. He said the merchants should set the proper example for the mechanics, just as the planters should for the farmers. And he would write nothing more about the mechanics, because they had "exerted themselves nobly . . . in . . . promoting the common cause at this crisis."

The nonimportation crisis prompted Gadsden to raise more positively than ever before the question of independence. He hoped that South Carolinians would again be able to apply "the endearing epithet, mother," to Great Britain, but he strongly suggested that they should seek independence if Parliament did not yield to the pressure of the association. He said that "no slavery can be so galling, so mortifying, as that of brother to brother." He thought that the ministers themselves did not believe it was possible for an independence movement to develop in America, but he said that the "oppressive measures pursued" by the king's treacherous and wicked counselors tended to bring on, rather than prevent, American "independency." If Americans were driven to independence, it would be the fault of the mother country herself because "the sons of *British America* . . . would think that to be independent of *Great-Britain*, would be the greatest misfortune that could befal[l] them, excepting that of losing their rights and liberties; that indeed is, and must be, confessedly greater."[38]

Wragg replied immediately, vowing to continue "to pray for the glory and long life of his Majesty, the honour of the parliament, the welfare of *Great-Britain*, and every one of her colonies, and in particular for the peace of *Jerusalem*" in his native South

Carolina. He thought that Gadsden's thousands of words were an "incoherent discourse in his own peculiar, I need not say barbarous, jargon." He agreed that there were perhaps incompetent politicians serving the king, but he doubted that the British government was any more corrupt now than it ever had been. Certainly it was no worse than in the days when Gadsden's father had served it as collector of customs and when Gadsden himself had served as a purser on a British vessel. Corrupt politicians should be impeached, proved guilty, condemned, and decapitated, but the British constitution should not be destroyed by an unlawful conspiracy such as the association. Wragg said that he himself would continue to serve His Majesty's government even "though Mr. G. may think I ought to be sent to the devil for it."[39]

Gadsden fired back at Wragg with 3,000 more words, a barrage of quotations from Jeremiah, Cato the Elder, and Cicero, but no essentially new arguments. In a brief rejoinder, Wragg said that he took no pleasure in touching upon the foibles of men or the fallacy of their reasoning; if he did, he would indulge himself "by ranging at large over Mr. *Christopher Gadsden's* literary exhibitions." Drayton then sent a petition to the Commons complaining that he could not sell his rice since his name had been published in the handbill and asking for protection from the injuries done to him by the association. His petition, as Drayton himself succinctly noted, "passed in the negative." Late in December 1769, Drayton published his final complaint. "'Tis not because a man is always bellowing, liberty! liberty! that he is to be exalted into the rank of patriots!" he wrote. The committee had exhibited a spirit of persecution, was violating laws with impunity, and was threatening to create a "galling tyranny . . . upon their ruins."[40]

Drayton sailed for England on January 3, 1770. Two years later he returned to South Carolina as a member of the Council, and by 1775 he completely rejected his position during the nonimportation crisis and became an ardent patriot and one of Gadsden's staunchest friends. William Wragg never recanted. He retired to his barony in disgust. When he refused to become a patriot after the declaration of independence, the South Carolina provincial assembly banished him in the summer of 1777. As his ship approached the coast of Holland, a storm blew his young son overboard. Wragg drowned trying to rescue the boy. Mackenzie died in South Carolina on May 30, 1771, at the age of thirty-three. Gadsden, age forty-five, was only a few years past the mid-point of his life, destined to see his darkest predictions come true and to fight many more battles for what he believed was liberty.

In 1769 and 1770 Gadsden was a hero to some people in Charleston. Writing in the *South-Carolina Gazette* on August 17, 1769, one "Pythagoras" compared Gadsden to John Hampden, a seventeenth-century English statesman who had defended the forces of Parliament against King Charles I in the name of constitutional liberty. In a 1770 broadside, a Charleston poet, "Rusticus," celebrated "our GADSDEN" as a zealous patriot: "And Truth came mended from his Pen refin'd; / . . . / The Man was valu'd, honour'd, and carest." Whatever pleasure Gadsden may have taken from the adulation of a few local poets, however, could not obscure the fact that the association could have never come into existence without the cooperation and help of many others.

Despite the vigorous and often intelligent complaints of Wragg and Drayton, the nonimportation association in South Carolina was overwhelmingly successful. The General Committee met frequently in August and September to receive the subscription papers. Gadsden and his fellows acquired the signatures of most of the planters, merchants, and mechanics, and some farmers. Many legislators and judges signed the agreement; at least one member of the Council, Henry Middleton, resigned for that purpose; and nonimportation generally met with the sanction of the public. Except for Crown officials, those who fell under the ban of the clause against nonsubscribers were neither numerous nor important.[41] In 1770 the city's most eminent citizens chaired the meetings under the Liberty Tree. Gadsden was first in January. Henry Laurens presided at the May meeting and again at the final session in December.

The meeting on January 30, 1770, over which Gadsden was elected to preside, witnessed more excitement than any other. The major item of business involved the case of Alexander Gillon, an ambitious, young, Dutch-born merchant who received his mercantile training in London and had moved to Charleston to seek his fortune. Gillon had imported 100 pipes of wine, which arrived after the association deadline. Rather than store or reship it, Gillon asked the general meeting for permission to sell it in

Charleston. After an extended discussion, the meeting voted unanimously against him. It demanded that he sign an agreement to store the wine until the boycott ended. Reluctantly, Gillon did so. Although he later became a patriot during the Revolution, he always regarded Gadsden as a personal enemy.[42]

The handling of Gillon's case was typical of the peaceful and unanimous decisions that the subscribers made at their monthly meetings. All was enthusiasm for the cause. When the South Carolinians heard a rumor that the northern colonies were about to abandon their associations, they sent a circular letter to all the colonies urging them to remain firm. In mid-July, Lieutenant Governor William Bull acknowledged that he had received the act of Parliament repealing all of the Townshend taxes except that on tea, but not even this news disrupted the association. South Carolina did finally abandon it in December 1770. She was the last colony to do so; her decision to end the boycott was not unanimous, and enough resistance remained in Charleston to prevent any general importation of British goods before May 1771. Christopher Gadsden, Thomas Lynch, and John Mackenzie had voted not to abandon it.[43]

The association had worked, because Parliament did repeal all of the Townshend duties except the tax on tea. In South Carolina something of a consensus had developed. The success of the association rested in part upon a groundswell of popular support. Although Virginia planters had been active with merchants in bringing about a nonimportation agreement in that province, the associations in the remainder of the colonies were primarily the work of the merchants. South Carolina alone incorporated the assistance of all of her social and economic groups, save the slaves, in the resistance to the Townshend duties.[44]

As he had done during the Stamp Act crisis, Gadsden had fought personally to establish the resistance on as broad a base as possible. And he revealed once again that underlying his emotional language he was also a skillful, practical politician. He had deliberately and carefully brought together the merchants, planters, farmers, and mechanics.

In the decade since Gadsden's first criticism of official decisions during and after the Cherokee wars, he had developed a distinctive political rhetoric. His language was typical of that of the English whigs who had supported the British Civil War and the

Glorious Revolution in the seventeenth century. His reading had been dominated by the classics, the Bible, and whig historians. His terminology was similar to that of the seventeenth-century British liberals and of the growing number of American rebels in the 1760s. The loss of civil freedom, he argued, would certainly bring a concurrent loss of religious freedom, an unusually persuasive argument in South Carolina where the citizens had always enjoyed religious freedom. He had appealed to the middle and lower classes for help in purifying a corrupt interpretation of the British constitution, but he was not asking for a new society based upon economic equality. He did not believe in social revolution.

But Gadsden had little appreciation for the practical problems of George III and his ministers. The very people whom he was attacking as defilers of the British constitution thought of themselves as friends of English liberty and guarantors of the rights Englishmen had won in their Civil War and Glorious Revolution of the previous century.[45] Gadsden's relatively frequent use of the words "slavery," "American," and "independence" suggested that he had already embarked upon a revolutionary course that foreshadowed the rending of the empire.

The irony of Gadsden's use of the word "slavery" to describe the colonists' total subordination to George III and his ministers was not entirely lost upon him. A slaveowner himself, he was troubled by the incongruity of his arguments and his actions and had said so once during the stamp crisis. Nevertheless, Gadsden understood that no harsher image could be found. It was a word used frequently by advocates of liberty in England, where slavery was illegal, and Gadsden seems to have simply borrowed the term from them. Apparently, he quickly rationalized his own practice of slavery, for he did not draw any more parallels between the treatment of the colonists by royal officials and wealthy South Carolinians who owned hundreds of Africans.

Gadsden also frequently used the word "American" in his writings of the 1760s. He often coupled it with the words "British" or "English," as did many other writers of the time, but he sometimes used it alone with a subtle implication that he was talking about a politically as well as geographically separate people.

The most significant word that Gadsden used for the first time in his public letter of June 22, 1769, was "independence." In that letter, signed "PRO GREGE ET REGE," and elsewhere in his writings,

Gadsden used the word like many other writers of 1769 and the early 1770s, namely, to refer to independence from Parliament and the ministry, not British rule as a whole. Yet he seemed also to go a step further in his "PRO GREGE" letter. His threat to use military force if necessary against the mother country, his contention that the only significant bond between Great Britain and her colonies was the tie of trade, and his assertion that the colonies could trade more profitably with other European countries suggest that the idea of total independence was already forming in his mind. Gadsden did not say frankly in 1769 that he wanted independence; he said that he wanted a return to the relationship the colonies had enjoyed with the parent country before the French and Indian War. If that could not be had, then he thought independence would be better than rule by George III and his ministers. Few people probably noticed Gadsden's unusual use of the word in 1769, and Gadsden himself apparently did not yet think of independence as the only alternative to what he thought of as ministerial corruption.

Resting beneath Gadsden's successful political maneuverings were the complex personal and economic motivations that had driven him to resist the Townshend duties. Certainly he was trying to protect his own economic and social interests. As the owner of a large wharf, he needed to establish goodwill with planters, merchants, and farmers. Since he was politically ambitious and unlikely ever to receive another royal appointment, Gadsden had to rely upon his local popularity to win new political offices. His leadership in previous crises exiled him from royal favor and generated a certain amount of social pressure to speak out in any crisis.

Gadsden understood, too, that the repeal of the Townshend duties, like the repeal of the Stamp Act, was only a temporary victory. The import tax on tea remained, and the Currency Act was still in force. No general reform in British politics had taken place. Gadsden saw no solution to the constitutional question that had created the dilemma, and he was suspicious of the real motives of the king's ministers. He also believed that he was fighting for what was right; the burdens of morality and his understanding of British history encouraged him to take the path from resistance to revolution.

CHAPTER FIVE

The Devil Take All

"Let . . . all *go to the Devil*," Gadsden exclaimed, when he realized that George III and his ministers intended to confound South Carolina's attempt to manage her own domestic affairs. The repeal of the Townshend duties did not restore calm to South Carolina as it did to the other American colonies, for by 1770 Gadsden and other Charlestonians were embroiled in another controversy with the king that made reconciliation unlikely. The point of contention was an old issue, the right of the Commons to control provincial fiscal policy without the approval of the Council and the governor. A new catalyst in that debate arose in the person of the English radical, John Wilkes, something of a devil himself, who was wildly celebrated in the American colonies and in Great Britain as a great friend of liberty. In this argument Gadsden was obsessed with the same commitment to constitutional freedom that had driven him to defy royal authority at the time of the Cherokee wars ten years earlier. Then, he had stood almost alone, but by 1773 his voice was only one among many in Charleston who cried out for the natural rights of Englishmen.

The well-educated John Wilkes, three years younger than Gadsden, was a journalist, whig politician, reformer, jokester, and libertine. Wilkes was elected to Parliament in 1757, the same year that Christopher Gadsden and Henry Laurens were first seated in the South Carolina Commons. Wilkes enjoyed the friendship of the Great Commoner William Pitt, the idolization of his Aylesbury constituency, and several positions of responsibility. In the meantime, however, Wilkes's personal life disintegrated into a shambles. He ended his unhappy marriage, indulged in indecent revelries, and borrowed money recklessly. After George III became king in 1760, Wilkes's political fortune also began to decline. Wilkes criticized the young monarch and soon alienated Pitt. In 1762 Wilkes and others launched *The North Briton* to excoriate the administration. Their principal target was the Scot, John Stuart, third Earl of Bute, who was the king's first minister from 1761 through 1763. Wilkes said that the king's advisers were "Butean rascals" and "Jacobites" who were destroying the liberties gained by the expulsion of King James II in 1688. In early issues of *The North Briton*, Wilkes wrote anonymous articles about the Scottish menace to British liberties, and once he accused Bute of having an affair with the king's mother. George III allowed this abuse to go unchallenged until Wilkes brazenly attacked the king himself.

On April 23, 1763, *The North Briton No. 45* rolled from the presses, stirring up a controversy that in South Carolina ultimately cleared the way for a revolution. In that issue Wilkes criticized a speech the king had made from the throne. Wilkes cagily pretended that the speech had been made by a leading minister, but his readers knew immediately that it was the king's speech. Wilkes was especially severe on Bute, who had recently resigned, and upon the new head of the ministry, George Grenville. While claiming respect for His Majesty, Wilkes lamented that the honor of the Crown had "sunk even to prostitution." Urgently prompted by his ministers, the outraged king ordered Wilkes thrown into the Tower of London on a charge of criminal libel. When the jailer showed him to his cell, Wilkes remarked that he hoped it had not been occupied previously by a Scot because he did not wish to catch the itch. But the king failed to win a conviction, and three days later Wilkes stepped out into the streets of London where he was greeted with cries of "Wilkes and Liberty!"

Before going to France for two months, Wilkes wrote a long poem, *Essay on Woman*, an obscene parody on Alexander Pope's *Essay on Man*. Wilkes privately printed twelve copies, complete with illustrations, for the amusement of his friends, but one copy fell into the hands of his enemies. While in France, he was charged with libel and blasphemy and declared an outlaw. The charge of outlawry was dropped when he returned to England, but he was sentenced to twenty-two months in prison and fined £1,000 on the other convictions. Four times Wilkes was elected to Parliament to represent Middlesex County, and four times the king ordered him expelled. Not until 1774 was he allowed to take his seat, and by then he had been elected lord mayor of London. Wilkes was the hero of the English middle class, mostly merchants who had pressured Parliament into repealing the Stamp Act. In 1769 his friends organized the Society for the Support of the Bill of Rights, both to assist Wilkes in the courts and to advocate a reform of government, including the abolition of general search warrants, freedom of press, freedom of elections, popular self-government, and the publication of parliamentary debates. Their cries of "Wilkes and Liberty!" in London were echoed in the colonies from Boston to Charleston.[1]

In 1763, the year Wilkes became internationally famous, Gadsden began to develop his land in Ansonborough as a small village adjacent to Charleston and thereby to find ways to honor the English radical. Gadsden divided the land into four wharf lots and 197 back lots, named the area Middlesex, and labeled the first four streets Virginia, Pitt, Wilkes, and Massachusetts. He designated the point at which Wilkes joined Boundary Street as Hand in Hand Corner. Other streets were named Corsican and Pal in honor of the Corsican advocate of liberty, Pascal Paoli. At the time of the Stamp Act crisis, Gadsden's friends the mechanics formed the John Wilkes Club, sometimes called Club No. 45, and adopted Wilkes and the number 45 as symbols of their own struggle against British tyranny. Gadsden had been supporting Wilkes for six years by the time the Society for the Support of the Bill of Rights was organized in London. When the society decided to appeal for help from friends of Wilkes in South Carolina, it contacted Christopher Gadsden.[2]

Although other American colonies sent various gifts to Wilkes, the South Carolina Commons House of Assembly was the only official governmental body to send him money. On December 8, 1769, at the peak of the nonimportation crisis, the Commons directed treasurer Jacob Motte to pay a local committee £1,500 sterling to be sent to Wilkes's attorneys in England "for the defense of British and American Liberty."[3] Gadsden was one of the eight members of this committee.

Gadsden's subdivision Middlesex, sometimes known as Ansonborough or Gadsdenboro, was named in honor of the English radical, John Wilkes. Charleston *Yearbook, 1880*, p. 257.

The House's action was a direct affront to George III, who took notice, ordered his ministers to investigate, and launched a controversy that lasted until the Revolution.[4] British Attorney General William De Grey ruled that the South Carolina Commons House of Assembly was coordinate with the Council and could not pass a money bill without the Council's approval. His decision shocked the South Carolinians who believed that their Assembly had the right to draw up money bills without the approval of the Council and governor. Since 1750 the Commons had routinely borrowed money from the treasury without prior consent from the Council. The money was then paid back through an appropriation written into the next tax bill. During his election controversy with Governor Boone in the early 1760s, Gadsden himself had written a long treatise on the powers of the Council. He had argued that since South Carolina had become a royal province in 1719, the Council had never had the right to amend money bills; there was absolutely nothing in the British constitution, the royal instructions, laws passed by the Commons, or provincial tradition that gave the Council such a right.[5]

Lieutenant Governor William Bull also believed that the Council had long ago surrendered control of financial legislation. As the king's officer, however, Bull was obliged to enforce the ruling by the attorney general. He instructed the Council to veto any tax bill that provided for reimbursement to the treasury of the £1,500 the House had sent to Wilkes.[6]

The popularity of Wilkes was such a threat to George III's rule that he could not afford to allow a remote province to side with Wilkes against the monarchy. After reviewing the situation in South Carolina, the king issued his Additional Instruction of April 14, 1770, in which he positively forbade the governor, the lieutenant governor, or the Council, in the most emphatic language possible and with the direst penalties, to allow to pass any tax bill that reimbursed the money sent to Wilkes. He commanded the eight private gentlemen who had sent the advance to Wilkes to repay the South Carolina treasury themselves.[7]

In his anxiety to restore the authority of the monarchy, perhaps George III was unaware of the magnitude of the resistance he was bound to confront in South Carolina. His Additional Instruction created an impasse from which neither the Council nor the Commons House could recede. The Commons would not pass any tax bill without the appropriation for Wilkes; the Council would not approve any bill with the appropriation.

The Commons promptly outlined the position it would cling to as long as the impasse lasted. A committee chaired by Thomas Lynch and including Christopher Gadsden, Henry Laurens, Thomas Ferguson, and Benjamin Dart informed the Council that it intended no disrespect for the king but would look upon any attempt by the Council to control money bills as a "Seditious Doctrine." The committee reviewed what it considered to be the right of British Americans under the British constitution to be taxed only by their chosen representatives. It pointed out that the Council's attempt to abide by the British attorney general's ruling was absurd and inconsistent with the traditions and laws of South Carolina. And the Commons would not back down in the face of the royal threat.[8]

Wednesday, April 18, 1770, four days after Bull received the Additional Instruction, was the day Wilkes was released from prison. The date of his release was announced in advance, and in Charleston it was a day of rejoicing. Church bells were tolled, flags were waved, and many homes were illuminated with forty-five lights. Members of Club No. 45 gathered at Dillon's Tavern at 7:45 P.M. They stayed until 12:45 A.M. and drank forty-five toasts, including several to John Wilkes and at least one each to John Rutledge and Christopher Gadsden.[9]

When the Commons House met in August, it openly defied the king's Additional Instruction. A committee chaired by Thomas Lynch and John Rutledge and including Christopher Gadsden, Henry Laurens, John Mackenzie, Rawlins Lowndes, and Charles Cotesworth Pinckney introduced five resolutions, which the House adopted. The House said that it had the exclusive right to grant money to the king for any purpose, that the appropriation for Wilkes was constitutional, that attempts by the British ministry to dictate how money bills should be framed in the province were illegal, that the king's Additional Instruction was based on misinformation, and that the colony's London agent should obtain the withdrawal of the king's instructions. A few days later the House passed a tax bill, with the reimbursement of the Wilkes Fund, but the Council and lieutenant governor disallowed the bill. Upon the request of the House, Lieutenant Governor William Bull adjourned the House until the following January.[10]

The tactful William Bull understood the depth of the crisis better than any other royal official. He enjoyed the goodwill of most people in the province and at the same time attempted to obey the royal instructions. When the Assembly reconvened in January, he calmly pleaded for a tax bill without the appropriation for Wilkes. Bull also urged the British ministry to soften the royal instructions. But neither the ministry nor the Commons would heed Bull's call for compromise. The lieutenant governor's efforts at mediation were all in vain; he must have greeted with relief the return of Governor Lord Charles Greville Montagu in September 1771.

Returning from a two-year stay in England, Governor Montagu intended to enforce the king's dictate. An inept politician and clumsy administrator, Montagu succeeded only at making the situation worse. For a full year he accomplished nothing. Then, unwisely imitating Governor Thomas Hutchinson of Massachusetts, Montagu dissolved the South Carolina Assembly, called for new elections, and ordered the new Assembly to meet at Beaufort, about seventy-five miles south of Charleston. Montagu hoped that the distance to Beaufort would cause the rebellious Charleston members to stay away, but he was disappointed. An angry electorate returned the same members to the Commons.

The House met in the Beaufort Court House on October 8, 1772, with an unusually large number of members present, and they were in an ill humor. Peter Manigault was reelected speaker, a clear indication that the Commons had not changed its mind. After keeping the delegates waiting for three days, Montagu gave them a lecture on the duties of legislators and his own fidelity to the law and the constitution. The Commons did not know it, but Montagu himself was under great pressure from the ministry to end the deadlock. Lord Hillsborough, secretary of state for the colonies, had ordered him to force the Commons to get back to business but had not told him how to accomplish such a miracle. As a conciliatory gesture, Montagu prorogued the Assembly to meet again in Charleston.

When the Commons met in Charleston on October 22, however, it was even angrier than the governor. It promptly appointed Christopher Gadsden to chair a committee on grievances to investigate the Beaufort affair. Gadsden demanded that the governor explain why he had called the Assembly to Beaufort. Then on October 29 Gadsden produced a report that eloquently expressed the House's reaction to the governor's unprecedented conduct. Gadsden feared that if Montagu were not reprimanded, future governors might put an end to freedom of debate by harassing the members of the Assembly. He offered resolutions severely condemning the governor's actions and recommending that the colonial agent be instructed to petition the Crown for Montagu's removal from office.[11]

Responding to Gadsden, Montagu growled that he had given his reasons in Beaufort for calling the Assembly to that distant site and would say no more about it. He then demanded to see the journals of the Assembly. In the meantime, Peter Manigault had resigned as speaker for reasons of health, and Gadsden had successfully moved that Rawlins Lowndes be elected in his place. A wealthy planter who believed that provincial and property rights should take precedence over royal prerogative, Lowndes delayed twenty-four hours before surrendering the journal to the governor. The infuriated Montagu refused to recognize Lowndes as the new speaker. When he read Gadsden's report in the journal, he summoned the House to appear before him immediately, hoping to prorogue it before it could adopt the report. The House, however, finished its discussions, adopted Gadsden's resolutions, and then appeared before the governor at its leisure.

Montagu at last exploded with anger. He condemned Lowndes for being reluctant to surrender the journal. He decided that the Commons must be punished for continuing "to sit, to put a Question, and to form Resolves and Orders" after it had been summoned into the governor's presence. The members of the Commons, he said, had violated the faith of their constituents by "Wantonly shewing how little they regard the Laws of Parliament." Then he prorogued the Assembly until November 9.[12]

The Committee of Correspondence, of which Gadsden was a member, promptly wrote its agent, Charles Garth, asking him to bring about Montagu's removal, or at least have him disciplined in some way. Garth replied that he was surprised to learn that the

Assembly had been called to meet at Beaufort. Furthermore, Garth said, the Earl of Dartmouth, who had replaced Hillsborough as colonial secretary in August 1772, hoped that the Assembly would stay in Charleston permanently and that a reconciliation between the governor and the Commons could be reached.[13] Before Garth received his instructions from the Commons, however, the ministry had already decided to remove Montagu because he was unable to govern the province. Montagu received his orders to depart and sailed for England on March 10, 1773.

Gadsden must have taken particular pleasure in Montagu's recall; the case was almost identical with the removal of Governor Thomas Boone a decade earlier, in which Gadsden had taken the leading role. The king appointed Lord William Campbell, the governor of Nova Scotia, to be Montagu's replacement, but Campbell did not arrive in the province until two years later. By then, nothing remained to be saved.[14]

Lieutenant Governor William Bull again assumed authority on March 11, 1773, but he was no more successful than Montagu had been in affirming the power of the Council. The Council had been reduced to a board of royal placemen who were ignored by the Assembly. The Commons launched attack after attack on the Council's money powers, often with Gadsden serving as its spokesman. Shortly after Bull took command, Gadsden assured him that the Commons would never obey the king's Additional Instruction of April 14, 1770. Again in August, Gadsden wrote a report denying that the Council had any right to approve local tax bills and attempting to prove that the economic stability of the colony did not depend upon the governor and the Council. In fact, Gadsden was able to offer abundant proof that the wealth of the province was increasing rapidly even though the Commons had passed no money bills or conducted any other business for more than four years. Finally, Bull reported to the Earl of Dartmouth in September 1773 that frequent attacks by the Assembly had "so degraded the Council in the eyes of the People" that service thereon "is now become rather humiliating and obnoxious."[15]

The decline of the Royal Council in South Carolina raised an important question about the nature of colonial constitutions.

The opinion of the king and his ministers was that the Council had the same relationship to the Commons in South Carolina as the House of Lords did to the House of Commons in the British Parliament. They thought that the Commons did not have the authority to pass any law unless it was approved by the Council and endorsed by the royal governor. Both Gadsden and other dissenters, both in the colonies and in Great Britain, were arguing that the province should be governed by a colonial constitution consisting of the accumulation of royal instructions, judicial decisions, and provincial traditions, including the established custom of allowing the lower house in South Carolina to exercise control over money bills. Neither the friends of the government nor the opposition was willing, or able, to understand the arguments of the other. The opposition believed that George III and his ministers were conspiring to subvert the British constitution, especially those rights to a limited monarchy that the British people had won in their Glorious Revolution of 1688.

Gadsden and his friends wanted to preserve the victory for representative government that had been achieved in 1688, but they were actually going a step beyond their British counterparts. By linking their demand for home rule with their cry for the restoration of the traditional rights of Britons, they were in reality claiming that an unwritten constitution had evolved for South Carolina that paralleled and imitated the British constitution, but was separate from it. While maintaining their loyalty to the British monarch, the stubborn Carolinians said that they had already accomplished a constitutional reform that gave the lower house, composed of the people's representatives, greater power than an appointed upper house and appointed chief executive.[16] The British rulers in the 1770s, however, would not recognize the existence of such a reform in South Carolina, and the Carolinians would not deny it. Ultimately the colonists would have to subjugate themselves to the king's will or choose separation.

In this painful and delayed birth of a new nation, the voice of Christopher Gadsden was rarely silent. During the five years that the Wilkes Fund dispute lasted, he was elected to every Assembly and appointed to every committee that dealt with the crisis. During a debate in March 1773, he was described by one observer as "plain, blunt, hot and incorrect, though very sensible." The subject of that debate was a new general duty law on the importation of slaves to replace an old law that had expired in 1772. When Gadsden realized that the deadlock over the Wilkes Fund would make it impossible for the Commons to implement a new law, he spoke out. "And Mr. Speaker, if the Governor and Council don't see fit to fall in with us, I say let the general duty law and all *go to the Devil*, and we go about our business."[17]

The majority of the members of the Commons House of Assembly agreed with Gadsden. The consensus that had formed during the nonimportation crisis held through the Wilkes Fund dispute. Even Henry Laurens, perhaps the richest man in the province at the time, found himself agreeing with Gadsden. Wealthy merchants, planters, and lawyers, most of whom dared not dream of independence, openly defied the king's orders and officers. Benjamin Dart and Henry Laurens were successful merchants; Thomas Ferguson, Thomas Lynch, and Rawlins Lowndes were great planters; and John Rutledge and Charles Pinckney were lawyers. All were very rich men. Many had been educated in England. They were so steeped in the British tradition of constitutional monarchy that none among them believed that their insistence upon controlling their domestic finances implied any desire to overthrow the king. They did not realize the full implication of their refusal to obey the Additional Instruction and allow the Council to function as an upper house of legislature.

Gadsden himself did not mention the possibility of separation, as he had done in earlier crises. Perhaps he thought that the friends of Wilkes in Great Britain would exert enough pressure to persuade the king to restore the political principles that had nourished the Glorious Revolution in 1688. Perhaps Gadsden also experienced fewer personal frustrations during the Wilkes Fund debate. Those years were spent busily expanding his wharf, an enterprise that brought him an enormous increase in wealth. And surely Gadsden took some pride in seeing men who had been his critics ten years earlier now using his own arguments. But the crisis was extremely serious and the provincial challenge to royal authority was still unresolved.

The debate over the Wilkes Fund was still at fever pitch when Parliament passed the Tea Act in May 1773. The public discussions shifted from Wilkes to the Townshend tax that Parliament had retained on tea as proof that it had the right to tax the colonies. Because of the tax, the American colonies had been boycotting English tea, and it had been piling up in the East India Company's warehouses in London. Prime Minister Lord North conceived the Tea Act in order to help the British East India Company out of financial difficulty. This law exempted the company from paying a tax in England on tea that would later be shipped to America. The company could thus reduce the price of its tea, but the Townshend tax of three pence per pound still must be collected. The Charlestonians who were already outraged by the Wilkes Fund dispute looked upon the Tea Act as a devious attempt by Parliament to trick the colonies into paying the Townshend tax by offering them cheap tea. They thought the Tea Act was the Crown's attempt to circumvent the intransigency of the Commons relative to tax bills and to emphasize Parliament's right to levy internal taxes upon the colonies.

On December 2, 1773, the ship *London* dropped anchor in Charleston harbor. Her cargo, "*clogg'd with a duty unconstitutionally imposed*," consisted of 257 chests of tea.[18] *London* was one of seven ships laden with tea that the British East India Company sent to American ports. From Boston to Charleston the colonial newspapers warned Americans that they were facing another crisis like the Stamp Act. "Junius Brutus" wrote in the *South-Carolina Gazette* on November 29 that Parliament was determined "to raise a revenue, out of your pockets, *against your consent* — and to render assemblies of your representatives *totally useless*." A week later Peter Timothy argued in his *Gazette* that soon England would be taxing the colonies even for the "light of heaven." On the very day *London* dropped anchor, handbills circulated through Charleston summoning the inhabitants to a meeting in the great hall over the Exchange.

The meeting at the Exchange on December 3, 1773, was one of the most significant events in the coming of the Revolution to South Carolina. It marked the beginning of the uninterrupted development of a legislative body for an independent state, one that was entirely free of British control. It became the voice of the people in South Carolina and assumed the legislative functions that the Commons had been unable to accomplish because of the impasse over the Wilkes Fund.[19] The meeting elected Gabriel

Powell chairman. He was a large planter from Prince George Winyah Parish who owned 3,500 acres in the backcountry. He had worked on the circuit court bill for the backcountry, signed the nonimportation association, served in the Commons, and since 1769 had sided with the critics of royal policy. The meeting then resolved to prevent Captain Alexander Curling of the *London* from unloading his cargo.

Christopher Gadsden was present at the meeting and apparently had much to say. Only planters and mechanics had attended; Gadsden was disturbed with the merchants for staying away and had harsh words for them. One observer reported that "many are offended at some severe reflections that Mr. G. Let drop against that Body in the Wrath of declamation yesterday."[20] Despite the alleged offense that some took to Gadsden's remarks, or perhaps because of it, Gadsden was appointed to chair a committee of five charged with responsibility for getting the merchants to sign a statement that they would not import the taxed tea.

Within Gadsden's committee, representatives of the South Carolina assemblies that had defied the Council and British ministry during the Wilkes dispute and representatives of the mechanics who had demonstrated in the streets and in the taverns came together with a single voice.[21] The four men serving with Gadsden were Charles Pinckney, Charles Cotesworth Pinckney, Thomas Ferguson, and Daniel Cannon. The Pinckneys and Ferguson had been members of the assemblies that had defied the king's Additional Instruction of April 14, 1770. They represented the planting class. Daniel Cannon was one of the most prominent mechanics in the province. He had never sat in the Assembly. A carpenter by trade, Cannon was no ordinary laborer. By 1770 he had amassed a great deal of property near the city, which he developed as Cannonsboro. He had led the group of mechanics who enforced the nonimportation association.

Gadsden's committee had to overcome some extraordinary obstacles. The merchants were not easily convinced that the tea crisis was as serious as the stamp and nonimportation crises had been. Nevertheless, Gadsden persuaded fifty of them to sign an agreement that they would import no more tea, but they demanded the privilege of selling during the next six months the tea they already had on hand.[22] Furthermore, Captain Curling refused to sail away with his cargo, and Lieutenant Governor Bull intended to collect the tax if the tea were sold in Charleston. Finally, the collector of customs seized *London*'s shipment and stored it in the basement of the Exchange Building. When Bull reported the events to the British ministry, the Earl of Dartmouth congratulated him in February for preventing the criminal actions from occurring in South Carolina that had marked the arrival of the tea ships in Boston.[23]

The South Carolinians were tardy in hearing about the great tea party that had occurred in Boston Harbor on December 16 when the friends of liberty there had disguised themselves as Indians and dumped the "cursed weed" overboard. At New York and Philadelphia, the tea ships were simply turned back. When the Charleston dissidents learned in mid-January that their province was the only one in which the tea had actually been landed, they were a bit chagrined. They held monthly meetings to plot their strategy and attempt to generate a stronger protest in South Carolina.

At those monthly meetings, business was conducted by the General Committee, the same committee that had been established in 1769 to enforce the nonimportation association. In January 1774, Gadsden was named chairman of the General Committee, and in March it was made permanent. It served both as the *de facto* legislature for the province and as South Carolina's Committee of Correspondence. The forty-five members included merchants, mechanics, planters, and lawyers, but planters were more numerous. Among the planters were Thomas Bee, Thomas Ferguson, Rawlins Lowndes, Thomas Lynch, William Moultrie, Jacob Motte, and Charles Pinckney. The merchants were represented by Gadsden, William Gibbs, Alexander Gillon, and others. Daniel Cannon, Peter Timothy, and five other mechanics were members. The lawyers included Thomas Heyward, Charles Cotesworth Pinckney, and Edward Rutledge. Many of these same men were also members of the Assembly that was now crippled because of the Wilkes Fund dispute. The General Committee made very little progress in stirring up the population to resist the taxed tea before June 1774.[24]

The news that Parliament had passed the Boston port bill

turned the tide of opinion in South Carolina in favor of the dissidents. In June, Peter Timothy printed an extra edition of his newspaper with the complete text of the Boston port bill surrounded by a heavy black border. The Crown had decreed that the Boston port be closed until the city paid for the destroyed tea. Shortly, Parliament passed other laws to punish Massachusetts. These laws, which the colonists called intolerable, virtually ended freedom of assembly in Massachusetts, required that British officials charged with murder while suppressing riots in America be transported to Great Britain for trial, and attempted to force Massachusetts to provide quarters for British soldiers stationed there. On May 13 a desperate Boston called upon all the colonies to ban all commerce between Great Britain and her West Indian possessions until the Boston port was reopened.

Responding to Boston's cry for help, the South Carolina General Committee met at Dillon's Tavern on June 13. The minds of some members were "now fermenting" and "for putting all at hazard."[25] Peter Timothy immediately reported to Samuel Adams that South Carolina would "raise something for our suffering brethren" in Massachusetts and that Carolina's cessation of commerce with Great Britain would depend in part upon what happened in New York and Philadelphia. "Even the Merchants *now* seem generally inclined to a Non-importation," he continued. In a second letter, Timothy told Adams that "my friend Gadsden" had "warmly pushed" for a boycott, but that decision has been postponed.[26] The South Carolina committee decided to publish a handbill calling a general meeting of representatives from every part of the province at the Exchange Building on July 6.

In the meantime, Gadsden exploded with outrage. In two letters written in rapid succession to Samuel Adams, he sneered that Mother England was now behaving like "our mother *in law*." He promised Adams that no pressure, not even the perennial fear of a slave insurrection, could deter him from prodding South Carolina to aid Massachusetts. He would rather see his family "reduced to the utmost Extremity and cut to pieces" than submit to the "damned Machinations" of Parliament. Although he had invested his entire fortune and seven years of hard labor greater than that of "any negroe in any of our swamps" in building his wharf, he would gladly see every inch of it destroyed rather than undermine the common cause of liberty. Gadsden promised that South Carolina would follow whatever plan of resistance Massachusetts adopted. And he bragged that there were "not a few Amongst us who are hopeful" that the coercive acts of Parliament "will Occasion many Bonny Rebels in America."[27]

Gadsden and the South Carolina General Committee then began to accept donations for the relief of the distressed people in Boston. Gadsden announced that any rice sent to his wharf for that purpose would be landed, shipped, and stored if necessary without charge. On June 28 he notified Samuel Adams and the Boston Committee of Correspondence that the sloop *Mary* with 194 whole and 21 half-barrels of rice had departed for Boston, and he predicted that South Carolina would ultimately send 1,000 barrels to the strangulated port. "We are thoroughly alarm'd here," he continued, "and will be ready to do every Thing in our Power. We depend on your Firmness, and that you will not pay for an ounce of the damn'd Tea."[28]

The shipment of rice got through safely, because on July 18 Samuel Adams wrote Gadsden thanking him for it. Adams added that the "noble and generous Part which all are taking & particularly South Carolina on this Occasion" must convince Lord North "that the British Colonists in North America are an inseparable Band of Brothers." Adams hoped that the "united Wisdom of the Colonists" would devise a peaceful way "for the Restoration of their own Rights and Liberties" and for "the Establishment of Harmony with Great Britain."[29]

Samuel Adams was already thinking beyond the immediate crisis of the closed port. On May 27 the Massachusetts Assembly had sent a letter to all the colonies asking that they send delegates to a continental congress that would meet in Philadelphia on September 1. Gadsden was enthusiastic about the idea. To the Boston Committee of Correspondence, he wrote, "A Congress seems to be much wish'd for here."[30] The major item of business at the general meeting in Charleston on July 6 now would be to choose delegates to the Continental Congress.

Both the tea crisis and the Wilkes Fund controversy confirmed an opinion that Christopher Gadsden had held for a dozen years. He thought that the current British Parliament and ministry were denying British Americans the natural rights of Englishmen, including the right to be represented only by men of their own choice. The establishment of a general meeting of citizens as a *de facto* legislature for the province in 1773 was for Gadsden a personal victory. He had worked both within the legal framework of the Commons House of Assembly and with the extralegal pressure of the mob. He welcomed the events that brought assemblymen and mechanics together into a kind of town meeting that now provided the only viable government in the province. The response to the tea crisis in the other colonies and the subsequent call for a continental congress would carry his point home to the mother country. As delegates from the American colonies prepared to go to Philadelphia, the British ministry should have seen evidence aplenty that insofar as royal control of America was concerned, all had indeed gone to the devil.

CHAPTER SIX

Business in Philadelphia

In Charleston on July 6, 7, and 8, 1774, a chaotic gathering of merchants, planters, mechanics, and backsettlers selected Christopher Gadsden and four others to attend the first session of the Continental Congress. The meeting in Charleston took place in the elegant new Exchange Building, which had been completed in the fall of 1771 at the eastern end of Broad Street. Gadsden was one of 104 men from the city and almost every part of the province who gathered there in response to the call from the General Committee for a meeting of all the inhabitants of South Carolina to discuss how to respond to the Crown's punitive action toward Massachusetts and to Boston's subsequent cry for help.

Gadsden was chairman of the General Committee that called the July meeting, and he knew precisely what action he wanted the meeting to take. Apparently he had worked behind the scenes to guarantee the presence of a majority of delegates who would see things his way. Although he had persuaded fifty merchants to sign an agreement that they would import no more tea, he thought that they were likely to be more interested in protecting their lucrative trade than protesting an unconstitutional tax on one item. Gadsden found more kindred minds among the planters, many of whom had been educated in England and who opposed Parliament's recent actions on constitutional grounds, but most were so rich and comfortable that they could well afford to be indifferent to the crisis. Gadsden knew that he could count upon the mechanics to defy the Crown, but they alone could not outvote the merchants and planters.

Therefore, Gadsden apparently made a deliberate effort to get men from the backcountry to the July meeting. Their presence in the Exchange marked the first time that the backcountry took an important role in provincial politics. Gadsden had needed their help in 1769 to win a nonimportation agreement, and he needed it even more in 1774. Although some merchants and planters would surely vote with him, he could not be certain of the majority. Since no property qualifications were necessary for membership in the general meeting, Gadsden was able to capitalize upon the democratic demands of the mechanics and backsettlers. The rise of democracy in South Carolina was not an incidental by-product of the Revolution; it was one of the causes of the war.[1]

The presence of backsettlers, mechanics, merchants, and planters in the general meeting inevitably caused the group to divide into political factions. Those who favored a boycott, a continental congress, and a defiant protest of the Intolerable Acts were called radicals. Those who favored a congress and only a mild form of protest were moderates. Gadsden, the mechanics, and some planters and backsettlers were radicals; the merchants and lawyers were moderates. The distinction between radicals and moderates, however, was not clear-cut. Individuals freely switched from one camp to the other. For example, John Rutledge had agreed with Gadsden and the radicals at the time of the Stamp Act, but in 1774 he became a leader of the moderates. And Edward Rutledge, his younger brother and a very ambitious politician, attempted to avoid becoming too closely identified with either group. Originally, the radicals simply wanted to claim for the British colonies the civil victories won in the English Civil War and the Glorious Revolution. When they learned that they could not do so under the rule of George III, they became advocates of independence.

On July 6, the first day of the meeting, the radicals scored a victory in the choice of George Gabriel Powell as chairman. Before 1772 Powell had had a distinguished career as a royal official. He had been a member of the Council from 1738 through 1741 and governor from 1741 through 1743. A planter with extensive landholdings in the backcountry, he had fought the Cherokee Indians with Governor Lyttelton. In 1769 he shifted his sympathies to the people in the backcountry and became their advocate in the nonimportation debate. In 1772 Lieutenant Governor

Bull had denounced him for his unconstitutional principles, and thereafter he was a hero of the dissidents in St. David and Prince George Winyah parishes. A radical himself, Powell announced rules for the July 6 meeting that favored his own faction. Voting would be by individuals present, rather than by parishes, he said. That decision gave the mechanics an advantage, because they could rush in their fellows from the streets in time to cast votes. Although there were only 104 legal delegates, Powell allowed anyone who was present to vote.[2] At times more than 400 people crowded into the hall.

Powell then announced four questions that had to be decided; whether or not to join Boston in a boycott of British goods, whether or not to send delegates to a continental congress, how many delegates to send, and what authority to give them. Both the radicals and moderates agreed that five delegates should be sent to Philadelphia, but the other questions were so controversial that they had to be put off until the next day.

On July 7 the moderates won a major victory. They defeated a proposal to join Boston in a boycott of British goods. South Carolina's merchants had unhappy memories of the distress they had suffered under the nonimportation association of 1769 and 1770. They did not want to relive it, and they had gone to the meeting at the Exchange primarily to block a new nonimportation agreement. A large number of planters must have voted with them, or they would not have won. There was in Charleston a certain feeling of jealousy toward Boston for seemingly always initiating the protests against Great Britain. There was also a lingering bitterness among South Carolinians who resented the fact that all of the New England and middle colonies had abandoned their nonimportation associations before South Carolina had. Perhaps a significant number of radicals even joined with the moderates on July 7 in order to postpone the decision about a boycott until the meeting of representatives from all the colonies could take place in Philadelphia.[3]

Greater excitement swirled around the choice of the five delegates to the Continental Congress. Both the moderates and radicals agreed upon the selection of Henry Middleton and John Rutledge. Middleton was a wealthy planter who had not joined the opposition to the Stamp Act but who had signed the nonimportation association in 1769. John Rutledge was both a lawyer and a planter. He had taken the side of Gadsden against Governor Thomas Boone in Gadsden's election controversy and had later served with Gadsden in the Stamp Act Congress. But in 1774 Rutledge was posing as a friend to the merchants and beginning to dissociate himself from Gadsden. Although Rutledge and Middleton had at one time or another in the past taken the radical veiw, in 1774 both were moderates. They did not favor a new boycott, and they were horrified by the very idea of independence. Their election to the Continental Congress was clearly a moderate victory.

A fierce struggle ensued over the choice of the other three delegates. The radicals proposed a ticket consisting of Christopher Gadsden, Thomas Lynch, and Edward Rutledge. The moderates suggested the names of Rawlins Lowndes, Charles Pinckney, and Miles Brewton. According to Edward Rutledge, the radical ticket won by a majority of 397 votes![4] Gadsden and Lynch were already established leaders of the radicals, but young Edward Rutledge was something of a mystery. Only twenty-five years old, he had read law under his older brother John and had studied in England. During the Wilkes dispute he had defended the Commons against the Council. Although the radicals claimed him as their own in 1774, he apparently saw himself as a mediator between them and the moderates. As the fifth man in the delegation, he was therefore in a unique position to determine South Carolina's vote in the Continental Congress.

The final issue to be settled on July 7 was the matter of instructions to the five delegates. On this vital point, the moderates again carried the day. The delegates were given unlimited power to agree upon "*legal measures . . . to obtain a repeal of the objectionable acts*" of Parliament. They were not given permission to vote for independence, which was illegal, and the implication seemed to be that they were not given permission to vote for a new boycott, which the moderates were also suggesting was illegal. Plainly, the South Carolina delegates were supposed to attempt to resolve their differences with Parliament within the empire. And even if they should be driven to take up arms, they were to do so not to win independence but to retrieve the ancient and natural rights of Englishmen.[5]

On July 8, for a third consecutive day, the crowd again gathered at the Exchange to discuss strategy for maintaining local self-government while the five delegates were in Philadelphia. It established a General Committee consisting of ninety-nine members that would function as the government of the province until the next general meeting. The General Committee was to correspond with committees in the other colonies and execute all resolutions that had been passed by the general meeting of July 6 through 8. The ninety-nine members included fifteen merchants, fifteen mechanics, and sixty-nine planters. Since most of the planters also owned homes in Charleston, the General Committee represented the city far more completely than it did the backcountry. The democratic gains won in the general meeting were greatly diluted in the General Committee. The sheer size of this committee suggests that it was intended to function more as a legislature than as a committee. Chairman Powell then dissolved the meeting.

Lieutenant Governor Bull had noted the proceedings at the Exchange with great apprehension. He hoped to maintain the status quo until the new governor arrived, and he intended to prohibit the Commons House of Assembly from giving legal sanction to the decisions made by the general public. But the Commons outsmarted him. It assembled at eight o'clock in the morning of August 2, claiming that the excessive heat had prompted the unusually early meeting. Within five minutes, before Bull could get dressed and prorogue it, the Commons approved the election of the five delegates to the Continental Congress and appropriated £1,500 sterling to pay their expenses.[6] A few days later, John and Edward Rutledge and Henry Middleton sailed for Philadelphia without much public display.

The sailing of Christopher Gadsden and Thomas Lynch on Sunday, August 14, 1774, however, attracted a great deal of attention. In his morning sermon the Reverend John Bullman, assistant rector of St. Michael's, condemned them as traitors. In the afternoon a riotous congregational meeting demanded his resignation, and Bullman later left the colony in 1775 with the unsettled case for his dismissal still charged against him. Despite the sermon, Gadsden and Lynch were accompanied by "prayers and every mark of respect" and saluted by cannon fire as they

walked along Market Wharf to board the brigantine *Sea Nymph*.
Nevertheless, their departure was marred by tragedy when some
powder was ignited by an unextinguished piece of wadding and
burned three men, one fatally. But the accident did not delay
them. Gadsden, still a widower, took his seventeen-year-old son
Thomas with him. Lynch was accompanied by his wife and
daughter. The Gadsdens and Lynches sailed on *Sea Nymph* for
eight days before she dropped anchor within sight of Philadelphia's Market Street Wharf.[7]

From the deck of *Sea Nymph* Gadsen surveyed the skyline of the
city where he had lived almost thirty years earlier. Fronting on the
Delaware River and flanked by the Schuylkill, Philadelphia rested
upon a hot, humid strip of land much like Charleston. Three
times the size of Charleston, it enjoyed the same religious diversity, cultural opportunities, and cosmopolitan atmosphere, but
on a grander scale. The society was dominated by a large number
of very wealthy merchants, but there were also more mechanics
and tradesmen than anywhere else in America. Absent were the
great planters and thousands of slaves who were to be found in
South Carolina. Although slaves and free blacks could be seen on
the streets of Philadelphia, they were not so numerous, and at
least three-fourths of the citizens already favored ending slavery.
Philadelphia was the center of the Enlightenment in North
America. A large scientific community gathered around Benjamin Franklin, printer of the *Pennsylvania Gazette* and mentor of
Charleston's Peter Timothy. Ideologically as well as geograph-
ically, the city was about halfway between Boston and Charleston.
But the Southerners who went to Philadelphia in the late summer
of 1774 probably felt a bit more at home than did the men from
Boston and New York.[8]

Gadsden arrived on August 22, two weeks before the Congress
convened. He had plenty of time to explore the city and to enjoy
an informal camaraderie with the other delegates who arrived
early. He and Thomas found lodging in the home of a Mrs.
House, a widow about forty, whom Silas Deane described as
"genteel and sensible."[9] The other lodgers included Eliphalet
Dyer and Silas Deane of Connecticut. Deane, thirteen years
younger than Gadsden, was a prosperous lawyer and merchant
from Wethersfield. Like Gadsden, he was prepared to sacrifice his

substantial fortune if necessary for the cause of liberty in America. Eliphalet Dyer, who had served with Gadsden in the Stamp Act Congress, was the principal leader of the revolutionary agitation in Connecticut.

The arrival of the Massachusetts delegation created something of a sensation. Since their province was being punished by the Crown, and since they had called for a congress, the other delegates seemed eager to greet them in person. Because they could not get safely out of the Boston port, John Adams, Samuel Adams, Thomas Cushing, and Robert Treat Paine were making the trip by coach, drawn by four horses. They reached Philadelphia late in the afternoon of August 29. Although tired and dirty, they went immediately to City Tavern where Christopher Gadsden, Thomas Lynch, and many others joined them for a supper that John Adams said was "as elegant as ever was laid upon a Table." After they had dined they circulated "the glass," wrote Silas Deane, "long enough to raise the spirits of everyone just to that nice point which is above disguise or suspicion." By the time they departed for their respective rooming houses at eleven o'clock, they were "in the highest possible spirits."[10]

Gadsden met the Adams cousins for the first time when they arrived in Philadelphia on August 29. He and Samuel Adams had become friends through their correspondence, and both were already identified as leading radicals. Both were students of the classics and outspoken critics of royal policies. Samuel Adams was two years older than Gadsden, Harvard-educated and notoriously incompetent at managing his private finances.[11] Gadsden did not have the literary polish that a Harvard education might have afforded, but he was thoroughly self-taught and a very successful businessman. As propagandists, he and Samuel Adams were equals, but in the other areas of their lives they had little in common.

Gadsden found John Adams more to his liking. Educated at Harvard in the classics, religion, and law, John Adams was eleven years younger than Gadsden. John Adams had been associated with James Otis in protest of the Stamp Act in 1765, but he had not won the reputation for being a master propagandist like Samuel Adams. As early as 1774, John Adams realized that independence was likely but dreaded it. He served on many committees with

Gadsden and usually agreed with him. He was a successful lawyer and prominent diplomat and politician, although he probably did not achieve the great wealth that Gadsden did. Like Gadsden, John Adams struggled to maintain a public stance of humility while nourishing a secret, seething ambition for fame.[12] He and Gadsden were both whigs, both radicals, and later both Federalists. In the four days remaining before the Congress convened, they became friends.

On September 4, 1774, the last of the fifty-six delegates from twelve colonies arrived. Georgia did not send anyone; she was far away, relatively young, and tightly controlled by the Crown. The Virginia delegation arrived last. Consisting of Richard Bland, Benjamin Harrison, Patrick Henry, Richard Henry Lee, Edmund Pendleton, Peyton Randolph, and George Washington, it contributed some of the most distinguished members to the Congress. Their late arrival did not allow them to get to know the other delegates before the meeting began, and apparently Gadsden did not form lasting friendships with any of the Virginians.[13]

When the delegates convened in Carpenter's Hall on September 5, the men from the northern and middle provinces were amazed by the enthusiasm of some of the southerners. Perhaps they had forgotten that Patrick Henry had denounced the Stamp Act more roundly than anyone, that South Carolina had been the only southern province to send delegates to New York in 1765, and that Christopher Gadsden had teamed with James Otis then to lead the radicals. At any rate, the delegates from Connecticut and Delaware were surprised that those from the South were so ready to be united with New England. Silas Deane said the southern delegates were men of "firmness, sensibility, spirit, and thorough knowledge of the interests of America." Another observer suggested that Bostonians were moderate men when compared to those from Virginia, South Carolina, and Rhode Island.[14] Stephen Hopkins and Samuel Ward of Rhode Island hated each other but joined with Christopher Gadsden, Samuel Adams, Patrick Henry, and Richard Henry Lee to form the nucleus of the radicals. When the credentials of all the delegates were read, however, it was clear that none had been sent to Philadelphia to start a revolution.[15]

On September 6 the Congress settled the question of how to vote so easily that the differences between the radicals and the conservatives were not readily apparent. Gadsden, following the lead of Patrick Henry, voted with the majority to give each colony one vote in the Congress.[16] The delegates who thought that population, property, and slaves should be considered were easily outvoted. Gadsden's position clearly indicated that he intended to take a broad rather than a provincial view. Unity was to him far more important than preferential treatment for South Carolina. Since the radical faction dominated the South Carolina delegation, Gadsden had a good chance to control South Carolina's vote.

Scarcely had the question of how to vote been settled before the Congress was electrified by a false report that the British had bombarded Boston, killing six people. Gadsden was on his feet immediately. He urged the others to join him in taking up weapons and marching directly to Boston. He announced that if his wife and children were in Boston, and if they should perish there by the sword, it would not change his commitment to American liberty. "Mr. Gadsden leaves all New England Sons of Liberty far behind," Silas Deane reported. Outside the hall, the "Bells toll muffled, & the people run as in a case of extremity, they know not where or why," Deane wrote.[17] "War! war! war! was the cry," wrote John Adams.[18] The Reverend Jacob Duché quoted Biblical sanction for taking up the sword and the spear against the wicked; he delivered a prayer that Deane thought was "worth riding one hundred miles to hear." The report of the disturbance in Boston was soon proved to be untrue, but the men assembled in Carpenters's Hall could now have little doubt about the position Gadsden would take in the debates.

Against this tense background the Congress went to work. Two committees were established. One, consisting of two members from each colony, was to draw up a list of the colonists' rights within the empire and of the infringements which had taken place since 1763; it was also supposed to recommend ways to restore those lost rights. The second committee, consisting of one member from each colony, was to report upon the statutes that affected trade and manufacturing in the colonies. Gadsden served on the latter, perhaps because the president thought that his experience in trade would make him a useful member. Gadsden himself, however, was as interested in political and constitutional affairs as he was in economic matters.[19]

The relative calm of the assembly was again interrupted on September 17 when someone from Boston presented the Suffolk Resolves to the Congress. The resolves were a resounding indictment of the actions that England had taken toward Massachusetts and a call for revolutionary resistance. Frightened by General Thomas Gage's movements to fortify Boston, her citizens appealed to the Congress for advice. They offered to abandon their homes in the city and, taking their wives, children, aged, and infirm, to seek refuge with country people or in primitive huts to be constructed in the woods; they would refuse to reenter Boston until their rights and liberties were restored.[20] Gadsden immediately proposed that General Gage be attacked and defeated in Boston before he could receive reinforcements. But cooler heads prevailed; Congress was unwilling to draw the sword while any other means of attaining redress remained.[21] The Congress only passed a resolution expressing support for Massachusetts and trust that the united efforts of North America would convince the "British nation . . . to introduce better men and wiser measures."[22]

The Suffolk Resolves also called for a general cessation of commerce with Great Britain. This issue, closely related to the work of Gadsden's committee, had been hotly debated in the Charleston general meeting on July 6, 7, and 8; in the discussion of it in Philadelphia, Gadsden and the entire South Carolina delegation played a controversial role. The hope that the colonies might agree to boycott all commerce with Great Britain had been a major reason that Massachusetts called for the Congress; the fear that such a boycott would be enacted had prompted moderate Carolinians to elect Henry Middleton and John Rutledge as their representatives. The issue was debated long and furiously during September and October. Some delegates argued that a boycott would not work because Virginia would not agree to ban the exportation of her tobacco before 1776. Gadsden promptly replied that he favored a boycott without the cooperation of Virginia. "Boston and New England cant hold out—the Country will be deluged with Blood, if We dont Act with Spirit," he proclaimed. "Dont let America look at this Mountain, and let it bring forth a Mouse."[23] By the end of September, Congress, including the Virginia delegation, resolved to prohibit all trade with Great Britain, effective December 1.

The subject of a complete boycott of trade with Great Britain was reopened in October because the delegates from South Carolina, with the exception of Gadsden, flatly refused to cooperate unless the exportation of rice and indigo were exempted. The Congress compromised and agreed to exempt rice, but not indigo, in order to prevent the assembly from dissolving without taking a stand. Gadsden disapproved of the compromise. "Take care, or your liberties will be traded away," he warned.[24]

After losing the battle over the exemption of rice, Gadsden then fought to have the boycott of all other goods put into effect quickly. And again he lost. He and Edward Rutledge argued that the boycott should become effective in November 1774, but the nonimportation association as finally approved by the Congress resolved not to import any goods, slaves, or duty-laden tea from Great Britain from December 1, 1774, through September 20, 1775. If by the latter date Great Britain had not repealed all objectionable laws, then all exportations, except rice, to her and her possessions would cease.[25]

Gadsden thought the Congress was being too timid. He joined Samuel Adams in a denial of all authority of Parliament whatsoever, including the right to regulate trade. The majority of the delegates, however, still thought of themselves as Englishmen who should submit peacefully to Parliament's right to regulate trade. That right had not been questioned at the time of the Stamp Act. But Gadsden and Samuel Adams apparently thought that the only way to guarantee that Parliament would not impose any unconstitutional taxes upon the colonies was to deny Parliament all rights of legislation with regard to the Americans. When John Adams visited Gadsden at his lodging on September 14, he found Gadsden in a violent mood on the subject. "Power of regulating Trade he says, " Adams wrote, "is Power of ruining us—as bad as acknowledging [Parliament] a Supreme Legislative, in all Cases whatsoever. A Right of regulating Trade is a Right of Legislation, and a Right of Legislation in one Case, is a Right in all." John Adams denied that Gadsden's argument was correct, but he could not persuade Gadsden to give it up.[26]

The brief references to Gadsden in the contemporary records reveal the fury with which he stated his opinions. John Adams described him as "rough, honest, impulsive, and energetic."[27] Certainly Gadsden was all of those things, especially impulsive. With the possible exception of Samuel Adams, Gadsden was more ready than any other man there to fight if necessary to win back the natural rights of Englishmen. Even Edward Rutledge, who often agreed with Gadsden, thought that Gadsden was an extremist. Rutledge wrote that Congress might have done much mischief if Gadsden had had his way. Gadsden was "more violent, more wrong-headed" than ever, he explained.[28]

Gadsden's comments on military preparedness were not quite as extreme as Rutledge contended. Gadsden wrote a private correspondent that "the only way to prevent the sword from being used is to have it ready."[29] During one debate, Gadsden said, "I am for being ready, but I am not for the sword." Later, he explained, "There are numbers of men who will risk their all. I shudder at the thought of the blood which will be spilled, and would be glad to avoid it."[30] On another occasion he argued that the fear of death and destruction should not prevent Americans from going to war. "Our seaport towns are composed of brick and wood. If they are destroyed we have clay and lumber enough to rebuild them. But if the liberties of our country are destroyed where shall we find the materials to replace them?"[31] But Gadsden, like the majority of the delegates, hoped that England would make the concessions that were needed to end the crisis.

The four documents that Congress approved represented a compromise between the radicals and the conservatives, but they were significantly milder than the language Gadsden had used in the public debates. The Declaration of Rights appealed to the laws of nature, British common law, colonial charters, and provincial laws to deny Parliament the right of internal taxation; but it carefully recognized the supremacy of the Crown and stated the colonists' desire for reconciliation with the mother country. The petition to the king sandwiched sharp accusations against his "designing and dangerous" ministers between prolific expressions of filial devotion. An address was sent to the people of England, many of whom were sympathetic with the American whigs. An address was also framed to the people of Canada, especially those in Quebec, to explain the business of the Continental Congress. All four documents were signed by conservative Henry Middleton, who served as president of the Congress for its last five days.

If they did not enjoy a complete victory, the radicals nonetheless made an impression upon the Congress. Conservative Joseph Galloway's plan for colonial unity within the empire was discussed briefly and abandoned.[32] The delegates were committed to the further pursuit of their liberties if Great Britain remained intransigent. Machinery for enforcing the nonimportation agreement had been implemented and plans for a second congress were made. Whether or not the final compromise between conservatives and radicals would be sufficient to redress grievances and maintain peace depended upon the response from England.

The Congress adjourned on October 26, 1774, and on Sunday morning, November 6, the brigantine carrying the South Carolina delegation arrived in Charleston. That evening the delegates presented extracts of the proceedings of the Continental Congress to the General Committee. The committee congratulated them and invited them to an elegant celebration to be held in their honor on Wednesday, November 9, at Ramage's Tavern. At that festival, Gadsden and Lynch both made speeches. Gadsden read from the address to the people of Canada and from the petition to the king. Thomas Lynch explained that he favored the exemption of rice and indigo from the nonexportation agreement in order to place rice and indigo, which by British law had to be sold in Great Britain, on an equal footing with commodities produced in the northern colonies such as fish, meat, and flour that could be sold outside the British Isles. His opinion was warmly received, but Gadsden courageously maintained that rice should not have been exempted from the nonexportation agreement.[33]

Lieutenant Governor Bull feared that the celebrations might erupt into violent defiance of British authority. He promised Lord Dartmouth that he would do all in his power to arrest, detain, and secure any gunpowder, arms, or ammunition that might be imported into the province.[34] The Carolinians, however, did not intend to allow any royal interference. On December 8 the General Committee resolved that no person engaged in transacting public business, or going to, or returning from, a meeting to elect delegates to a provincial congress could be "arrested, imprisoned, summoned or otherwise molested by any Civil Process." The committee then resolved that an election would be held throughout the province on December 19 to choose delegates to a General Provincial Committee that would meet on January 11, 1775.[35]

When the General Provincial Committee met on January 11, it declared itself to be a Provincial Congress and proceeded to act as the independent government of the colony. It consisted of 184 delegates, 11 of whom did not attend. Gadsden was one of the 30 representatives from the city; 13 of the 30 were mechanics who had supported Gadsden since 1764. The backcountry was generously represented, and 40 of the 48 members of the Commons were present. In fact, the election apparently had been rigged to guarantee that a large number of mechanics and backcountrymen would be chosen. The Provincial Congress brought planters, merchants, backcountrymen, and artisans together as equals. It was almost as democratic as the chaotic general meeting that had chosen the delegates to the Continental Congress the previous summer. Disagreements were certain to flare, but the very existence of the Provincial Congress indicated that sectional and class differences in South Carolina were not so great as to prevent the colony from taking unified action against a common enemy.[36] The major items of business were to approve or disapprove the actions taken by the Continental Congress and to choose delegates to the second meeting of the Continental Congress.

Gadsden described the debates in the Provincial Congress as a series of "long Disputes and Heats."[37] The assembly divided loosely into two factions, one led by Gadsden and the other led by John Rutledge. As they had done in Philadelphia, Gadsden and Rutledge again took opposite sides on the question of the exportation of rice. This disagreement was the first of many between Gadsden and Rutledge, and it marked the culmination of Rutledge's conversion to the moderate viewpoint. Gadsden established himself as the spokesman for the small farmers who produced no rice. He argued that the exemption of rice favored one group in South Carolina over the rest and favored the southern province over their northern brethren. The words in the association, "except rice to Europe," which had nearly wrecked the

Continental Congress, should be removed in the interest of the common good, he said. William Tennent, a clergyman and spokesman for the backcountry, agreed with him, as did Rawlins Lowndes, a wealthy planter who wanted colonial unity and reconciliation with the mother country.

John Rutledge used the same arguments that Thomas Lynch had given at Ramage's Tavern on November 9. Rutledge begged the South Carolinians to allow the clause as written by the Continental Congress to stand. Rice should be excluded from the nonexportation agreement, he said, because the northern colonies could export flour and fish to countries other than Great Britain and thus would suffer little from the agreement. Since nearly all South Carolina indigo and about two-thirds of her rice went to British ports, South Carolina would be carrying an unfair proportion of the burden of nonexportation.

After listing to the arguments of both Gadsden and Rutledge, the members of the Provincial Congress fell into "downright uproar and confusion." Finally, after all were weary and the hour was late, the "question was put by candlelight." On an intimidating roll-call vote the moderates won by 87 to 75.[38] The resolutions of the Continental Congress were thus approved intact; Gadsden did not dominate his home province.

The other actions taken by the Provincial Congress were thoroughly rebellious. Since the majority of its members represented the debtor class, it easily forbade suit for debt in the local courts unless the full Congress approved; thus it ended the authority of the judicial branch of the royal government.[39] Henry Laurens's motion that debts owed to the Crown should be excepted was seconded by John Rutledge but soundly defeated.[40] The Congress then recommended that the inhabitants of the province give diligent attention "in learning the use of arms." It set aside February 17 "as a day of fasting, humiliation and prayer, before Almighty God, devoutly to petition him to inspire the King . . . to avert . . . the impending calamities of civil war."[41] Before adjourning on January 17, 1775, the Provincial Congress reelected all five delegates, including Gadsden, to the next session of the Continental Congress.

Henry Laurens did not vote to send Gadsden back to Philadelphia. "Unhappy Choice," he wrote to his son about Gadsden.

"How will posterity curse the projector of our present troubles & those who are forwarding his designs by machinations of their own." Laurens had agreed with Rutledge that the exportation of rice should be exempted from the association. He thought that by arguing to the contrary, Gadsden had been motivated by self-interest, insulting to his colleagues, and "an uncouth figure." Laurens was horrified by Gadsden's scheme not to pay debts owed to Great Britain and was dismayed by Gadsden's telling the Provincial Congress that in Philadelphia he had favored marching to Boston and sending General Gage and his soldiers back to England. But Laurens added that he might have expected such an irrational outburst from Gadsden because he remembered "how easy it was for that Gentleman to march through the Cherokee Mountains[,] Kill every Indian & return unscalped to Charles Town without moving one Step from his Fire Side." One who could do that could ship "off a veteran British General & three thousand regular troops with less trouble than he would Ship a Cargo of Rice." That, according to Laurens, was "an enterprising Reverie fit only to be laughed at—."[42]

When the Commons met at the end of January, however, it praised Gadsden, Lynch, Middleton, and the Rutledges for their services in Philadelphia. "Posterity will pay a just tribute to your Memories, and will revere the Names of the Members of the Continental Congress," Speaker Rawlins Lowndes proclaimed.[43] But the Commons had not been able to function legally since the Wilkes Fund dispute; its brief session was only ceremonial. Real power rested in the hands of the General Committee now charged with enforcing the new boycott.

On January 18, the very day after the Provincial Congress adjourned, the General Committee got to work. The first item for discussion was what to do about Georgia. Georgia had not sent delegates to Phialdelphia and had not signed the association. A little less than half a century earlier, the South Carolinians had welcomed the founding of Georgia as a buffer zone between them and the hostile Spaniards to the south. Now they feared that Georgia as a stronghold of British authority might jeopardize their chances to win back their liberties. The committee urged South Carolinians to have no dealings with Georgians "as unworthy of the freemen, and as inimical to the liberties, of their country."[44] Gadsden and his son Thomas were serving as agents, probably at a commission, to sell for a Philadelphia printer copies of the proceedings of the Continental Congress and various propaganda pamphlets. Following the will of the General Committee, Gadsden decided that he would not sell such literature to the uncooperative Georgians.[45]

The General Committee did its work well. The value of imports at Charleston fell from £378,116 in 1774 to £6,245 in 1775. Early in 1775 *Charming Martha* arrived with a cargo of British goods which were dumped into the harbor; a cargo of slaves was turned back. In March, a Carolina family residing in England requested permission to bring back to South Carolina their furniture and horses which they had previously owned in the province. After a long debate the General Committee granted their request by a narrow margin. A near riot broke out among people who were too poor to own horses and furniture that they could transport back and forth between Charleston and England. They looked to Gadsden for help. As a member of the General Committee, Gadsden moved that its decision be reversed. A second vote was taken, and Gadsden's motion carried to 35 to 34; neither the furniture nor the horses were allowed reentry.[46]

The prohibition against importing goods which Carolinians already owned struck the wealthier classes hardest and was a sure indication of the increasing power of Gadsden and his followers.[47] Laurens's son John was as dismayed by the actions of his countrymen as his father was. Citing a lesson from Roman history, the example of the third century B.C. dictator Fabius Maximus, who by a strategy of delay and avoidance of battle successfully harassed and annoyed Hannibal in the Second Punic War, John Laurens suggested that Carolinians should "emulate that noblest of all Patriots the Dictator Fabius. Let Mr. Gadsden read the Conduct of this great Man, and blush."[48]

Gadsden did not blush; he was not embarrassed to be a thorn in the sides of the royal officials. Lieutenant Governor Bull reported sadly that "Authority and reason unsupported by real Power are too weak to stem the torrent of popular prejudices." He hoped, but not very optimistically, that the "Men of property" who suffered most from the association would ultimately be able to break the "many headed power of the People."[49] Bull's hopes were shattered by the news in April that Parliament had ignored the petition from the Continental Congress and had granted the king's request for additional troops to enforce the laws of the empire in America.

Something approaching a state of war already existed in South Carolina. In accord with the directions of the Provincial Congress, troops were being organized and drilled. On the night of April 20, five members of the Provincial Congress, calling themselves the Secret Committee, stole the public supply of gunpowder from the Hobcaw and Charleston Neck magazines and from the weapons in the State House. They delivered it the next morning to Gadsden's Wharf for storage. Not bothering to wear disguises, they did the deed at night to avoid embarrassing the lieutenant governor. The next day Bull reported to the Commons the "extraordinary and alarming" disappearance of 800 guns, 200 cutlasses, and 1,600 pounds of powder. The House responded that its investigation had failed to reveal the culprits, but it had "reason to suppose that some of the inhabitants of this colony may have been induced to take so extraordinary and uncommon a step in consequence of the late alarming accounts from Great Britain."[50]

The Carolinians did not know that in Massachusetts on the very day before, April 19, 1775, a similar controversy had resulted in the firing of the first shot in the Revolution. Gadsden himself would hear about it only after he arrived again in Philadelphia.

CHAPTER SEVEN

"DONT TREAD ON ME"

After sailing for five days without incident, Christopher Gadsden arrived in Philadelphia on May 8, 1775. He found the city near the point of hysteria. The news of the fighting at Lexington and Concord had, for the times, spread like wildfire. It had reached Philadelphia in only five days, Charleston on the very day Gadsden disembarked at Philadelphia, and distant Savannah on May 10. Gadsden's immediate reaction was irrational excitement and a total willingness to fight. Adopting a firm stance to the left of the majority, he threw himself into the work with the passion of a man obsessed. He had but a day and a half to wait before the second session of the Continental Congress convened.

When Gadsden surveyed the gathering on May 10, he saw many of the same men who had been there in 1774. Among the more significant additions were John Hancock of Massachusetts and Benjamin Franklin of Pennsylvania. Lyman Hall, elected by St. John's Parish in Georgia, appeared on May 13, marking the first time ever that that province had participated in a continental gathering. Thomas Jefferson of Virginia took his seat on June 21. Despite the presence of men from all thirteen colonies and the appearance of unanimity, the majority of delegates were more interested in the welfare of their individual provinces than that of the united colonies. Among the southerners, only Christopher Gadsden, Patrick Henry, and Richard Henry Lee placed the needs of the united colonies above sectional interests. A whole month passed before the Congress decided to organize a Continental Army. Five days later, June 15, it appointed George Washington as commander in chief. No doubt many members, including Gadsden, had privately come to the conclusion that independence was the only way for the American colonies to win their rights, but none dared to make a public demand for such a radical solution.[1]

The majority of the members still wished to patch up the disagreement with the mother country, and even the radical minority wanted to make Great Britain appear to be the aggressor. Hence, on July 8, 1775, Gadsden joined forty-five others in signing the famed "Olive Branch Petition." Addressed to the king in the form of a last desperate request for autonomy within the empire, the document was written largely by conservative John Dickinson of Pennsylvania. It was a necessary concession to the majority and good propaganda to prove to the people at home and abroad that the Americans were doing their share to halt hostilities. But King George III had already decided to bring the rebels to submission; he rejected the olive branch and thus drove the Americans deeper into the world of armed resistance.[2]

Gadsden assumed a significantly more important role than he had in the first session of the Continental Congress. The balance between conservatives and radicals rested with the members from South Carolina, thus increasing the interest others took in the opinions of Gadsden. Henry Middleton and Thomas Lynch, both old and very wealthy, did not want war. Moderate John Rutledge was still inclined to put the needs of South Carolina before those of the unified colonies. His brother Edward was less moderate but still far behind Gadsden. Gadsden was clearly the most independent thinker from his home province. After the Congress had been in session for four months, John Adams wrote that Christopher Gadsden was more committed to the American cause than any other person there. In fact, Adams implied that the other delegates understood so well that Gadsden was already in favor of independence that they did not even attempt to change his mind.[3]

In his leisure hours, Gadsden sought the congenial company of the most radical delegates. He passed the afternoon of September 20 drinking coffee and enjoying "free conversation" with a group of men who welcomed war after the king had rejected the olive branch.[4] The group included John Adams, Samuel Adams, Samuel Ward, and Christopher Marshall. Ward, one year younger than Gadsden, was a farmer, former governor of Rhode Island, and ex-conservative who had become indignant over the tea crisis and had shifted to the radical perspective. He died of smallpox in Philadelphia three months before independence was declared. Christopher Marshall was a Quaker intellectual who scoffed at the notion of pacifism; he was excluded from Quaker fellowship when he openly advocated war with Great Britain. His home was a salon where the delegates could talk about religion and politics. A prolific diarist and freethinker, he was eventually converted to unitarianism.[5] Gadsden enjoyed his company.

Although the majority of Southern delegates distrusted the radicalism of the New Englanders, Gadsden was quick to defend them. He argued vigorously for colonial unity before it was a popular idea in Charleston. Four years later, when South Carolina was in imminent danger of an invasion and desperately needed the help of New England, Gadsden reminded Samuel Adams that he had attempted to allay the "insinuating distrusts of the New England States" during the Congress. "How often I stood up in their Defense," Gadsden wrote. "I bless'd God there was such a People in America," he said, "and only wish we wou'd imitate instead of abusing them." Any danger for Boston or Providence was also a danger for Charleston and Savannah, he thought.[6]

If some members of the Congress did not appreciate Gadsden's radicalism, others realized that his limited military experience and extensive trade connections made him a valuable member. John Hancock, president of the Congress, appointed him to a committee to put the militia in a proper state for the defense of the colonies.[7] This committee appealed to each colony to send ammunition and supplies to the Continental Congress, the cost to be borne by having the delegates personally sign certificates of public credit. The debt would be repaid through each colony's normal program of taxation. The entire burden was distributed among all the cooperating colonies proportionately to population.

For South Carolina, Gadsden, Edward Rutledge, and Thomas Lynch each signed eighty-four £50 certificates. On July 1, Gadsden and the others from South Carolina sent an urgent letter to their local Secret Committee in Charleston requesting gunpowder. They suggested that it be hidden among bushels of rice and shipped immediately to Philadelphia.[8] The Secret Committee did its work well; on July 19 the Council of Safety reported that 5,000 pounds of gunpowder, which had been borrowed from Georgia, was loaded and ready to sail. Its safe arrival enabled the patriots to continue the siege of Boston that had been under way since the fighting at Lexington and Concord, and some of it was later used in the American invasion of Canada.[9] Gadsden also served on a committee that investigated ways to collect, smelt, and refine lead, and he assisted in raising a company of artillerymen in Philadelphia to be sent to Boston.[10]

The demand for military preparedness forced the Congress to move quickly to protect the trade of the colonies. Hancock appointed Christopher Gadsden, John Jay, Benjamin Franklin, Silas Deane, and Richard Henry Lee to think up ways to do so. This committee was immediately concerned with the problem of how to import munitions and export produce to pay for them, but what conclusions it reached went unrecorded.[11] The very existence of the committee, however, raised enormous questions about which the delegates could not agree. For a group of colonies locked into a mercantile economic system to develop new patterns of trade implied a declaration of independence.

Gadsden welcomed the opportunity for change; he envisioned the conflict as partly a struggle for free trade. Such an attitude set him apart from merchants who still seemed to desire no more than a return to the status quo before 1763. At the first session of the Continental Congress, during the debates over the association, Gadsden had argued that it would be stupid for the Americans to tax their own trade, and after the war was over he insisted that the new nation should be founded upon the principle of free trade.[12]

In the trade committee meetings during the summer of 1775, Gadsden argued violently against any arrangement that would give one or more of the colonies preferential treatment. "Let the Point be whether We shall shut up all our Ports, and be all on a footing," he debated. He adamantly opposed giving South Carolina special privileges to export rice to any of Great Britain's possessions. "One colony will envy another, and be jealous. Mankind act by their feelings," he said. He insisted that all American ports should be closed to all trade with Great Britain. And he hoped that closing the ports would create a demand for a continental navy.[13]

The Continental Navy was finally born amid scenes of bewildering confusion. The lack of records, the casualness with which the relevant committees went about their work, and the general neglect which the navy suffered during the war and for many decades afterward all served to obscure its beginnings and importance. The scraps of evidence in John Adams's diary, however, suggest that Gadsden's part in the creation of the navy may have been profound, perhaps even his greatest contribution to the second session of the Continental Congress. Although John Adams has traditionally been given the credit for suggesting a navy, Adams himself clearly said that he had never thought about the need for a fleet until Gadsden urged him to consider it. Since childhood, Gadsden had been associated with naval affairs. He had served actively in the Royal Navy thirty years earlier, and he probably knew more about British sea power than any other member of Congress.[14]

Gadsden was certain that a few American vessels could protect the North American coast from the British navy. He attempted to convince John Adams that it would be easy to take the small British sloops, schooners, and cutters that sailed near the coast. With these captured vessels, the Americans could then attack Great Britain's larger ships, upon which lived many impressed and discontented men. Gadsden thought that these sailors would not resist because they would understand that an American victory would restore their liberty and happiness. Gadsden "has several Times taken Pains to convince me," John Adams wrote, "that the [British] Fleet is not so formidable to America as we fear. . . . He thinks the Men would not fight on board the large ships with their fellow subjects but would certainly kill their own officers." If the Americans acquired a fleet of their own, Gadsden continued, this development would "give great Spirit to the Continent, as well as little Spirit to the Ministry." But Gadsden's plan apparently never made it to the floor for discussion.[15]

Inspired by Gadsden's enthusiasm, John Adams talked about his plan with other New Englanders and thus cleared the way for Stephen Hopkins and Samuel Ward of Rhode Island to present an ambitious plan to the Congress on October 7. New England had more to gain from a navy than the southern provinces did, because the ships would be built in northern shipyards and largely manned by Yankee sailors. Rhode Island, more exposed to the sea, especially needed the protection of a navy. Following their instructions, Ward and Hopkins introduced a resolution calling for a complete American fleet.[16]

A lively debate erupted over the Rhode Island plan. Samuel Chase of Maryland thought it was "the maddest Idea in the World" to think that the colonies could afford such a navy. Edward Rutledge declared it was like "an infant taking a mad bull by the horns." But the Reverend John Joachim Zubly from Georgia, who had joined the Congress only three weeks earlier, attempted to defend the Rhode Island idea. Gadsden was at first against the "Extensiveness of the Rhode Island Plan," but he thought it was "absolutely necessary that some Plan of Defence by Sea should be adopted." Then John Rutledge confused the issue by proposing that a committee be appointed to study the cost of a fleet. Both Samuel Adams and John Adams thought it foolish to appoint such a committee before the Congress decided how many ships should be built. While this stage of the debate raged, Zubly, Rutledge, Robert Treat Paine, and Gadsden were, according to John Adams, "lightly skirmishing." Gadsden said that the appointment of the committee suggested by Rutledge would throw the Rhode Island plan to build a fleet "into Ridicule." At this point in the debate, he appeared to be in complete agreement with the Rhode Island plan and no doubt was pleased when the Congress defeated John Rutledge's motion. The original proposal of Stephen Hopkins was then approved by a narrow margin.[17]

A Naval Committee then evolved from several smaller committees. Congress first appointed Silas Deane, John Langdon, and John Adams to acquire two armed ships from Massachusetts. On October 13 Congress asked Silas Deane, John Langdon, and Christopher Gadsden to estimate the cost of fitting out two armed vessels that could be used to intercept British vessels laden with military supplies. The replacement of John Adams with Christopher Gadsden was partly an attempt to win southern support, but it was also a recognition of Gadsden's enthusiasm for the project and his own naval and trade experiences that would make him a very useful member of the committee. Before the end of the month, Congress expanded the three-man committee to seven by adding John Adams, Stephen Hopkins, Joseph Hewes of North Carolina, and Richard Henry Lee. The committee was now called the Naval Committee, but early in 1776, it was renamed the Marine Committee.[18]

The Naval Committee immediately purchased the merchant vessel *Black Prince*, rechristened her *Alfred*, and outfitted her as the flagship of the Continental Navy. By the end of the year, *Columbus, Andrew Doria*, and *Cabot* were added. *Alfred* and *Columbus* were large, clumsy vessels which had been originally built to haul 300 tons of cargo. They required extensive internal bracing to withstand the weight of their armaments. *Cabot* was a fourteen-gun brig about 75 feet long, but nothing is known of the dimensions of *Andrew Doria*.[19]

The Naval Committee proceeded to recruit and direct the Continental Navy. It gave specific instructions to merchants Silas Deane and Dudley Saltonstall to outfit ships and recruit sailors. It appointed fifty-seven-year-old, rugged Commodore Esek Hopkins of Rhode Island as commander in chief, instructed him to direct all the captains, correspond with the committee, equip vessels and appoint officers, issue all orders in writing, take care that all men in his command were properly fed and clothed, protect his weapons, and see that prisoners "be well and humanely treated." Hopkins was to "dispose of all the Men you make Prisoners in such manner as you may judge safe for North America and will least retard the Service you are upon." Whenever he though it expedient, Hopkins could hand his prisoners over to the nearest local Council of Public Safety. Since Congress supplied the financing for the navy, rewards for extraordinary individual exertions were not to be paid out of the continental share of the captures; Congress was always to receive two-thirds of the value of all cargoes taken, the other one-third going to the sailors.[20]

The Naval Committee often met at night and sometimes mixed pleasure with business. John Adams thought that his service on that committee was the "pleasantest part of my Labours." He described Christopher Gadsden and Richard Henry Lee as "sensible men, and very chearful." But Stephen Hopkins, more than

Christopher Gadsden's Flag. The bright yellow flag that Gadsden designed was an appropriate symbol of the Revolution.

seventy years old, was the life of the party. At about eight o'clock in the evening, Hopkins began to consume "Jamaica Spirit and water," which gave him "Wit, Humour, Anecdotes, Science and Learning." He engaged the others, all "very temperate" gentlemen, in lively conversation until eleven or twelve in the evening. Adams hastened to add that Hopkins did not drink to excess but only enough to get into a "good humour" and inspire the others "with similar qualities."[21]

Perhaps in one of their sessions someone suggested that they ought to create a special flag for the navy. The weight of tradition and circumstantial evidence attributes the creation of the famed rattlesnake flag to Christopher Gadsden. It consisted of a coiled rattlesnake, painted gray on a bright yellow backgound, with the words "DONT TREAD ON ME" inscribed beneath. The snake had long been a political symbol in America; at the time of the Albany Congress in 1754 Benjamin Franklin had drawn a disconnected serpent and given it the caption, "Join or Die." The coiled, threatening rattlesnake in 1775 was a symbol of the unity that the colonies had achieved. As a resident of the lowcountry of South Carolina, Gadsden would have seen many rattlesnakes and have learned to treat them with respect. In Charleston the rattlesnake was regarded as a noble and useful creature who warned his enemies before he struck. He attacked only in self-defense but was always deadly. No more fitting symbol could have been found to express the mood of the Continental Congress. A drummer parading through the streets of Philadelphia to attract recruits painted the emblem on the side of his drum, and the design was probably intended to be used to decorate all of the arms of North America.[22]

Gadsden's Flag was first seen unfurled from the main mast of *Alfred* on December 20, 1775, when she rested at anchor in the Chesapeake Bay opposite Philadelphia. Gadsden had sent the flag as a gift to Commander Esek Hopkins. Hopkins used it as his personal flag and always flew it from the mainmast of the flagship when he was on board. Two other flags were also displayed. From *Alfred*'s bow flew the navy jack, a small square flag with alternate red and white stripes, a crawling snake, and the words "DONT TREAD ON ME." From the stern drifted the Grand Union Flag, composed of the old British jack in the canton and thirteen red and white stripes in the field.[23] The Grand Union Flag was the official flag of the Continental Navy, but Gadsden's Flag became the most popular symbol of the American Revolution.

The brilliant color of Gadsden's Flag with the brazen warning to Great Britain that she had better not trample upon the liberties of her subjects was a perfect symbol of its creator's participation in the Continental Congress. Not content to be a quiet committeeman, Gadsden seized every chance to stir up emotions against the mother country, or to praise a patriot leader. Three days before Christmas 1775, he persuaded Congress to publish that part of a letter from an American officer quoting an Indian who said a British official "invited them to take up the Hatchet against the Colonists and . . . feast on the Flesh and Blood of a New England man." After the aborted attack on Quebec in the winter of 1775 and 1776, a campaign which Congress never tried to reconcile with its contention that it was fighting only for the colonists' rights within the empire, Gadsden moved, and the other delegates concurred, that Benedict Arnold be promoted to brigadier general and receive the thanks of Congress for his heroism.[24] John Adams noted that Gadsden was unapproachable by John Dickinson, whom Gadsden later called a "Tiptoe Gentleman" who wanted to remain in the empire.[25]

In the meantime the hostility between Gadsden's native South Carolina and Great Britain mounted to such a point that the Provincial Congress called him home. By the winter of 1775, the South Carolina Provincial Congress expected a British invasion at Charleston, and it asked Gadsden to return and command the provincial troops. On January 2, 1776, Gadsden asked permission from Congress to leave. His request at first was refused, perhaps indicating the importance which his colleagues attached to his services; but by January 14 he had received his orders from the South Carolina Provincial Congress and permission from the Continental Congress to depart.[26]

Before leaving Philadelphia, Gadsden recruited troops in the northern colonies to aid against the anticipated British attack at Charleston. Upon the recommendation of his "very worthy Friend Col. Gadsden," Samuel Ward, three times governor of Rhode Island and a member of the Naval Committee, urged his brother to assist Captain Robert Cochran in getting sailors for

South Carolina.[27] Cochran, now in Rhode Island recruiting for the navy, had been the powder receiver in Charleston who on the night of April 20, 1775, had assisted the Carolina rebels in stealing ammunition from the public supply. His mission to gather sailors was equally successful, and he apparently departed for the southern province about the same time Gadsden did. Congress ordered Commander Esek Hopkins to sail to Charleston to ascertain the number and sizes of British ships that might be cruising along the southern coast. Gadsden immediately sent Hopkins a list of all the officers he would find in South Carolina. "I flatter myself we shall have your assistance at Carolina," Gadsden continued, "where you may depend on an easy Conquest." Gadsden assured Hopkins that if he did run into trouble he could count upon assistance from the Carolinians. A few days later Gadsden suggested a system of flag signals that Hopkins might use to announce his approach to Charleston. But the signals were never used, for ice sealed over the Delaware River before any of the continental ships could sail. Gadsden himself would take passage in a small pilot boat before the river iced over.[28]

Gadsden's imminent departure from Philadelphia brought a flurry of comments from his colleagues. Moderate Thomas Lynch drily noted, "My Colleague Gadsden is gone home, to Command our Troops, God save them."[29] Within several weeks after Gadsden left on January 18, another delegate wrote, "You would be surprised to see with how much dispatch we have done business since . . . Gaddesden [*sic*] left us."[30] On the other hand, Richard Henry Lee remembered Gadsden "with much affection";[31] George Washington trusted him;[32] and John Adams thought that he was the most trustworthy and patriotic American at the Congress and that he had one of the purest hearts in America. Gadsden, according to John Adams, "had less influence than many others, who had neither so considerable parts, nor any share at all of [his] purity of intention."[33]

Gadsden's impact upon the Congress may not have been immediately apparent to John Adams, but the Congress had scarcely made a decision that Gadsden disapproved. On blank pages interleaved in his personal copy of the journal, he took copious notes in shorthand on issues that impressed him.[34] He copied a letter which had been written in New York, intercepted, and read to the Continental Congress on June 25, 1775. The letter described the real danger that the rebellion in New York might lapse into a bloody civil war because of the presence of so many loyalists, a situation which Gadsden knew also existed in South Carolina. Gadsden took extensive notes on John Adams's speech against Parliament's right to legislate for the colonies without their approval. He transcribed the speech William Pitt made in Parliament defending the rights of the North American colonists; and in a note on the cover of his journal that recalled the Albany Congress of 1754, Gadsden wrote, "Government itself called a Congress in the last war to apportion the quotas of men and troops." Still thinking like a whig politician, Gadsden wanted his actions and those of the Congress to be recognized as being within the realm of British law and tradition. But Gadsden was irked by the delegates who were lukewarm in the resistance. He copied a letter that John Adams wrote to his wife Abigail and apparently handed to Gadsden to read, in which Adams bemoaned the fact that so many of their colleagues did not seem to appreciate the urgency and importance of the Congress.[35] Gadsden probably intended to use these notes to help win his fellow South Carolinians over to his viewpoint as well as to impress upon them the great importance of the assembly in Philadelphia.

During the eight months that Gadsden spent in Philadelphia, the revolution in South Carolina had leaped ahead. The last royal governor, Lord William Campbell, had arrived in Charleston on June 18, 1775, but he had been denied the joyous and colorful fanfare that had greeted his predecessors. He was unable to exercise the royal prerogative, for political power now resided in the Provincial Congress of which Gadsden was a member in absentia. Patriot mobs carrying buckets of tar and bags of feathers often terrorized loyalists in the streets. In August a mob hanged Jerry, a free Negro pilot, and burned his corpse because allegedly he had offered to guide British warships across the bar. Two Roman Catholic loyalists, James Dealy and Laughlin Martin, who reportedly favored arming Catholics, Indians, and Negroes, were stripped, tarred, feathered, carted through the streets, and banished. A gunner at Fort Johnson was tarred, feathered, and exhibited in front of the home of the most obnoxious British officials. The Provincial Congress sent a successful expedition against the loyalists in the backcountry. Lord Campbell feared for his own safety; he slipped out into the harbor where he took shelter on board H. M. S. *Tamar*. From there he encouraged the loyalists to continue to fight and occasionally exchanged ineffectual shots with a patriot schooner. Finally, on November 12, 1775, the last royal governor of South Carolina fled to the high seas. "They have dipt their hands in Blood," Campbell wrote. "God Almighty knows where it will end."[36]

CHAPTER EIGHT

A Man on Revolution Bent

On the cold, icy day of January 18, 1776, Gadsden, his son Thomas, and several other passengers boarded the small pilot boat *Hawke* for the trip from Philadelphia to Charleston. Since *Hawke*'s captain intended to seek a harbor quickly if spotted by a British warship, he hoped to slide through the stormy Atlantic as close to the shoreline as safely possible. The captain and his passengers were acutely aware that a state of war existed between Great Britain and her North American colonies. Some commander of one of His Majesty's ships might be all too pleased to capture the notorious Christopher Gadsden en route to his home in Charleston. Gadsden knew that he risked his first personal experience in the military conflict, but he probably never dreamed that in the course of his passage he would undergo the emotional and intellectual transformation that marked his final, violent commitment to independence in North America. The catalyst that brought about this change was *Common Sense*.

On January 9, nine days before Gadsden sailed, the first copies of *Common Sense* appeared for sale in Philadelphia. This pamphlet had been written by a young Englishman, Thomas Paine, who had been in America less than two years. He had arrived in America with no money, but with a valuable introduction to Benjamin Franklin. Paine's immediate interest was to earn a decent living, not to fuel a revolution. But he wrote about precisely the right topics at the right time. A radical English whig who had weathered the Wilkes dispute on the side of Wilkes, Paine attacked King George III with the strongest language imaginable. With dramatic words that could be easily understood by all

147

people, he urged Americans to declare their independence and to establish a republican government without a king. Within a few months, thousands of copies were distributed from New Hampshire to Georgia.[1]

Gadsden purchased three copies—one for himself, one to present to the South Carolina Provincial Congress, and one to send to Savannah as an antidote to the loyalism that still gripped Georgia. No doubt he read it before leaving Philadelphia, but he intended to pass his days on board *Hawke* studying it closely. Gadsden learned nothing from *Common Sense* that he did not already know. He found no new political philosophy, no additional details in the whig interpretation of British history, and no fresh revelations of the merits of republican government. Paine's violent attack against the king himself, however, went to excesses beyond Gadsden's imagination. What Gadsden acquired from his reading of *Common Sense* was the courage to be the first man in South Carolina to stand up in a public assembly filled with loyalists and doubters and speak out in favor of independence.

As Gadsden read the pamphlet, he became increasingly excited; he liberally underlined Paine's sentences and phrases that were critical of the British monarchy's destruction of the natural rights of man.[2] Paine appealed to European history, the Bible, nature, and common sense to prove that a monarchy was the most absurd form of government that man could devise. "Holland, without a king," Paine wrote, "enjoyed more peace for the last century than any of the monarchical governments in Europe." Those who approved of a monarchy, Paine continued, were as unprepared to choose a new system of government "as a man who is attached to a prostitute is unfitted to choose or judge of a wife." The history of the Hebrews proved that "the Almighty hath entered his protest against monarchical government." Nature herself registered disapproval of "the folly of hereditary rights in kings" by frequently turning it into "ridicule by giving mankind an *ass for a lion*." An hereditary monarchy might mean that in the next generation the king would be a "rogue or fool." In fact, the current monarch of Great Britain was descended from "a French bastard" who had landed in 1066 "with an armed banditti" and established "himself king of England against the consent of the natives."

Gadsden became ecstatic when he read Paine's analysis of the situation in North America. The new world, Paine wrote, was "the asylum for the persecuted lovers of civil and religious liberty from every part of Europe." Since not more than one-third of the inhabitants of America were British, the phrase "parent or mother country, applied to England only" was "false, selfish, narrow, and ungenerous." Paine declared, "The next war . . . will be . . . for separation." He concluded that "until an independence is declared, the continent will feel itself like a man who continues putting off some unpleasant business from day to day, yet knows it must be done, hates to set about it, wishes it over, and is continually haunted with the thoughts of its necessity."

Gadsden was so engrossed in his reading that he temporarily forgot the danger that accompanied *Hawke*'s voyage toward Charleston. But suddenly he was reminded, for the British man-of-war *Syren* appeared upon the horizon and bore down upon the small pilot boat. *Hawke* veered dangerously inward upon the coast of North Carolina, finally coming to rest near the state's southern boundary. Her passengers, captain, and crew scrambled overboard and fled into the nearby swamp. Gadsden clutched his copies of *Common Sense* and his annotated copy of the journal of the Continental Congress as he scurried to safety. In the meantime, a second British man-of-war, *Tender*, appeared upon the scene. She sailed in close to *Hawke* only to find her a drifting ghost ship.[3] The travelers apparently made the rest of their journey over land, for they did not arrive in Charleston until February 8. A trip that should have required only four or five days of easy sailing had taken twenty-one days, many of them difficult and terrifying.

On Friday, February 9, 1776, Gadsden made a triumphal entry into the meeting of the South Carolina Provincial Congress. He was carrying the bright yellow flag with the emblem of a rattlesnake coiled and ready to strike, and beneath that the warning "DONT TREAD ON ME." Some members cheered as he walked to the front of the room and presented it to the president of the Congress. The president ordered it displayed at the left side of his chair. The Congress promptly approved a resolution thanking Gadsden for his service in Philadelphia. Since Gadsden had been called home to command the First South Carolina Regiment, the president then appointed him to a committee on defense. Before the end of the day, Gadsden's name was also added to a list of men charged with drawing up a temporary form of government to be used until the dispute with Great Britain ended.[4] Not a man there yet knew what had transpired in Gadsden's mind during his long trip home. He enjoyed a brief moment of glory.

The man who occupied the president's chair was none other than Gadsden's old adversary, William Henry Drayton. Drayton had undergone a dramatic transformation from defender of the Crown to the most ardent patriot in the province except for Gadsden. Drayton had sailed for London in January 1770 in disgust over the harsh treatment he had received for refusing to sign the nonimportation agreement of 1769. But he had returned in 1771 to accept a succession of temporary appointments to the Royal Council, as deputy postmaster general for the Southern District in North America, and to the South Carolina Circuit Court. He was quickly removed from the latter two positions to make room for English placemen. Realizing that there was little hope for natives of the province to hold top offices, Drayton was converted into a radical revolutionary. He violently attacked the Intolerable Acts of 1774, warmly endorsed the first two sessions of the Continental Congress, led a successful expedition against the loyalists in the Carolina backcountry in 1775, and fired several shots at the fleeing Governor Campbell in November 1775. Probably as a reward for his patriotism, he had been elected president of the Provincial Congress, but very few of the other members agreed with his or Gadsden's radicalism.[5]

Drayton was presiding over the Provincial Congress on Saturday, February 10, 1776, when Gadsden threw it into chaos by announcing publicly for the first time that he was in favor of independence. Gadsden read from *Common Sense*, probably the very passages that he had underlined on board *Hawke*. His precise words were not recorded, but apparently he then expressed his approval of Paine and declared that the time had come for the American colonies to declare their independence. Gadsden's speech, Drayton said, fell upon the Congress "like an explosion of thunder." Its members were horrified by such a harsh denunciation of their king and frightened by the specter of independence. John Rutledge shouted that Gadsden was guilty of treason and declared that he himself would ride post day and night to Philadelphia to prevent separation from the mother country. Henry Laurens later said privately that the notorious pamphlet was filled with "indecent expressions" that Paine had plagiarized from an "Apology for the Revolt of the Low Countries." Rawlins Lowndes cursed Paine soundly in front of the full Congress. And one Charleston loyalist sadly noted, "Gadsden is as mad with [*Common Sense*], as ever he was without it."[6]

Gadsden's madness prompted the Provincial Congress to meet in a special session the next day, a Sunday afternoon, to blunt his impact. Gadsden was particularly dangerous, because the day before his outburst he had already been appointed to a committee to draw up some plan of government for South Carolina. This government was to last only while the dispute with Great Britain lasted; it was not supposed to be permanently independent of the mother country. Therefore, on Sunday afternoon, the committee was stacked with moderates who would mute Gadsden's demand for independence. Gadsden's incendiary speech created such apprehension among the members that they probably would have abandoned any plan to write even a temporary constitution if ominous news had not arrived from England. Parliament had declared the Americans to be in a state of rebellion and had authorized the seizure of their cargo vessels. This news diminished the dissension among the committee members sufficiently for them to proceed to write a constitution.[7]

The South Carolina Constitution of 1776 was the epitome of vagueness; it could have been written only by a group of people who were fighting for their independence but still afraid to admit what they were doing. The preamble timidly stated that since "Lord William Campbell, late Governor," had attempted to destroy their "lives, liberties and properties," they were forced to assume the management of their own domestic affairs. Although they had been "traduced and treated as rebels" by their parent country, they still earnestly desired "an accommodation of the unhappy differences between Great Britain and America." Nevertheless, they created a president, vice president, General Assembly, and Legislative Council to replace the governor, lieutenant governor, Provincial Congress, and Privy Council. The 202 members of the General Assembly were to be elected every two years; they were to vote each year to elect the president. He would have very little appointive power. The judiciary would be severely crippled; judges would be nominated by the General Assembly and commissioned by the president. He could remove them at his pleasure.[8]

The document was carefully planned to allow the native elite to occupy offices formerly held by placemen, but it was just as carefully designed to prevent the intrusion of the unpropertied masses into local politics. Two-thirds of the members of the General Assembly were apportioned to the lowcountry, and thirty of those to Charleston. All officers had to own significant property to be eligible for election. In order to vote, a man had to own at least 50 acres of land. The document was not submitted to the people for ratification; the Provincial Congress simply declared it to be in effect on March 26, 1776. In the first election, John Rutledge and Henry Laurens were named president and vice president. Neither man favored independence. In his inaugural address, Rutledge flatly stated "that no Man would embrace a Just & equitable Accommodation with Great Britain more gladly" than himself.[9] Gadsden thought Rutledge "perverted" the constitution by viewing it as temporary until reconciliation could be achieved.[10] Gadsden and Drayton both were elected to the General Assembly, but they were so outnumbered by moderates that they were not likely to have much influence.

The safest place in the new government to shelve dangerous radicals like Gadsden and Drayton was the judiciary. The General Assembly nominated them both for judgeships. John Rutledge granted them their commissions, but he could remove them any time he wished. Gadsden and Drayton both understood quite well what had been done to them. Drayton used his post as a forum to follow Gadsden's example and declare for independence. While expounding upon the new constitution before a grand jury, he reviewed a century of British history and concluded that "the Almighty created America to be independent of Britain."[11] Gadsden knew that there was nothing he could accomplish as a powerless judge; he decided to search for some extraconstitutional means to mount his drive for independence.

The issue that Gadsden used was the disestablishment of the Anglican Church; a bill calling for it was already being circulated throughout the province. By working for disestablishment, Gadsden could win political support from the lower middle class in Charleston and the numerous Baptists, Presbyterians, and other Protestants, many of whom lived in the backcountry. He was appealing to the same groups he had courted during the Stamp and Townshend crises. But Gadsden was completely unsuccessful in 1776. The people in the backcountry had very little power under the new constitution, and even the revolutionaries in Charleston did not wish to separate the church from the state. The Anglican clergymen in South Carolina were usually patriots. Of the twenty-six Sons of Liberty whom Gadsden had rallied beneath the Liberty Tree in 1766, ten were members of St. Philip's.[12] Gadsden may have gained some political clout by fighting for disestablishment in 1776, but it was an idea whose time had not yet come.

Religious freedom stemmed from political freedom and was equal to it, Gadsden thought. In the margin of *Common Sense* next to Paine's argument for freedom of religion, Gadsden wrote "Noble Sentiments." At the Continental Congress, he had been fascinated by Christopher Marshall's discussions of unitarianism. Gadsden was not converted to unitarianism, but he seemed to like its toleration of many theological viewpoints and emphasis upon human virtue. He accepted dissenters and counted clergymen of several denominations among his friends. Gadsden's personal theology was almost pietistic. He had an unshakable faith in the sovereignty of a benevolent God. Twenty years earlier he had belonged to a religious and literary discussion group organized by Richard Clarke, a rabid, evangelistic Anglican clergyman in Charleston who had once predicted the end of the world. Silas Deane, who first met Gadsden in Philadelphia in 1774, found Gadsden to be a "regularly, religious" man.[13] His service as a vestryman at St. Philip's, habitual attendance, and persistent use of the church's ministries sprang as certainly from the sincerity of his faith as it did from the prominence of his position in Charleston society.

Despite the busyness of Gadsden's public life in the first four months of 1776, he found time to court the woman who would become his third wife. She was Ann Wragg, a spinster, age forty-five, and a member of one of the wealthiest and most prominent families in South Carolina. Gadsden had probably known her for all of her life and perhaps had enjoyed many social events with her in the eight years since his second wife had died. Gadsden had always relished the company and affection of his immediate family. He was still hale and vigorous at the age of fifty-two. He did not seem to mind that his new love came from a family of loyalists. Ann was a double first cousin to William Wragg, Gadsden's antagonist during the nonimportation debate who was banished in 1777 for his refusal to support the war for independence, and who subsequently drowned at sea.[14] Ann herself was probably apolitical, for it was not customary for women to discuss politics. And she was worth a small fortune. According to her marriage contract, which required that her property remain in her family, she owned fifty slaves, bonds worth £21,700, two lots and a dwelling in Charleston, and half of the 3,000 acres, stock, and tools in Dockon Plantation.[15]

Christopher Gadsden and Ann Wragg were married in St. Philip's Church on April 14, 1776. Despite their own personal maturity, they must have felt something of the excitement that the unsettled times would certainly impose upon them. Perhaps the chance of an imminent political upheaval deepened their commitment to each other, like that of a young couple at the threshold of an unknown life together. They made a good marriage that endured long separations and severe hardships. But on April 14 that fate was still in their future. After their wedding ceremony, according to Henry Laurens, the happy couple went to "Mr. Wragg's Seat near the Quarter House to celebrate & consummate—."[16]

The British, however, were not likely to delay their planned invasion of the southern colonies to suit the convenience of the celebrating and consummating commander of the First South Carolina Regiment. Since December 6, 1775, they had planned to attack Charleston, and their intent was known in Philadelphia by January 1776. The British commanders anticipated a light struggle after which they would restore South Carolina to royal control and promptly return to New York. But they were not thoroughly acquainted with the fortifications of Charleston harbor, and they had underestimated the strength of the patriot resistance and overestimated the numbers of loyalists who would be in close

Ann Wragg Gadsden (date unknown but probably about the time of her marriage to Christopher Gadsden in 1776). Henry Benbridge, artist. Collection of the Honorable John Grimball. Photograph courtesy of the Frick Art Reference Library.

enough range to give them aid. They were ill prepared to accomplish their mission.[17]

Upon his return on February 18, 1776, Gadsden assumed command from Colonel William Moultrie, who had been in charge during his absence. While Gadsden was in Philadelphia, the Provincial Congress had elected him colonel of the First Regiment and Moultrie colonel of the Second. Moultrie reported that Gadsden's regiment contained 263 men; his own, 207. Every officer in the First Regiment had provided himself with a "blue cloth coatee, faced and cuffed with scarlet cloth, and lined with scarlet." White buttons, a white waistcoat, and breeches were part of the costume; headgear consisted of a cap with a black feather. The caps of the Second Regiment were of black leather with a small white thread tassel at the top; the front was ornamented with a silver or white metal crescent on which was engraved the initials of its owner and the motto "Liberty or Death." When the men were in service they replaced the short black gaiters and linen breeches with long linen overalls.[18]

Gadsden's job as commander of the First South Carolina Regiment was far more difficult than the sight of his officers parading in striking red, white, and blue uniforms would suggest. The officers came from prominent families, often held political positions, and in general could be trusted. The enlisted men, however, frequently came from the dregs of society. The last royal governor was telling the truth when he reported that many of the rebel troops consisted "of Vagabonds & Thieves of all Countries."[19] At first, the officers simply implored the men to behave like gentlemen, but as the war progressed they resorted to severe punishments to maintain discipline. Maximum punishments were established by acts of the Provincial and Continental congresses. Between December 1777 and April 1778, half of the men in the South Carolina First, Second, Third, and Fourth regiments were court-martialed. Their crimes included stealing from the officers, sleeping on duty, losing their weapons, drinking, gambling, and beating women. One fellow was court-martialed for threatening to shoot the company's fifer for disturbing his rest. The typical punishment was one hundred lashes. Deserters and traitors were sentenced to be shot or hanged. Within a few months in 1777 and 1778 at least seven men in Gadsden's regiment were sentenced to die. There is a gruesome eyewitness account of the execution of one of them, a Sergeant Malcom who had to be shot four times before he finally died.[20] Gadsden undoubtedly knew and approved of the punishments, but the fragmented records do not reveal whether he ever personally demanded or commuted a sentence for any of his men.

The task of fortifying the harbor and city was somewhat easier than that of raising an army. Two forts guarded the channel that provided access to the harbor. A small unfinished fort on Sullivan's Island was under the command of Colonel William Moultrie. The older and sturdier Fort Johnson was located on James Island to the south, about two miles from the city and within close range of the channel. Its lower battery was at water level and armed with fifteen eighteen-pounder cannon; the upper part had three projections toward the water, all well armed with cannon. A gate, ditches, and bridges separated the fort from the land. Within the fort were barracks for fifty men, but upon the approach of the enemy, the militia on the island could easily march into the shelter. The town itself was protected by seven batteries, including one on Gadsden's Wharf. A total of about one hundred cannon were mounted on all seven. The storage areas on Gadsden's Wharf were converted into barracks, and one section was used to incarcerate loyalist prisoners.[21]

Gadsden not only had to command his troops, who were stationed in Fort Johnson, but he also advised the Provincial Congress on a variety of military matters. He recommended that South Carolina pay 1,500 men to be held in readiness to march at a moment's notice to the aid of North Carolina. He inspected a ship that South Carolina was considering for her navy, outlined the duties of a muster-master general, and recommended the addition of another regiment of riflemen to the provincial troops. The Congress gave him a blank check to draw upon the Commission of Public Accounts to buy supplies. Gadsden went about his work in a level-headed way, avoiding the panicky purchase of inadequate equipment but accepting his duty with confident authority. He ordered all of South Carolina's recruiting officers in Georgia to return home where they were desperately needed. He made himself available to confer with any officer between the hours of six and eight-thirty each morning.[22]

On March 2 Gadsden ordered William Moultrie to complete the fort capable of holding 1,000 men on Sullivan's Island, then little more than a wilderness covered with myrtle, live oak, and palmetto trees. He ordered eighteen men aboard the armed schooner *Peggy*, placed advertisements for Negroes to labor on public works near Fort Johnson, offered reprieves to deserters if they returned within three weeks, and threatened to prosecute those who harbored deserters. He approved the use of vagrant Negroes to work upon an additional battery that was being constructed on his wharf. He placed a sentinel to guard the artillery and ammunition that was stored in a depot behind his own house. The depot was accessible to the two regiments of provincials commanded by Gadsden and Moultrie, one company of artillery, six of militia, and two of riflemen that had been organized by the eve of the battle.[23]

Gadsden devised a series of flag signals to warn the town of the arrival of the British, their exact location, and the number and types of their vessels. A narrow blue pendant would signal the appearance of a sloop or schooner; the blue "jack or flagg" marked the sighting of a brigantine or snow; and a red pendant warned that a ship of three masts had been spotted. Small white flags would indicate the number of ships seen. "If Men of War" were sighted, "the New Provincial Flagg will be hoisted and lowered as many times as there are Men of War seen." That flag was a field of blue with a silver crescent, adapted from the caps of the patriots' uniforms, in the upper left corner. A small pendant flying from Gadsden's Wharf indicated that the troops were to look for other signals flying from Fort Johnson, the lighthouse, or Sullivan's Island. If a gun were fired from "the Battery of Col. Laurens's Wharf and at the same time a Jack or Flagg hoisted on the Barracks at Gadsden['s] Wharf . . . [,] all officers and others in the Provincial Service" were to "repair immediately to their respective Posts."[24]

To prepare for the onslaught, President Rutledge appealed to the Continental Congress to send General Charles Lee, recently named military commander of the southern colonies. Lee's arrival on June 4, wrote William Moultrie, "was equal to a reinforcement of 1000 men . . . because he taught us to think lightly of the enemy, and gave a spur to all our actions."[25] Lee assumed command of all troops in South Carolina, but Rutledge retained the right to veto any of his decisions. Reinforcements poured in from Georgia, North Carolina, and Virginia, swelling the ranks to 4,500. Moultrie, with 435 men, was stationed inside the incomplete fort on Sullivan's Island at the northern side of the harbor. Gadsden, with 380 men plus a small detachment of artillery, was in command of Fort Johnson at the opposite side of the harbor. On June 18 the Continental Congress resolved that the battalions under Gadsden and Moultrie be considered as Continental forces.[26] Gadsden thus became a colonel in the Continental Army. His elevation to Continental status, however, actually diminished his authority. He was now equal to Moultrie and subordinate to both Lee and Rutledge.

But there was no time to worry about rank. On June 10, 1776, the provincial flag was hoisted and lowered nine times to signal that nine British warships had been sighted. Admiral Sir Peter Parker commanded two ships of fifty guns and six frigates. Sir Henry Clinton, in command of more than 2,000 redcoats, accompanied him. They had been joined on the high seas by the ship carrying Lord William Campbell, who hoped to regain the governorship. The British officers ordered the rebels to declare their allegiance to the Crown and thus avoid a conflict. But the Americans refused, and both sides spent two more weeks planning their strategies.

The British decided to concentrate upon the small, unfinished fort on Sullivan's Island, which they believed would fall quickly and give them easy access to the city. Clinton landed his men on Long Island, just to the north of Sullivan's. He thought the water between the two islands was shallow enough for his troops to wade across and attack the unfinished side of the fort. But the unexpected deepness of the water foiled his plan; after some hard fighting and many casualties on both sides, his troops were turned back by the Provincials. General Charles Lee feared that the men inside the fort would be trapped and destroyed when the British fleet moved in. He wanted to abandon it, but Moultrie preferred to hold it. President Rutledge vetoed Lee, and Moultrie had his way.

On the morning of June 28, the nine vessels in Sir Peter Parker's fleet sailed up the channel, taking care to stay beyond the range of the guns of Fort Johnson. *Syren, Sphinx,* and *Acteon* moved into dangerously shallow waters between Sullivan's Island and the mainland in order to bombard the unfinished fort at close range. The other vessels planned to attack from deeper waters in the harbor, but they were not likely to get close enough to inflict much damage. The three daring frigates ran upon shoals where they sat as easy targets for the cannon inside the fort. *Acteon* was destroyed. The other two managed to get free and limp away badly damaged. Their cannon balls had merely sunk into the spongy palmetto logs out of which the fort was built. William Moultrie, short on powder and suffering from a painful attack of gout, took maximum advantage of the situation. He ordered his men to fire slowly in order to increase their accuracy and to stretch their ammunition. The loyalty of his men, the geographical accident of his location, some very hard fighting, and the shrewdness of his use of resources gave Moultrie the victory. The British remained in the harbor for more than a month, tending their wounded and waiting for a tide to take them out to sea.[27]

Gadsden was extremely frustrated because his position inside Fort Johnson had precluded his participation in the battle. He and his men wished that they could have picked up Fort Johnson and moved it within range of the battle. Gadsden did fire three cannon at *Syren,* but the shots fell far short, as he had expected. He proposed to General Lee that the patriots launch a sneak attack at night against the crippled British ships still in the harbor, but Lee rejected his plan as "repugnant to common prudence." But Gadsden's ardor was not dampened. A few days later he wrote Moultrie, "I most heartily congratulate the Colony on the drubbing you gave those fellows the other day. . . . We admired your behaviour, but could do no more. My compliments to all your corps; we drink to their health every day."[28]

After the Battle of Sullivan's Island, the leadership of the Revolution in South Carolina shifted solidly and swiftly from the hands of Gadsden and his mechanics into those of powerful planters and merchants who only a few months earlier had been appalled by Gadsden's declaration for independence. The armed invasion, bloodshed, and victory did more to convert the doubters in South Carolina to the idea of independence than *Common Sense* did. Honest merchants who had been insulted by British efforts to discover and destroy illicit trade longed for the advantage of reopening the ports on a free-trade basis, and planters began to think that separation would bring the only permanent end to the nonexportation of their crops. As Gadsden's allies, however, they neither shared his enthusiasm nor trusted his judgment. Nevertheless, something approaching a consensus had emerged among the colony's leaders. The majority favored independence, but they did not agree among themselves upon the details of how to pursue it.

The new consensus was the natural result of the political changes that had taken place in South Carolina since 1762. In that year, as a result of Gadsden's election controversy, the locally elected Commons House of Assembly had begun its successful struggle for power with the Royal Council and governor. Since the Wilkes Fund dispute in 1769, the royal prerogative had not been effectively exercised in South Carolina. The reins of government had gradually shifted from the hands of royal agents into those of extralegal committees and assemblies of the native elite. But the trappings of royal government remained. By 1776 a majority of the colonial elite understood that the only way they would ever have free access to the positions of governor, lieutenant governor, judge, and customs collector was to throw off entirely all symbols of royal control. From the Stamp Act Congress through the first two sessions of the Continental Congress they had offered their parent country the opportunity to recant, but they had stubbornly refused to retract their own demands for the rights to which they thought the laws of nature and the weight of British tradition entitled them. The Battle of Sullivan's Island brought into focus a change that had been more than a dozen years in the making. Parliament's decree of the Intolerable Acts and the appearance of Mother England's soldiers ready to do battle with her children convinced the colonial elite that responsibility for the war for separation rested with the parent.[29]

The realization that they were indeed in a war for independence caused some of the reluctant rebels to experience a severe psychological trauma. With tears trickling down his cheeks, Henry Laurens said that he felt like a dutiful son driven "by the hand of violence out of his father's house."[30] Although the American provincials were extraordinarily mature people, in their relationship to England they were experiencing the pains of their transition from adolescence to adulthood. The mother country looked upon them as adolescents who were not living up to her standards; they thought of themselves as mature enough to manage their own political and economic affairs. Yet there was within them the terrible conflict of a people who yearned to have both the security of home and the freedom of adulthood. To resolve that conflict, they quietly embraced the horror of regicide. As certainly as their seventeenth-century whig ancestors in Great Britain had decapitated Charles I and expelled James II, they themselves were ready to let the figurative axe drop upon the neck of George III.[31]

Gadsden did not share in the psychological trauma of separation from Great Britain. He shed no tears over the bloodless execution of the king. For two years he had already judged the parent country to be a meddlesome mother-in-law rather than a doting mother. He had long ago forgotten whatever pains he might have personally experienced in his own passage into adulthood. He had been separated from his natural parents at the age of seven or eight. Although he spent the next eight years living with relatives in England while attending grammar school, he probably learned very early in life that the time for a child to depend upon his parents is short. At the age of sixteen he was alone in Philadelphia learning the mercantile business from Thomas Lawrence. He went into trade for himself at eighteen. His drive to reach the top in Charleston had overridden any natural tendency to cling to the indecisive years of youth. He had encouraged his own children to accept the responsibilities of adulthood as quickly and smoothly as possible. Thinking of himself as the equal to any citizen in the British empire, he had, step by step, bravely and brazenly defied a royal officer, a royal governor, the British Parliament, the royal ministry, and now the king himself. Since 1762 his expressions of filial affection had always been coupled with a more urgent demand for constitutional freedom. The fact that he welcomed so openly the passage of North America from colony to nation was a distinguishing characteristic of his radicalism.

The desire of the South Carolina elite to rid the province of English placemen, however, was as real with Gadsden as with anyone. As one of the ruling group, Gadsden himself would have a chance to win election to the top offices once they became available to natives. But Gadsden knew that his unpopularity among his peers would diminish the likelihood of his winning an office higher than membership in the General Assembly. For him to achieve more, the franchise would have to be extended to the lower middle-class groups who had supported him since the Stamp Act crisis. And he knew that such a democratic reform was probably still far away. In 1776 Gadsden seemed indifferent to his own political future. For the moment, he was content to secure the right to live as a private citizen in a constitutional republic that guaranteed freedom of religion, free trade, and the natural rights of man. His early belief in an absolute difference between charter rights and natural rights, an idea that even John Adams and Thomas Jefferson did not grasp fully when they wrote the Declaration of Independence and attempted to blend the two, was another distinguishing characteristic of his radicalism.

On August 2, 1776, a courier from Philadelphia spread the news in Charleston that the Continental Congress had declared independence on July 2. The news arrived on the very day the last of the defeated British ships cleared the bar. The South Carolinians in Philadelphia had not been eager to inform Charleston that they had cast South Carolina's vote for independence. Edward Rutledge, Arthur Middleton, Thomas Lynch, junior, and Thomas Heyward, junior, feared that their decision would be very unpopular at home. If they had known the mood of the city immediately after the Battle of Sullivan's Island, however, they would have understood that they had nothing to fear. On August 5, President John Rutledge, Colonel Christopher Gadsden, all civil and military officers in the state, and a crowd of thousands gathered at the Liberty Tree. There they listened to Major Barnard Elliott read the Declaration of Independence. The crowd generally approved the document, but lines of anxiety creased the faces of some who watched the "Sword of State . . . Unsheath'd . . . in a Declaration of War" against their king.[32]

Gadsden was touched by both the joy and solemnity of the occasion. Bent upon pressing the Revolution to its conclusion, he was not so lost in celebration that he could not see the difficult path ahead.

CHAPTER NINE

The Challenge of Independence

The looming of a long, complex war for independence posed enormous challenges for Christopher Gadsden. He was neither a great military commander nor a shrewd politician. His training, experience, and interest resided in the world of trade, but the times that Tom Paine said tried men's souls thrust upon him difficult military and political assignments. The war with England, the disunity among the thirteen provinces, and the civil war between patriots and loyalists were all intensified by the political factionalism within South Carolina. The patriots themselves were divided into radicals and moderates. Gadsden and Drayton led the radicals; Laurens and John Rutledge led the moderates. But the moderates had greater power in Charleston; they were willing to use Gadsden for unpopular tasks and ready to block any radical's attempt to grasp power.

Gadsden's first job after the British left the harbor on August 2, 1776, was to build a bridge connecting Sullivan's Island with the mainland. General Charles Lee had ordered a flimsy structure built there on the eve of the battle as an escape route for the patriots inside the fort. William Moultrie, however, had refused to use the bridge and had even condemned it as being more useful to the British than to the Carolinians. But Gadsden agreed with Lee that a permanent bridge should now be built to help fortify the harbor. Such a bridge would enable the patriots to move men and ammunition quickly into the fort if the enemy again approached.

Early in September, Gadsden got to work. He was assisted by Daniel Cannon, a wealthy carpenter and one of his mechanic friends. They planned a structure with an eighteen-foot-wide roadbed that would rest upon pillars 25 feet apart at the channel and 14 feet apart elsewhere.[1] Wooden piles anchored in sea shells became the pillars. The bridge was basically wood overlaid with iron sheets. It was designed to withstand the weight of hundreds of men and heavy cannon, resist fire and ramming, allow small vessels to pass underneath in the channel, and be unaffected by the ebb and flow of the tide. The finished product zigzagged curiously for almost three-fourths of a mile across the water. The zigzag apparently resulted from the lack of skill of the engineers, the necessity to put down the pillars in shallow water, the pattern of the water currents, and perhaps even the effect of rum upon the workers.

The construction workers were the men in Gadsden's regiment plus a large number of hired Negroes and carpenters. In a climate where "Drunkenness may be called an endemic vice,"[2] rum for these men was the first necessity. Even before construction began, Gadsden sent an urgent note to Colonel John Lewis Gervais, the commissary officer: "We are out of rum, of which for the Work I am about[,] I am obliged to use a great deal." Two weeks later, Gadsden pleaded with Gervais to send him "a Hogshead of Rum for the Regiment by first Opportunity. I am oblig'd to give a great deal of Rum to the Labourers *etc.* about the Bridge."[3] In addition to the rum, the workers were paid small wages.

After nine months of steady work, Gadsden announced on June 7, 1777, that the bridge was almost complete. Some sections of the roadbed had not yet been built, but Gadsden claimed that he could have those planks installed on twenty-four hours' notice if necessary. He said that the bridge was 3,517 feet long, wide enough for ten or twelve men to march across abreast, and as capable of withstanding the tides below as London Bridge.[4] The General Assembly thanked him for his work and officially named the edifice Gadsden's Bridge. An observer from Philadelphia reported, "This harbor is well fortified, and their bridge from Sullivan's Island is an amazing work; nothing like it on the continent." Gadsden himself proudly wrote that the harbor was now "almost as strong as Gibraltar. Thank God we seem to be in a fine Way to drive the Tyrants from America."[5]

The question of who had financed Gadsden's Bridge, however,

became a matter of controversy. Gadsden liked to present himself as the unselfish friend of the public who frequently spent his personal fortune for the general good. He may have started the unsubstantiated legend that he himself had paid for the bridge. A second legend, that he paid one-third of the cost, cannot be proved. The rum and wages for the workers were certainly supplied by the state. President Rutledge granted Gadsden's requests for hands and materials. The General Assembly supplied boats and other materials and, after the bridge was completed, appropriated many thousands of pounds to hire workers and pay for iron work to keep the bridge in good repair. The commissioners of the South Carolina Navy sent the cable, anchors, carpenters, and boats that Gadsden requested. Gadsden himself earned pay for being both a member of the General Assembly and a military officer while he was constructing the bridge.[6] The demand for supplies to be used in construction and the increased safety of the harbor enhanced the flow of trade. As the largest wharf in the harbor, Gadsden's business was certain to flourish when trade increased, but other merchants and wharfowners also shared the same opportunity.

Gadsden understood, however, that whatever military advantage might be gained from the bridge would be meaningless without cooperation between Provincial and Continental troops. Since June the South Carolina Provincial troops had been part of the Continental system. On September 17, 1776, the Continental Congress rewarded Gadsden and Moultrie for their roles in the Battle of Sullivan's Island by appointing them brigadier generals in the Continental Army. Gadsden was proud of his promotion; he trusted George Washington and believed that the continuing presence of Continental troops and generals in Charleston would help cement South Carolina to the other states as well as tighten her own security. The moderate Edward Rutledge, however, distrusted the Continental commanders. He argued that men of "low cunning" and without character or fortune would be promoted to positions of responsibility. He wanted only native South Carolinians to command troops in South Carolina.[7] Gadsden disagreed. On March 20, 1777, using the *South Carolina and American General Gazette* as his medium, he praised George Washington and the New England troops. He argued that South Carolina could expect to receive quick assistance and able leadership from a Continental establishment that was devoted to peace and union for all America. Gadsden foresaw that strife between Continental and Provincial troops would handicap the patriots, but he did not foresee the magnitude of the problem of disagreement that would eventually become a painful reality.

Gadsden's debate with the moderate leaders in South Carolina over military affairs may have been related to a larger struggle over the role and structure of state government. After the declaration of independence, the South Carolina Constitution of 1776, only four months old, was obsolete. That constitution implied that the South Carolinians were working for reconciliation within the empire, but after July 2 they were fighting for independence. Hence, on October 12, 1776, the General Assembly appointed a committee to study the constitution and report on ways that it should be revised. Gadsden was named to the committee, but he was counterbalanced by a majority of moderates, including Rawlins Lowndes and John Mathews, who were not likely to favor dramatic innovations. Lowndes was a successful planter who had become a moderate after the nonimportation crisis, but he was still a cautious man who doubted the efficacy of independence. John Mathews was a young lawyer and planter whose political views were about midway between those of Lowndes and Gadsden. His political ambition had led him to take a strong stand in favor of the Revolution, but he was not the hothead that Gadsden was. After a long delay, caused by the necessity for new elections and general indifference to the constitution, in January 1777 the General Assembly went to work very slowly on the new document.[8]

The Assembly's first debate was over the question of the disestablishment of the Anglican Church, an issue in which Gadsden was intensely interested. In April 1776 he had met at the High Hills of Santee with William Tennent, the leading Presbyterian clergyman in the province, and Richard Furman and Oliver Hart, the leading Baptists, and the four of them had drawn up a petition asking for disestablishment. Thousands of people in the backcountry and in Charleston, including many Anglicans, had signed it. Gadsden, revealing the breadth of character that underlay his colorful challenges to autocratic authority, now presented that petition to the Assembly. Tennent, well known for his patriotism, made a powerful speech on January 11 calling for disestablishment and religious equality.

Gadsden and Tennent acted at an opportune moment. Many moderate patriots, such as John Rutledge, who did not favor disestablishment, were anxious to make concessions to the backcountry. Rutledge knew that loyalist sentiment was rampant there, but he hoped to persuade as many of the backcountrymen as possible to support the war effort. Yielding to the backcountry on the question of disestablishment might be a small price to pay for its help in winning the war.

After hearing the petition and Tennent's speech, the General Assembly fell into a heated debate. Rawlins Lowndes and Charles Pinckney arose to defend the state's support of the church. Edward Rutledge thought the issue was not worth the Assembly's time. Reluctantly submitting to the dissenters, he lamented that "Religion is now become the subject of dispute & will I am afraid play the Devil with us."[9] Gadsden and Charles Cotesworth Pinckney both made speeches in favor of disestablishment. Ultimately they won, for the Assembly voted unanimously to separate the church from the state. The Anglican Church retained its property, and Protestantism was declared to be the "established religion" of South Carolina.[10]

When the Assembly moved on to discuss other changes in the constitution, Gadsden apparently had a great deal to say. He thought that the executive, legislative, and judicial branches ought to be "altogether separate."[11] He argued that judges should not be eligible for concurrent membership in the General Assembly, but he lost on that point. He attempted to have included a provision to guarantee that all resolutions of the Continental Congress should be enforced in South Carolina, but the General Assembly in Charleston did not trust the weak congress in Philadelphia and voted against it.

The remaining items on the new South Carolina constitution met with Gadsden's approval. It contained minor democratic innovations but still favored the propertied class. An adult male had to own 50 acres of land or pay the equivalent tax in order to vote. The governor, lieutenant governor, senators, and representatives all had to own substantial property to be eligible for office.

But for the first time, senators were to be chosen by popular election rather than by the lower house. Since Charleston contained two parishes, it was allotted two senators; every other district was given only one. There was a provision for redistricting on the basis of wealth and property at the end of seven years and every fourteen years thereafter. The president, now to be designated governor, was stripped of veto power. He was to be elected by the legislature every two years and was given only minimal appointive power. The Privy Council retained chief judicial authority, but probate courts were created in seven judicial districts, not just one in Charleston as previously.[12]

The General Assembly ordered the constitution printed and circulated through the state, but it took more than a year to get it adopted. John Rutledge opposed it. Moderate patriots who had helped to write it seemed less than enthusiastic. William Tennent, an advocate, died in August 1777. Gadsden argued that it should be adopted promptly, but he was generally ignored. Finally, developments in Philadelphia drove the South Carolinians to action; in March 1778, without submitting it to the people for ratification, the Assembly declared it to be in effect after a majority of its own members approved. Fearing that the Continental Congress would approve the Articles of Confederation creating a general government for the continent, the South Carolina General Assembly moved quickly to protect its local autonomy.

During the debates in Philadelphia over the Articles of Confederation, South Carolina argued against any continental constitution that would weaken the power of the individual states. South Carolina offered more amendments than any other state, all of which were rejected. The fear of central tyranny and disagreement over whether slaves should be counted as population or taxable property caused the southern states to move with extreme caution toward continental unity on every issue except military defense. And South Carolina even favored putting the army under state control.[13]

The fate of the Articles of Confederation was uppermost in the minds of the men in the South Carolina General Assembly on January 31, 1778, when they elected a new slate of delegates to the Continental Congress. They chose Christopher Gadsden, William Henry Drayton, Arthur Middleton, and Henry Laurens.

Gadsden and Laurens favored adoption of the Articles, but Drayton and Middleton did not. Gadsden and Middleton asked to be excused from service, thus leaving the bitter enemies Laurens and Drayton to represent South Carolina in Philadelphia. Gadsden did not give his reasons for wanting to be excused, but probably he foresaw a greater political drama unfolding in South Carolina, felt needed at home to command the troops, and perhaps did not care to leave his wife of two years. Once they arrived in Philadelphia, Drayton and Laurens signed the Articles in July 1778. Three more years were needed, however, before a majority of the other states signed.[14]

Gadsden was delighted when he heard that Drayton and Laurens had signed the Articles. He wrote his friend Drayton that this display of American unity would discourage foreign powers from intervening in the war for their own purposes. Less risk was involved in trusting future congresses to correct mistakes in the Articles than in letting "this matter lay any longer open," he wrote. He dreaded the "restless Ambition of a few Individuals in each State" ten thousand times more than he feared the power of the collective whole.[15]

One of the restless individuals whom Gadsden distrusted was John Rutledge of South Carolina. In March 1778, Rutledge had made an impassioned speech against the new state constitution. He objected to the popular election of senators, arguing that the voters, if given the opportunity, would reject democratic power as "arbitrary, severe, and destructive." He still dreamed of reconciliation with the parent country and argued that adoption of the new constitution would postpone even longer the day when peace would return to the empire. When the General Assembly approved the document anyway, Rutledge vetoed its decision, was overridden, and resigned in a huff. He remained separated from the executive branch of the government until 1779, when he finally embraced independence and again agreed to serve as chief executive.[16]

After Rutledge's resignation, the Assembly elected Rawlins Lowndes governor. Lowndes chose to use the title of president, implying continuity with the previous government and that he thought of himself chiefly as a presiding officer among a group of peers. Lowndes knew that he was taking on a most difficult job.

Rutledge's resignation was not popular with either the General Assembly or the general population. Many members of the new Assembly stayed away to protest the fact that Rutledge was no longer their president. Lowndes faced the awesome task of governing the state in wartime with the aid of a sparsely attended legislature that was in a bad mood.

Under these extraordinary circumstances, the General Assembly elected Christopher Gadsden vice president of South Carolina, a "safe" position in which he was not supposed to have much influence. The General Assembly of 1778 trusted Gadsden no more than it had trusted him in 1776. Then, it had placed him and Drayton in the powerless judicial branch of the government; now, it was putting him into a job almost equally insignificant. Gadsden understood what was happening; he complained bitterly to William Henry Drayton that he had been "dubbed" vice president in "the *last Hour*" by the "plenitude of the Wanton Power of a bare house." He accepted the appointment only because he thought it was in the best interest of the state, but he told the Assembly that he "perceiv'd their Motive—To get rid of me at the next meeting and to make me ineligible at next Election."[17]

When Gadsden complained about being "dubbed" vice president, he did not know that that office would soon thrust him into a major political crisis. In June 1778 the city fell into riot and chaos over a loyalty oath that the government was trying to enforce. On March 28, 1778, the General Assembly had imposed an oath of loyalty to the state upon pain of disfranchisement and complete loss of legal rights to anyone who refused to sign. A growing number of radical democrats in the city disliked the Constitution of 1778 because they thought it favored the propertied class, and they decided to protest the constitution by refusing to sign the oath. One of their leaders was Alexander Gillon, fast growing wealthy from prize money he was collecting as a commander in the South Carolina navy, but still harboring a grudge against the affluent elite. Some of the radical democrats were poor whites who were unemployed or worked for low wages, including several mechanics who had once supported Gadsden. Seeing trouble coming, President Rawlins Lowndes postponed the enforcement date until June 10.

Before a large crowd on June 5, the sheriff attempted to read a proclamation from the Privy Council that all must conform to the law. Before he could read it, however, the radical democrats snatched it from his hands. Physician John Budd and lawyer Joshua Ward were the principal leaders of the dissidents. Both of them had gained the confidence of the mechanics and were actively working for independence, but they feared aristocratic rule as much as they loathed British tyranny. Budd, Ward, and several others then dashed through the streets with the proclamation in their hands shouting that the government was going to ruin their liberties. When they reached the State House where both President Lowndes and Vice President Gadsden were waiting, they barged in and rudely tossed the hated document to Lowndes. Gadsden must have said something in defense of the oath and probably harshly critical of the democrats, for Ward turned to the vice president and called him a madman. "He told me I was a Madman," Gadsden reported later, "but first took Care to sneak out of my reach; however had he not, I should have done nothing more . . . than what I did, laugh in his face."[18]

Lowndes attempted to quiet the protesters, but in vain. They called another public meeting later the same evening, June 5. Gadsden attended. Budd presided, and the crowd cheered when he warned printers not to publish copies of the proclamation. Gadsden became so infuriated that he stormed to the front and took the platform. "I Don Quixote Secundus," he later reported to Drayton, declared "that I would give the Oath of Fidelity and Certificates to any applicants by the 10th." Gadsden looked straight into the faces of some of his old friends among the mechanics. "I told them I advised the Measure," he continued, "and that they should put a Halter about my neck and hang me at once if they thought it wrong That they had a Constitutional Remedy; they might impeach the President and Council if they acted improperly and that they had better do that. But all to no purpose."[19]

Gadsden thought that the crowd was "chiefly a Mere Mob," and that the running of "restless flighty Men . . . upon every Fancy to the Meetings of liberty tree" was "a Disease . . . more dangerous than . . . the whole present Herd of contemptible exportable Tories." He was angry and embittered to see "here and there some who ought not to have been." He suspected that the mechanics had been duped by evil-minded men who hated him. "In my Opinion," he wrote Drayton, "if they were not set on [by] the old Leven, [it] was at least not sorry for it as it was echoed amongst the people, I am told, that had Mr. R[utledge] been president Nothing of this Sort would have happen'd."[20] The "old Leven" no doubt took delight in Gadsden's embarrassment before his former friends, but they probably did not cause the riot. Nevertheless, Gadsden would be intimidated "neither by the Many nor few"; he determined to administer the oath to all who would take it.

Gadsden then had trouble finding someone to print the proclamation. John Wells, junior, owned the only working press, and he supported the "old Leven." Although Gadsden promised him protection, Wells laughed that he "had not the Smallest idea of being a *Scape Goat*."[21] Gadsden then turned for help to his old friend Peter Timothy. He asked the aging Son of Liberty to print fifty to one hundred copies for North America and "to undeceive the Misled Inhabitants of Chas. Town."[22] Timothy was sympathetic but in no position to be of immediate help. His press had been destroyed in a fire that had swept through Charleston on January 15, 1778, and he had not fully restored it. Although he had been in retirement for about a year, his "natural Eyes being almost worn out," he promised to try to repair his press and print the document.[23]

On June 10, the final day for taking the oath, the crowd again gathered to hear Dr. John Budd. Budd harangued the crowd until it was about ready to demand the impeachment of the president and the Privy Council. But Edward Rutledge stepped forward and offered an acceptable compromise. Rutledge recognized that the dispute revolved upon the crowd's fear that the executive branch of the new government was too powerful. In the turmoil the people had forgotten that the loyalty oath had been imposed by an act of the General Assembly, not by an executive and judicial decision. Lowndes and the Privy Council were only carrying out a law of the Assembly, which they were bound by the constitution to do. The Privy Council's proclamation said that the oath of allegiance would be enforced, but Rutledge suggested that the words "an *act of assembly*" requiring every adult male to take the oath be added to the proclamation in order that everyone would understand that the origin of the law resided with the Assembly, not with the Privy Council. The crowd unanimously accepted the compromise, and on June 24 Timothy got his press together sufficiently to print the copies Gadsden had ordered.[24]

Faithfully reporting the episode to Drayton, Gadsden questioned Edward Rutledge's motivation. "I plainly see into Mischief," he said. He mistakenly thought that Rutledge was attempting to discredit the oath, and he was "full persuaded" that Rutledge hoped to undercut the authority of himself and Lowndes and to restore his brother to power. And he feared that the riots in Charleston would be an invitation to the British to return and try to take the city.[25]

But Gadsden did not understand Edward Rutledge. Gadsden was so apprehensive of a loyalist takeover in the state that he did not realize that Rutledge was attempting to bring about an honest compromise between the government and the dissidents. That compromise did not weaken Gadsden or Lowndes, nor did it give comfort to the loyalists. The crowd who approved the settlement was composed of patriots who hated the British as much as Gadsden did.

The spectacle of his former friends' rioting against him saddened Gadsden. Although the mechanics gave their allegiance to other leaders, Gadsden did not reject them. He thought they were innocent victims of evil men. After the Revolution he thanked them warmly for their support during the war, and for the rest of his days he worked to honor the commitments he had made to them under the Liberty Tree in 1766. But the mechanics, who had first put Gadsden into power, had broken with him. The agreement between them and Gadsden before the war was on constitutional rather than economic grounds. For Gadsden to advocate boycotts and home manufactures in order to break the economic hold of Great Britain was a simple matter of self-denial; for the mechanics it was a matter of survival. Gadsden had led the mechanics for fifteen years, but he was never one of them. Economically he was among the elite, but politically he had sympathized with the lower middle class. When they turned away from him in 1778, he became a man without a party.[26]

Gadsden's sad denunciation of the flighty men who rushed too quickly to meetings at the Liberty Tree in 1778 does not represent a major change in his political thinking. He was a strict constitutionalist. He had advocated mob action against British rulers who were destroying the British constitution, but as a member of the state government in 1778 he was determined to enforce the law. Within the confines of whig thinking, mob action against Great Britain was justified, but against the South Carolina government it was not. King George III and his ministers were undermining their constitution and denying legitimate rights to the people, but Rawlins Lowndes and Christopher Gadsden were attempting to enforce a constitution that guaranteed the people their rights. Gadsden underwent no sudden transformation from radical to conservative; in the relative political spectrum the appearance of a new group more radical than he merely made it appear that his views had moderated.

In 1778 Gadsden was defending a state constitution that rested upon a concept of republicanism that was quite different from the English model. The Americans had failed to retrieve the constitution which had been established by the Glorious Revolution of 1688, had declared independence, and were attempting to launch a government in which all power flowed from the people and none from a king or entrenched nobility.[27] Gadsden himself had fought to establish the South Carolina Constitution of 1778 on the broadest feasible popular base. His traditional belief that the right to vote and to hold office should be reserved for men of property was in the interest of good government and totally different from the British idea that power should flow in part from those who inherited titles of nobility. Gadsden's confrontation with the Charleston mob in 1778 was based upon a misunderstanding and less important than the immediate excitement suggested. As soon as Edward Rutledge had reminded the rioters that the oath was the work of the Assembly, not the executive and judicial officers, they had backed down. The defection of the mechanics cost Gadsden a severe loss of political power, but both he and they still believed in a constitutional system based upon the principle of representative government.

Gadsden's contemporary reputation did not change as a result of the stand he took before the mob in the summer of 1778. The radical patriots still counted him among their own, and the moderates continued to view him with suspicion. When the second anniversary of independence was celebrated on July 4, 1778, less than a month after the riots, David Ramsay dedicated his oration to Christopher Gadsden, "who, fearless of danger, undaunted by opposition, uninfluenced by the hopes of reward, in the worst of times, has stood among the foremost, an early, active, zealous, disinterested champion in the cause of American liberty and independence—." Both Gadsden and Lowndes were present. The words of Ramsay were but hollow praise, however, for neither Gadsden nor Lowndes could look to the moderates or to the radical democrats for comfort.[28]

Although appropriate toasts had been drunk and quietness prevailed in the streets, no one had yet signed the loyalty oath. When the General Assembly convened in September, Lowndes sent it a full report on the riots. The Assembly procrastinated and finally extended the deadline for signing until 1779. By then the military situation had become more urgent and the oath was never universally enforced. South Carolina was plunged into a civil struggle between the signers and nonsigners that lasted until the end of the Revolution.

Gadsden was again infuriated because the General Assembly did not order the oath to be enforced immediately. On October 5, 1778, he wrote an angry letter resigning the vice presidency. If the legislature would not censure a group of men "who called themselves the Flint Club," Gadsden explained, then he would no longer serve that legislature. If the constitution were held in contempt, he argued, "none but dastardly Trimmers, ambitious Caballers, [and] interested Jobbers will serve in a Department rendered so low, suspicious, and despicable."[29] Gadsden had not wanted to accept the vice presidency in the first place, and he was glad for the chance to quit it. But he would have been naive to think that his resignation would be accepted. The moderates felt safer with Gadsden as vice president than with him free perchance to win the presidency. Two members of the Assembly appealed to his patriotism, always a weak spot, and urged him to stay. Gadsden meekly agreed.[30]

In the first two and one-half years of independence, the long lull in the military conflict was a trying time for Christopher Gadsden. The lack of military activity in South Carolina provided so much time for debate over the new constitution and the loyalty oath that popular violence and conflict among rival political factions threatened to jeopardize independence itself. The events during the summer of 1778 were pivotal in Gadsden's career. The political and popular forces that had lifted him to power had crumbled beneath him, and the powerful moderate patriots were glad to see him fall. But Gadsden knew that the fluid morass of South Carolina politics could easily be changed by military events. Simmering beneath the local political fracas, and inseparable from it, was an uneasy alliance between Continental and Provincial troops and a fearful expectation that the British would soon return to Charleston harbor. David Ramsay was mistaken when he said that Gadsden had already seen the worst of times.

CHAPTER TEN

An Affair of Honor

On August 30, 1778, Christopher Gadsden fought a duel, or an *"Ecclaircisement en Militaire"* as he later jokingly called it, with Major General Robert Howe. Perhaps it was the fitting and inevitable climax to the domestic violence of that summer. The duel grew out of the uneasy relationship between individual states and the shadowy central government in Philadelphia; it was caused directly by a contest between Gadsden, a native of the province, and Howe, an outsider, for command of the Continental troops in South Carolina. It sprang, too, from the characters of the principals. Howe was a man with questionable virtue and little patience, and Gadsden had all of the personality traits that were likely to irritate him. Gadsden transformed a political issue into a personal vendetta, allowed his emotions to run away with him, labored under an exaggerated notion of his own virtue, and publicly slandered Howe's character until Howe could tolerate it no more. The events that compelled these two gentlemen to the field of honor began three weeks before independence.

Brigadier General Robert Howe had arrived in Charleston on June 11, 1776, in the company of General Charles Lee and Brigadier General James Moore. All three had been sent by the Continental Congress to help defend the major southern port from British attack. After the Battle of Sullivan's Island, Gadsden and Moultrie had been rewarded by elevation to the rank of brigadier general in the Continental Army. In the fall of 1776, Lee had departed on an unsuccessful campaign to liberate St. Augustine, Florida. He left Howe and Moore, both North Carolinians, in Charleston. Moore left shortly thereafter, and Howe assumed command of the Continental troops in the Southern Department.

Howe was a man of recognized military expertise but doubtful character. Six years younger than Gadsden, he had been born the son of a prosperous rice planter in what became Brunswick County, North Carolina.[1] Before beginning a military career, he had been charged by a governor of North Carolina with "misapplication of the public money" and endeavoring "to establish a new reputation by patriotism."[2] Howe's mismanagement of public money apparently was not proved, but he became celebrated for his mistreatment of women. Separated from his wife Sarah, he was a womanizer. A "Lady of Quality" thought he was "a horrid animal, a sort of woman-eater that devours everything that comes in his way."[3] Eventually the delegates to the Continental Congress from South Carolina and Georgia demanded that he be recalled from the South because of "the little ridiculous matter he has been concerned in S. C.—with regard to a female."[4]

Upon Howe's first arrival in South Carolina, however, the natives were more interested in his skills as a military commander. Howe liked Gadsden and was so pleased with his work on the bridge that he exempted him from all other duties. When Howe left for a campaign in Georgia in November 1776, he placed William Moultrie in command in South Carolina so that Gadsden could continue his work. Moultrie eventually joined the Georgia campaign, and Gadsden assume command in South Carolina because he was now the senior brigadier general there.

Upon his return from Georgia, Howe again took command in South Carolina. He looked upon Gadsden's command as no more than a temporary precaution that had been taken during his absence. Howe had been a brigadier general longer than Gadsden and technically should have taken command, especially since he had received no specific orders to the contrary. But Howe was now very unpopular in South Carolina. Many South Carolina officers asked his permission to resign their commissions. Howe called upon Gadsden and Moultrie for an explanation. What they said is unknown, but it was probably that Howe had left so many South Carolina troops in Georgia, as well as ordering North Carolina troops to return home, that the inhabitants of Charleston no longer trusted his judgment. Gadsden certainly did not trust Howe; he was angry because the mission to St. Augustine had failed, and he refused to relinquish the right to command in South Carolina to someone whom he considered to be incompetent. He avoided personal contact with Howe. Whatever messages passed between the rival officers were delivered by Moultrie. "Gen. Howe and Gadsden were not upon the best footing," Moultrie noted dryly.[5]

Claiming to be motivated only by "Affection to the Noble Cause we are engaged in," Gadsden appealed to President John Rutledge for help. He asked for an exact list of the Continental officers with the dates of their commissions. Gadsden argued that he did not "deserve to be affronted" by Howe, and he hoped that the list would prove that Howe had not been a brigadier general longer than he. He hoped also that the list would prove that Howe had never been ordered to leave Georgia and resume command in South Carolina.[6] But Rutledge was no friend of Gadsden's; he probably enjoyed watching Gadsden squirm. Whether he supplied the list or not is unknown, but the list would have proved that Howe had been a brigadier general for six months longer than Gadsden and therefore was entitled to the command. Rutledge gave Gadsden no help.

Gadsden then took the matter up with the South Carolina General Assembly. William Henry Drayton introduced a resolution to inquire into Howe's right to command. Rawlins Lowndes and Gadsden himself both seconded the motion. The Assembly, however, was packed with moderates who disliked Gadsden, Drayton, and Lowndes. Gadsden knew that he had no chance of winning there, but at least he could tell the Continental Congress that he had already exhausted the lower levels of appeal. When the Assembly quickly defeated Drayton's motion on August 21, 1777, Gadsden angrily resigned his commission. Howe at first refused to accept his resignation but finally did so when Gadsden roughly thrust it into his hat and demanded that it be conveyed to the Continental Congress.[7]

On August 28, 1777, Howe sent a cold, formal report to the Continental Congress. He used no abusive language against Gadsden but offered a temperate, balanced description of the debate between Gadsden and himself, the refusal of the South Carolina General Assembly to back Gadsden, and Gadsden's subsequent resignation. Howe did not understand the political alignments in the South Carolina Assembly that would have automatically determined that it would vote against Gadsden. Howe took the Assembly's action as proof enough that he was right. Howe defended himself as a native American who was "connected with the first families" of South Carolina and who enjoyed the confidence of the army and the general public. The fact that Howe went to such lengths to justify himself perhaps reflects some anxiety about his unpopularity in Charleston. Nevertheless, he told the congress that he had tried to persuade Gadsden not to resign his commission, but Gadsden had physically thrust it upon him.[8]

When the Continental Congress received Howe's letter containing Gadsden's resignation, one anonymous member cried, "Accept it! accept it." On October 2, 1777, the Continental Congress did just that. Inundated by resignations of Continental officers, it did not attempt even the slightest investigation of Gadsden's case. Some members, however, were aware that a problem existed in South Carolina. The Board of War voted to promote Howe to major general and discussed recalling him to George Washington's headquarters. Henry Laurens, now a member of the Congress, wrote John Rutledge that this arrangement "will probably afford satisfaction to the General & at the same time remove from our State a bone of contention, everybody here as far as I have been able to learn are surprised his Command in South Carolina has given offense to any one." The next day Laurens wrote Howe congratulating him upon his promotion and noting that he had withdrawn his own recommendation to remove him from South Carolina.[9]

Bitter and angry over Congress's decision, Gadsden bided his time until January 1778, when his friend Drayton was elected to Congress. Gadsden then took up the issue again. "I should be glad the Congress *collectively* were acquainted fully and candidly with my Affairs with Howe," he wrote to Drayton. He complained that Howe's letter had deliberately been presented to the Congress, perhaps by his "Arch Enemy" Henry Laurens, at a moment when it was irritated by the resignations of other officers. Therefore, the delegates in Philadelphia had mistakenly interpreted his resignation as a defiance of Congress. This impression was patently untrue, Gadsden explained, because he had been the first man in America "to bring about a Congress in 1765 and then to support it *ever* afterwards." If he had seen any authority from Congress in support of Howe's right to command, he would have withdrawn his question no matter what his personal opinion of Howe. Now that he had "some Friends among our Delegates," he hoped that his case could at last be fairly represented in the Congress.[10]

At Gadsden's request, Drayton acquired a copy of Howe's letter of August 28, 1777, to the Congress and sent it to Gadsden. It arrived on June 27, 1778, when Gadsden was deeply involved in the public furor over the oath of allegiance. On July 4, 1778, the very day he was being extolled by David Ramsay for being a great patriot, Gadsden wrote a long letter to Drayton, which he intended to be a public response to Howe's letter of August 28, 1777.[11] Gadsden complained bitterly that he "never saw or heard a Tittle of" Howe's letter for ten months. Then he proceeded to a lively defense of his loyalty to all the American congresses since 1765 and condemnation of Laurens's misrepresentation of him before the Congress.

Annotating Howe's letter paragraph by paragraph, Gadsden attacked the beleaguered North Carolinian with the same fervor, turgid prose, and rashness that he had once leveled against a parliament and a king who had dared to trample upon the basic rights of Americans. Calling Howe a liar, Gadsden denied that he had been issued any order from General Howe after the Battle of Sullivan's Island or that Howe had the authority to give him orders. He contended that it had been General Lee who had instructed him to build the bridge from Sullivan's Island to the mainland. The gist of Gadsden's argument was that Howe had been sent to Georgia to launch a campaign against St. Augustine. When that campaign was abandoned, Howe had returned to South Carolina without receiving orders to do so. Since Howe was in Charleston without orders, there was no reason why Brigadier General Gadsden should surrender command to him. Gadsden was attempting to prove that Howe, not himself, had acted in defiance of Congress. Such an allegation was difficult for Gadsden to prove, however, for Howe's decision to leave Georgia was an intelligent military decision that was not challenged by his superiors.

Gadsden then piled numerous personal insults upon his enemy. He called Howe a man of "downright low cunning, Jockeying and sharping, and . . . of low Ambition indeed." He accused Howe of attempting to cover his lack of character with "those *'advantages'* he puffs away with," such as "connections, blood relationship to first families, confidence of the army and public in general and what not." If a brigadier general assigned to a particular state could move legally into other states without orders and seize command, "Might he not as well have taken an opportunity in the absence of superior officers to [be] . . . the light, Itinerant Brigadier General Knight Errant to General Lee's whole Department." Howe was "dextrous in the Political intriguing way." His deliberate obfuscation of the chain of command among Lee, Moore, himself, and Gadsden was designed to confuse Congress. "Perhaps this thick mud is purposely thrown up to escape like a crab under it," Gadsden sneered.

Gadsden rationalized the South Carolina Assembly's refusal to investigate the dispute and perhaps succeeded in buttressing his point. He explained that Drayton's motion in the South Carolina Assembly on August 20, 1777, had been to establish a committee to inquire into Howe's right to command the South Carolina continentals. Gadsden thought the committee was necessary to determine "whether the American Military Command should be such a sacred Arcanum that any General, provided that he was on the list should, at his pleasure go out of one State into another." Since the beginning of the dispute, Gadsden had feared the power of a standing army. In 1775 he had joined John Adams, Thomas Jefferson, and others to sponsor the publication in America of a pamphlet by an English whig who argued that in time a nation with a standing army would lose its liberties.[12]

If Howe's conduct went unchecked, Gadsden continued, he feared that military commanders would have greater power than elected civil leaders. He argued that his political enemies in South Carolina had deliberately misrepresented Drayton's motion to make certain that it would be defeated. Only 89 of the 200 members were present when the vote was taken, he said, and those were "sorry for it very soon afterwards." They had been duped by Howe into believing that if they approved the motion they would be defying the Continental Congress. Gadsden was certain that if a new vote could be taken ten months later he would win.

Gadsden angrily blamed Henry Laurens for Congress's instant acceptance of his resignation. As president of the Continental Congress, Laurens might have appointed a committee to investigate the Gadsden-Howe feud, but he did not. Because of his previous disagreements with Gadsden, Laurens was inclined to dismiss Gadsden as a hothead and perhaps automatically take the side of his opponent. Gadsden thought it was unfortunate that his resignation had been laid before Laurens, "the greatest and most inveterate Enemy I have in the world." And he suspected that Laurens was gratified to see Howe oust him.

Interspersed with the vindictive attacks upon Henry Laurens and Robert Howe, Gadsden celebrated his own character, commitment, and unselfishness. He exaggerated his role in the Battle of Sullivan's Island and begged for recognition from Congress. He was so extremely proud of having been present at the Stamp Act Congress, which he thought was the dawn of American independence, that he was willing to do almost anything to preserve an untarnished continental reputation. He urged Drayton to read his long, explanatory, derogatory letter to Congress.

Drayton decided not to make the letter public. Gadsden's attack on Henry Laurens would not be especially welcomed in Philadelphia, and Drayton no doubt realized that the majority of the members of Congress would not be interested in reopening an old argument that would merely add to their burdensome talk of keeping peace between the local and Continental officers. But Gadsden kept his promise to send a copy of his letter to Howe and to circulate it in Charleston, where it was widely discussed in the summer of 1778. Public opinion in South Carolina was not entirely favorable to Gadsden, but it was strongly against Howe. Howe apparently disliked being there as much as the army under his command disliked having him there. John Wells, junior, wrote President Henry Laurens that "removing him from Carolina would be highly acceptable to the Army; nor would one think very disagreeable to himself."[13]

Laurens possibly would have taken Wells's advice more seriously had he known that Howe was more popular in Philadelphia than he was in Charleston. Laurens denied Gadsden's charges against himself. "General Gadsden has again endeavor'd to injure me," he wrote President Rawlins Lowndes, "by a groundless charge or insinuation, that I had presented the Letter intimating the resignation of his Commission . . . at an important time." He reminded Lowndes that Gadsden's resignation had been submitted to Congress on October 2 by John Hancock and that he himself had not assumed the presidency until November 1. Laurens urged Lowndes to explain to Gadsden that he had "never attempted to under value or depreciate" Gadsden's contributions to the war, and that he had only learned of Gadsden's "discourteous, injurious, attempts" by mere accident.[14]

Gadsden was genuinely worried about his reputation in the Continental Congress; he had been a member of the first two sessions and a champion of its decisions. He did not want the present members to think that he was disloyal. Therefore, on August 15 he again wrote Drayton urging him to inform the Congress "that my resignation was [not] intended as an Insult to them." The following day he wrote Thomas Heyward, retelling his story and saying that "to offend Congress is such a Sin Against America" that he would never be guilty of it. He merely wanted Congress to learn his version of the truth, and he did not trust Henry Laurens to tell it.[15]

Gadsden's letters created scarcely a ripple in Philadelphia, but they stirred up considerable excitement in Charleston. In a city already restless from the riots of June, the heat, the boredom created by a lull in battle, and the fear of a new British attack, the feud between Gadsden and Howe provided a popular diversion. "Some think arms will decide the contest," reported Henry Laurens's correspondent, "but it appears to me most probably, that a gray goose quill dipt in gall & bitterness will be the end chiefly employed on the occasion."[16]

For Gentleman Robert Howe, "a gray goose quill" was not nearly a deadly enough weapon to expiate the slander which Gadsden had heaped upon him in his letter of July 4. Remission could be won only by public apology, or upon the field of honor. On August 17, 1778, Howe sent a letter to Gadsden demanding satisfaction for the words Gadsden had written about him on July 4. Gadsden immediately replied that he "was ready to give him any Satisfaction he thought proper where when and how he pleased." He accused Howe of being the aggressor for not letting him see the letter which had directly affected his fortune "for 10 *Months*" before Gadsden even knew it existed.[17] Despite attempts by friends of both men to dissuade them, neither would retract. The date was set for August 30; the weapons, pistols; and the place, under the Liberty Tree.

When Gadsden and Howe and their seconds arrived for their appointment that Sunday morning at about eleven o'clock, they discovered that a large crowd had gathered, some of whom had climbed into the Liberty Tree to get a better view.[18] Gadsden and Howe decided to move to a safer and more private spot on the Reverend Mr. William Percy's land. Gadsden and his second, Colonel Barnard Elliott, rode to the new location in a carriage; Howe and his second, Charles Cotesworth Pinckney, followed on horseback.

The combatants alighted, "paid each other the usual compliment of hat and hand," and declared that they had come there only to settle a point of honor. They took their stations, which, according to Gadsden, were only "eight very small paces" apart. Neither knew what the other intended.

"Fire, Sir," Howe said to Gadsden.

"Do you fire first, Sir," Gadsden replied.

"We will both fire together," Howe announced.

Gadsden did not answer, but both presented their weapons.

For several very long seconds, they stared at each other through the sights of their pistols. But neither man pulled the trigger. General Howe lowered his pistol and said with a smile, "Why won't you fire, General Gadsden?"

"You brought me out, General Howe, to this ball play, and ought to begin the entertainment."

Howe raised his pistol steadily. He squeezed the trigger. His bullet lightly scratched Gadsden's ear.[19] Perhaps he had intended to miss, but it was a close call nevertheless.

Gadsden stood immobile for a few moments. He raised his pistol, placed it over his left arm at right angles with Howe, and fired deliberately wide of his target. He called upon Howe to fire again.

"No, General Gadsden, I cannot after this," Howe replied.

Colonel Barnard Elliott, Gadsden's second, said that he did not think Gadsden could have made a handsomer apology, or Howe shown a higher degree of honor. Walking up to Howe after the duel, Gadsden explained that he had not apologized for having challenged Howe's right to command, but only for publicly having used abusive language toward him. Howe replied that he was happy that he had missed Gadsden, and they then shook hands and parted.

After the duel was over, Gadsden seemed embarrassed about the whole affair. He wrote Drayton that his fight with Howe was *"private* and *personal,"* and he complained that the newspaper had printed the account of it "against my Opinion."[20] More than a generation later, in 1804, after Aaron Burr had killed Alexander Hamilton in a duel, Gadsden was one of the members of the South Carolina Society of the Cincinnati who addressed a petition to the New York society urging that "throughout the Union this absurd and barbarous custom" be abolished.[21]

The British officer John André, who delighted in writing ribald poems about the American commanders, made great sport of Gadsden's duel. In an eighteen-stanza poem, "On the Affair between the Rebel Generals Howe and Gadsden," set to the tune of "Yankee Doodle," he told the story in memorable style:

> It was on Mr. Percy's land,
>   At Squire Rugely's corner,
> Great H. and G. met, sword in hand,
>   Upon a point of honor.
>   . . . .
> They paused awhile, these gallant foes,
>   By turns politely grinning:
> 'Till after many cons and pros,
>   H. made a brisk beginning.
>   . . . .
> Such honor did they both display
>   They highly were commended;
> And thus, in short, this gallant fray
>   Without mischance ended.
>
> Chorus: Yankee Doodle, doodle, doo, etc.[22]

But Robert Howe got the last laugh on John André. Howe later served on the military tribunal that sentenced André to be hanged for his attempt to acquire West Point through the treason of Benedict Arnold.

The erratic plunge of Howe's career in the South during the three months after the duel seemed to reinforce Gadsden's estimation of him. In November he went to Savannah, where the British were about to attack, and he quickly got into an argument with the natives of that province over whether he or their governor had the right to command the Continental troops there. He suffered a major defeat in December 1778 when Savannah fell. Howe then made his way north, joined the main Continental Army under George Washington, and saw very little action. He was later court-martialed upon the initiative of the Georgians in the Continental Congress for his incompetency at Savannah, but he was acquitted "with Highest Honor."[23]

Gadsden emerged from the duel with his reputation for patriotism intact. As vice president of South Carolina, he went about his duties. On the night of September 6, 1778, French sailors on board *Comte de Narbonne* in Charleston harbor raked the shore with grapeshot, and the Carolinians fired the cannon mounted on Burns's Wharf back at the French. Gadsden called out the militia, and a number of men were killed before the disturbance ended early the next morning. Gadsden was dismayed by the spectacle of Americans fighting their principal European ally; he thought that the riot had been "set on by the Tories in Town."[24]

Gadsden caught a cold the evening of the riot and suffered with a fever for several days thereafter.[25] Gadsden may have had many colds during his long life, but his mention of this one is perhaps significant. It was unusual for him to complain about his health; he was more likely to comment upon how healthy he was than to mention some malady. Perhaps he suffered from sheer exhaustion, or contact with germs during the melee, or overexposure to the sea air as he watched the riot during the night. His passing reference to the cold carries the melancholy ring of a man who was very tired and perhaps a little depressed.

Gadsden scarcely had time to recover before he was grief-stricken by the death of his friend Barnard Elliott.[26] Fourteen years younger than Gadsden, the youthful Elliott was much like the older patriot. A wealthy planter, educated in England, he had a fiery temper that he vented against British placemen and

American loyalists. He had fought with Moultrie's Second Regiment during the Battle of Sullivan's Island, and later he had been given command of Fort Johnson. Apparently, Gadsden was his hero. As Gadsden's second in the duel with Howe, he had been willing to die for Gadsden if necessary. Gadsden sadly honored his deceased friend by marching in his funeral procession.

But Gadsden had no time to languish in his grief. Shortly before Elliott's death, Gadsden had received a communication that 10,000 British soldiers were ready for a massive invasion at Charleston or Beaufort. "We are going to fortify in all haste and make no doubt shall persist," he wrote Drayton.[27] The pressures of partisan bitterness that had erupted so violently in the summer and fall of 1778 and the excitement of Gadsden's affair of honor could no longer blind the Carolina leaders to the steadily approaching greater war with Britain. When the war in the North drifted into a stalemate in 1778, the British decided once again to concentrate upon taking the southern provinces. After the fall of Savannah on December 29, 1778, the patriots in Charleston began to prepare frantically for the inevitable beginning of their greatest trials.

CHAPTER ELEVEN

War and Exile

In the last days of 1778, Charleston was a melancholy place. It looked more like a city that had already been devastated in battle than one that was fearfully awaiting conquest. Most of the damage from a great fire that had swept through the city on January 15 had not been repaired. The fire had occurred at the very time the state and Continental currencies had begun to deteriorate. Although some of the victims had been able to rebuild, most had not. Gadsden himself did not suffer any losses, but he could look out of his windows and see weeds growing around blackened foundations upon which had once rested the homes of his neighbors. Of the 1,700 dwellings, 252 had been destroyed, the majority of them on the bay, or on Broad, Elliott, and Tradd streets. Gadsden estimated their value, exclusive of contents, at more than half a million pounds.[1]

The morale of the people was dangerously low. The effects of the fire, Rutledge's controversial resignation over the new constitution in the spring, the riots of the radical democrats in June, Gadsden's duel with Howe in August, the battle between American troops and their French allies in September, and the miserably hot, humid climate nourished a growing apathy. Some of the inhabitants would welcome the return of a royal governor. Even some moderate patriots were having second thoughts about the wisdom of independence. They had little confidence in their government headed by Rawlins Lowndes and Christopher Gadsden, and they doubted the ability of their troops to defend the city. The majority preferred the cool judgment of John Rutledge and Henry Laurens to the radicalism of Christopher Gadsden and William Henry Drayton.

On November 30, 1778, the moderates won a sweeping victory in the elections to the General Assembly. The winners included four Pinckneys, three Rutledges, two Middletons, two Laurenses, and one Gadsden. In January 1779 this Assembly chose the new executive and judicial officers. The tenures of Rawlins Lowndes and Christopher Gadsden had been so troubled that there was no chance they could be reelected to the top offices. By a wide margin the Assembly named John Rutledge governor. His veto of the Constitution of 1778 had not diminished his popularity, and he now agreed to serve as chief executive under the very constitution he had shunned because it did not allow for reconciliation with the mother country. The second highest office went to Thomas Bee, a wealthy planter whose political views were almost identical with those of Rutledge.[2]

Gadsden was one of eight men elected to the Privy Council. He, Thomas Ferguson, and John Edwards were radicals; the other five members were moderates. The Privy Council was a part of the executive branch of the government and subordinated to the General Assembly. The governor was required by the constitution to consult the Privy Council when appointing temporary officials normally elected by the legislature, making executive appointments, placing embargoes on trade, and convening the legislature earlier than scheduled or changing its place of meeting.[3] As a member of the Privy Council, Gadsden retained a voice in executive decisions; concurrently as a member of the General Assembly he had a vote in the more powerful arm of the government.

While the General Assembly of South Carolina was choosing the state's officers, Augusta, Georgia, fell to the British. They now prepared to march toward Charleston from both the south and the west. The new government not only had to cope with internal dissent and indifference, but also to prepare for an imminent attack. "Our town, once the seat of pleasure and amusement," wrote Charles Pinckney, junior, "is now dull and insipid. . . . We have very few men left here . . . and should a fleet and army appear at our bar, God knows what we should do."[4]

The Howe affair had damaged the strength of the Continentals in South Carolina and Georgia. In January 1779, Congress replaced Howe with General Benjamin Lincoln of Massachusetts.

He was lame from an ankle wound and excessively fat, but calm, practical, and hard working.[5] Governor Rutledge attempted to cooperate with him, but both men faced awesome obstacles. The state militia would not recognize the authority of the Continental officers, and many militiamen opposed the state government they served. Their attempts to mutiny were so common that Rutledge and Lincoln often were not in control of their own troops. In April, Lincoln decided to take about 4,000 Continentals and move into Georgia near Augusta; he hoped to prevent the British forces near Savannah from getting supplies from the Indians and loyalists in the backcountry. His departure left William Moultrie second to him in command with only 600 men to defend Charleston.

Gadsden was panicked by Lincoln's decision. He knew that South Carolina could not withstand a British assault with most of the Continental troops out of the state and only two ships in South Carolina's navy to defend the harbor. On April 4, 1779, "with the Overflowing of an anxious Heart," he wrote a desperate letter to Samuel Adams, begging for help. If Congress could not help South Carolina in this emergency, "what advantage have we by the Confederacy?" Gadsden asked. He reminded Adams that he, Gadsden, was "the same Man my Friend with the same Principles I set out with at first," still dedicated to the freedom and independence of *all* the states. He feared that Congress was so divided "into Cabals and Parties" that it would let South Carolina fall without a fight. He recalled that when "Massachusetts sounded the Trumpet" in 1765, Carolina had instantly leaped "to the appointed Rendezvous." He hoped that Massachusetts would now return the favor. All South Carolina needed, he said, was "four, five, or six Frigates at most, under an *honest* Man," to be stationed along her coast.

Gadsden was indignant over the handling of the Continental Navy since he had left Philadelphia early in 1776. There were fewer than a dozen vessels in service, and they were more interested in prize money than winning the war. The American force was weakened, he argued, by scattering the ships. "In short no prodigal ever squander'd his Inheritance more stupidly away than we have our Frigates to make Fortunes . . . in deba[u]chment." He contended that if the American vessels had remained together, the enemy's cruisers could have been captured quickly or at least the enemy would have been forced to pay the great expense of always sailing in fleets. Pridefully he told Samuel Adams that while he wrote he heard the guns of two of South Carolina's brigs chasing a British cruiser. But unless South Carolina received naval reinforcements, he threatened, New England could not count upon receiving provisions from the southern states.[6]

There was no hope that Congress could get Continental ships to Charleston in time to help. And even if it were possible for the ships to arrive in time, they would probably have been neither numerous nor strong enough to do much good. The navy was Gadsden's pet creation, and he had an inflated opinion of its ability to defeat the British. He would never admit that the British had a superior force, but his optimism did not change the respective power of the opposing forces. Even as he wrote, the future of the patriots became gloomier and gloomier.

Early in May 1779, General Augustine Prévost, principal British conqueror of Georgia, began to march from Savannah toward Charleston. He had about 2,400 troops with him. On May 10 he reached Ashley's Ferry, a few miles upriver from Charleston. Prévost put his men to digging parallel and zigzag rows of trenches through which they moved to within a few hundred yards of the city. On May 11 a rebel horseman bearing a white flag of truce rode into Prévost's camp. He brought a message from Governor Rutledge and General Moultrie asking what terms Prévost would grant if the Carolinians should decide to surrender. Prévost replied promptly that he would give protection to all who would declare their fealty to the king, but he would take the others as prisoners of war.

Rutledge was not particularly alarmed by Prévost's response. He probably still thought that life as a British citizen under the freest government in the world was preferable to independence. He could find many men in the state government who agreed with him. Even General Moultrie, who was usually an avid advocate of independence, temporarily succumbed to Rutledge's reasoning. Rutledge ordered Moultrie to raise a white flag over the city. Then he summoned the eight members of the Privy Council and the leading military officers to his home to help him prepare an answer for Prévost.

Gadsden was horrified by the sight of a white flag flying over the city; he was determined not to surrender when he rushed to Rutledge's house. He did not trust the governor, and he knew that five of the other members of the Privy Council would go along with whatever Rutledge wanted. Rutledge presented a shocking plan to the small group: he would evade the terms offered by Prévost and suggest more favorable terms of his own. He would offer to surrender the town provided that the state and harbor be neutral during the war, no prisoners be taken, and the fate of South Carolina after the war be exactly the same as that granted to the other states. Rutledge was ready to take South Carolina out of the war, destroy continental unity, risk the place-ment of tories in power, and repudiate the declaration of inde-pendence! The Privy Council voted 5 to 3 in favor of Rutledge's proposal. Christopher Gadsden, Thomas Ferguson, and John Edwards cast the three negative votes.

Gadsden disrupted the meeting. He shouted that he would not accept the decision of the majority. John Edwards wept. He was a wealthy merchant who had supported the Revolution since the first nonimportation crisis. His daughter Catherine had married Gadsden's son Philip. Edwards was, in a quieter manner, as radi-cal as Gadsden and Drayton. Ferguson, a planter, was Gadsden's son-in-law. He had agreed with Gadsden from his dispute with Governor Boone through the present crisis, and he was as deter-mined as Gadsden to stop Rutledge's neutrality proposal. Gadsden violated Rutledge's order of secrecy; he rushed out of the meeting to tell members of the Assembly about Rutledge's plan. Apparently Gadsden himself returned to inform the gover-nor that some men in town were demanding that all who favored neutrality should be handed over to the British.[7]

Rutledge fearlessly sent the message anyway. He, the Privy Council, and Moultrie remained at his house waiting for Prévost's reply. Prévost rejected his proposal and demanded that the gov-ernor, the Privy Council, and the garrison surrender. Before Rutledge or anyone else could speak, Moultrie regained his com-posure. He went back over to the radicals and once again spoke like the tough officer that had made him the hero of the Battle of Sullivan's Island. "We will fight it out," he proclaimed. No one disagreed with him. Even John Rutledge, who wanted to be a free citizen under the British constitution, did not wish to become the prisoner of a British officer. As the men left Rutledge's house, Gadsden and Ferguson were close on Moultrie's heels. "Act according to your own judgment," they told Moultrie, "and we will support you."[8]

Moultrie lowered the flag of truce, but nothing happened. Prévost was so afraid that General Lincoln was moving in with reinforcements that he did not go forward to take the city. Instead, he waited until dark, drew his troops back from the trenches surrounding Charleston, and decided to wait for reinforcements himself.

Gadsden was afraid of both the tories in the city and the redcoats outside. He was badly shaken by the willingness of Carolina's leaders to capitulate and accept neutrality. Almost two months later he wrote Samuel Adams, "As to Charles Town we have had a narrow, very narrow, escape indeed, more from the treacherous Whispers and Insinuation of *internal* Enemies than from what our external and open Foes were able to do against us here." But Gadsden knew that the British had not gone away. Prévost had established a garrison of 900 men on Port Royal Island at Beaufort. Gadsden again begged Samuel Adams to use his influence to get Congress to send four or five frigates to Charleston. The frigates, he said, would "do us more service than as many Thousand Troops."[9]

Instead of sending the navy, Congress, prodded by South Carolina's own delegates John Laurens and Isaac Huger, sent a message that South Carolina should arm 3,000 able-bodied slaves. John Laurens and his father Henry both favored emancipation. As president of the Continental Congress, Henry Laurens attempted to use the war crisis to end slavery completely in South Carolina. Under his leadership, Congress offered to pay each South Carolina master for the terms of his slaves' service and guarantee that every slave who served would be given his freedom and $50 at the end of the war. But the South Carolina Privy Council and the House of Representatives defeated the motion soundly. "The measure for embodying the negroes had about twelve votes," wrote David Ramsay; "it was received with horror by the planters, who figured to themselves terrible consequences." Gadsden agreed with the planters. "We are much disgusted here at the Congress recommending us to arm our Slaves, it was received with great resentment, as a very dangerous and impolitic Step," he informed Samuel Adams. Despite their indignation over Congress's recommendation in 1779, however, South Carolina did in 1780 take about 1,000 blacks into her armed forces. They were not given weapons but were used in menial capacities.[10]

The summer of 1779 was more wretched than the summer of 1778 had been. There were no riots, and Gadsden did not fight any more duels, but only the severe heat seemed to stop the British from taking Charleston. "The Enemy are within a few days March of the Town and if not sooner, when the sickly months are over I make no doubt they will be at us again," Gadsden wrote.[11] On September 1, David Ramsay sent a bleak report to William Henry Drayton. Even the enticements of "a negro bounty" and extra pay could not persuade men to volunteer for military duty, he lamented. If the British should take Charleston, he continued, no honest whig would be able to survive "southward of Santee." And profiteers abounded everywhere. "A spirit of money-making has eaten up our patriotism," Ramsay complained. "Our morals are more depreciated than our currency."[12] But Drayton never saw the letter; on September 3, at the age of thirty-six, he died in Philadelphia. Gadsden had no time to ponder the loss, because in the very same month of Drayton's death, the British, in a bloody fight, turned back the Americans and their French allies from their attempt to take Savannah. The Continentals fell back toward Charleston.[13]

The failure to break the power of the British at Savannah meant that South Carolina, save for whatever defense her own patriots and the depleted Continental force could muster, now lay open to British attack. Sir Henry Clinton, commander of the British army in the rebellious colonies, seized the opportunity to launch a massive attack at Charleston. Accompanied by Admiral Marriott Arbuthnot in command of five ships and nine frigates, Clinton and 8,500 troops left their base at New York in December 1779. By proclamation he promised severe punishment for all who had taken up arms against the king and protection and prosperity for those who had not.

> Hark, Rebels hark! Sir Henry comes,
> With proclamation, sword and drums!

So the Carolinians were warned by a patriot in Boston.[14]

"Sir Harry" and his troops landed at John's Island, about thirty miles south of Charleston, on February 11, 1780. By April, hundreds more redcoats had come from New York to join him, swelling his ranks to 10,000. Clinton moved his troops in closer around the city, while Admiral Arbuthnot sealed off the harbor and placed his vessels in position to fire into the city. The siege of Charleston had begun.

Even Governor Rutledge, his dream of neutrality smashed, knew that he must fight. The General Assembly gave him broad emergency powers. He could direct military matters without their consent, and he did not have to get the approval of a quorum of the members of the Privy Council. Rutledge begged Spanish officials in Havana to send him aid, but they were unable to do so. George Washington, attentive to Rutledge's distress, ordered 3,000 Continental troops from Virginia and North Carolina to join the 2,500 already in Lincoln's command.

The British still had almost twice as many troops as the patriots, and there was little hope that Charleston could withstand the siege. Rutledge removed his family to the High Hills of Santee in the central part of the state near the confluence of the Wateree and Congaree rivers. Other civilians, who could find a place to go, began to abandon the city. Lincoln urged Rutledge himself to take several members of the Privy Council with him and set up a government in exile at some distance from the doomed capital. On April 12, Rutledge and three members of the Privy Council sought refuge a few miles south of the High Hills between the Cooper and Santee rivers, nearly 100 miles from the beleaguered city.[15]

Before leaving Charleston, Rutledge set up a civilian government to stay behind. Lieutenant Governor Thomas Bee, a member of the Continental Congress, was in Philadelphia, and according to the Constitution of 1778, in the absence of the lieutenant governor the governor could appoint a member of the Privy Council to act in his stead. Therefore, Rutledge appointed

Gadsden because Gadsden wanted to remain in the city and confront the enemy. Lieutenant Governor Gadsden was joined by the four other members of the Privy Council. The old partisan factions held; the moderate officers moved to the safety of the High Hills, but the radicals remained to fight the British. Gadsden was thus the highest ranking official in the city during the last month of the siege.

One can imagine that Gadsden considered his appointment a distinct honor and savored the chance to stand personally before the British bayonets. He had said many times that he would give his life for the cause of American liberty, and he probably believed that the city still might survive the attack. In reality there was no hope for success; by accepting the appointment Gadsden was in effect submitting to almost certain capture and imprisonment. He may have secretly thought of himself as a braver man than Rutledge. His willingness to stay behind was dramatic proof to the British, the moderates, and perhaps even to himself that he was a man of his word and that his commitment to American independence was absolute. But Gadsden was not seeking martyrdom. He expected to get out alive and ultimately taste the victory.

The men who headed for the High Hills, however, thought that those who stayed behind were foolhardy. John Lewis Gervais, a member of the Privy Council who went with Rutledge, said that the decision for Gadsden and the others to stay behind was "more to Satisfy the Citizen[s], than the propriety of the measure."[16]

Gadsden went about his work. He was a member of the state militia as well as lieutenant governor. He ran around frantically performing military and civil duties. On April 19 the British fleet sailed past Fort Moultrie on Sullivan's Island. Colonel Charles Cotesworth Pinckney, thirty-two-year-old son of Charles and Eliza Lucas Pinckney, gamely ordered his men inside the fort to fire upon the British ships. But the ships were out of range. One of them, however, ran aground near Haddrell's Point, later renamed Mount Pleasant. Gadsden rushed to the area of the beached ship, personally fired two fieldpieces at the stranded vessel, and succeeded in making things difficult enough for the sailors that they set the ship on fire and escaped in small boats.[17]

Gadsden did not want to keep any British prisoners in Charleston. There would be too much chance that they would receive help from the loyalists or be rescued by their own troops and return to battle. He arranged to send them to North Carolina to be kept until the war was over. He also desperately appealed to America's foreign allies for help. In 1779 Spain had signed an alliance with France, thus indirectly entering the American war. Gadsden ordered one boat to Havana to seek help from the Spaniards and another to Cape François for help from the French.[18] The French and Spaniards sent a few volunteers, but they were not numerous enough to be of any real help. Gadsden and the city would have to depend upon the local militia and Lincoln's Continentals.

Lincoln was nonplussed by Gadsden's frenzied activities. He thought that his duty was to win the best terms of surrender possible; he knew that his forces were inferior and that all of Gadsden's mad dashing about was futile. But Gadsden assumed that as lieutenant governor and the chief civil officer in the city he had greater authority than Lincoln. He distrusted military leaders and attempted to limit Lincoln's power. Gadsden often bullied Lincoln into submission. But the Continentals trusted Lincoln more than they trusted Gadsden. His field officers at Fort Moultrie urged him to avoid the danger of allowing a civil authority to interfere with the deliberations of the military officers. They pledged to support Lincoln if he would take absolute command of the garrison and govern them strictly by his own judgment.[19] But Gadsden would not allow Lincoln to ignore him.

When General Lincoln called a council of his officers on April 20 and 21, Gadsden was present. Gadsden was not entitled by law or tradition to be there, but he had demanded that Lincoln allow him to attend. The officers were meeting to discuss when to surrender. They looked upon their problem as a military question to be decided by the commander of the Continental troops, who was under the jurisdiction of the Continental Congress, not that of a local civil officer. Gadsden was certain that the officers would be ready to surrender, and he was determined to prevent it if possible. The officers did vote to send Clinton an offer of capitulation. Gadsden, who apparently had more to say than Lincoln during the meeting, said that he would rather die than surrender.[20] He did promise, however, to consult the four remaining members of the Privy Council.

Gadsden knew that he could count upon the Privy Council to agree with him. Thomas Ferguson, Richard Hutson, Benjamin Cattell, and David Ramsay all thought that Gadsden was right, and they refused to surrender. Gadsden and his faithful councilors scoured the town and organized public demonstrations against any plan to withdraw the Continental troops. Thomas Ferguson rounded up a mob which went with him to confront General Lincoln. Ferguson angrily warned Lincoln that if he attempted to withdraw they would open the gates to the enemy and cut off his retreat. Gadsden, who apparently witnessed and approved the whole scene, declared that the militia was willing to live upon rice alone and that even the old women of Charleston would walk unterrified among the shells rather than give up the city.[21]

Lincoln ignored Gadsden and Ferguson and went quietly about discussing terms with the enemy. The British had destroyed Fort Johnson, and on May 5 they captured Fort Moultrie without a fight. The Continentals were ready to surrender. They were out of meat, rice, sugar, and coffee. Some blacks were beginning to help the British, and desertions from both the militia and the Continental forces were rampant. On May 6 Clinton offered terms to Lincoln, who had no choice but to accept, although he did not immediately tell the lieutenant governor what he had done.[22]

On May 8 Gadsden himself finally gave up. Unaware that Lincoln had already surrendered, Gadsden spent the evening writing out his proposals for surrender. He asked for generous terms that would guarantee the safety of the persons and property of the patriots and of the French and Spanish citizens who had helped them. He asked that those who chose not to live under the British government be given twelve months to dispose of their property and to move to some other location of their choice. Gadsden sent his proposals to Lincoln and instructed him to insert them into any agreement he made with the British.[23]

When Lieutenant Governor Gadsden learned the next morning, May 9, that Lincoln had already discussed terms with the British without his knowledge, he went wild with anger. He wrote a very nasty letter to Lincoln protesting his not having been consulted. But Gadsden's temper cooled before he sent the message, and he decided not to send it.[24] Within twenty-four hours the British themselves ended the dispute between Gadsden and Lincoln. On May 10 they began to bombard the city. After only a few hours, 300 citizens signed a petition asking to be surrendered because they could endure no more. "Surely," wrote one of the women, "if the British knew the Misery they occasion they would abate their rigor, and blush to think that the name of Englishman (once so famous among the Fair) should now produce terror and dismay in every female breast."[25]

On May 11, 1780, Gadsden wrote Lincoln that he and all members of the Privy Council had agreed that Lincoln should renew negotiations with Clinton. Gadsden urged Lincoln to agree only to a conference to discuss terms. The next day Lincoln notified him that he intended to accept Clinton's harsh terms before noon. Gadsden did not protest. Disoriented and depressed by the defeat, he simply asked Lincoln to tell him what manner of etiquette "Custom and propriety" demanded on this occasion. Surrender was a new experience for him.[26]

The first two days of surrender were filled with grief and nightmarish violence. Redcoats seemed to be everywhere. The patriots had five or six hundred sick and wounded in houses that had been converted into emergency hospitals. Clinton ordered the Continentals to march before his officers at eleven o'clock in the morning of May 12 and lay down their weapons. He ordered the South Carolina militia to do likewise on the following day. Anyone who did not comply would be shot. Some, however, loaded and cocked their guns before surrendering them. The British piled the weapons into wagons and hauled them to a warehouse containing 4,000 pounds of ammunition. Several of the guns discharged and set off an explosion that rattled windows throughout the town. The explosion blew the British guards to bits and scattered their torsos, arms, legs, and heads for hundreds of feet. An angry Hessian officer blamed Moultrie for the explosion. He rushed up to Moultrie, pounded him with his fists in the face and chest, and growled, "You, Gen. Moultrie, [and] your rebels have done this on purpose, as they did at New-York."[27] Moultrie denied it in order to escape from the Hessian, but he knew that the explosion was no accident.

The terms of the surrender were harsh. All property, including weapons and ammunition, went to the victor. Clinton declared that all militiamen, Continentals, and citizens of the town were prisoners on parole. The citizens and militiamen could return to their homes, but the Continentals were held in barracks until they could be exchanged for British prisoners elsewhere in America. The estates of the political prisoners were sequestered. Clinton made no effort to prevent his men from plundering private property. He ordered them to chop down the Liberty Tree. More than 5,000 grim-faced Continental and state troops helplessly accepted these terms. The men who sullenly deposited their weapons before Clinton included Benjamin Lincoln, William Moultrie, Edward Rutledge, Charles Cotesworth Pinckney, and Christopher Gadsden.[28] Gadsden himself, acting as lieutenant governor, signed the terms of surrender. It was the most difficult task he ever had to perform.

It was a sad and angry Gadsden who retreated to his home at the corner of Front and Washington streets to seek the comfort of his family and wait for better times. Thomas, age twenty-three, was a captain in the militia; he, too, had become a prisoner on parole. At age eighteen, Philip had met the same fate. The British eventually removed Thomas and Philip to a prison ship, probably because they feared the sons would attempt to help the father. Mary, still unmarried at twenty-one, lived at home. The youngest child, Ann, age sixteen, had married merchant Andrew Lord. Gadsden's oldest daughter, Elizabeth Rutledge Ferguson, had died more than three years earlier before her thirtieth birthday. Gadsden had only Mary and his wife Ann at home to comfort him during the defeat.

In the meantime, the British were finding it difficult to hold on to their prize. Since the lieutenant governor had signed the capitulation, General Clinton thought that the entire state had surrendered. But Governor Rutledge intended to continue the fight from his country hideaway. To their dismay, the British soon learned that their occupation of Charleston did not mean that they controlled South Carolina. In July, Clinton sailed for New York, and Lord Cornwallis took up the task of conquering the rest of the state.

The British did gradually claim an arc of forts across the state from Ninety-Six to Georgetown, but they were rarely able to retain control of the territory they conquered. Moving north-westward out of Charleston, Lord Cornwallis met heavy resistance. In August 1780 at Camden, he confronted and defeated the army of Horatio Gates, the hero of Saratoga who had been sent south to assume command after the surrender of Benjamin Lincoln. But most of the other battles or skirmishes went against the British. On October 7, 1,400 patriots subdued a band of tories at King's Mountain near the North Carolina border. Shaken by the news of defeat at King's Mountain and irritated by the stubborn resistance of guerrillas led by Francis Marion and Thomas Sumter, Cornwallis turned due north from Camden, hoping to transfer the theater of war to North Carolina. Lieutenant Colonel Nisbit Balfour, commandant of Charleston, attempted to prevent his prisoners from knowing how badly the war was going for the British, because he feared that such news would cause them to rebel.

The Charleston prisoners themselves delighted in irritating the redcoats in petty ways. One royal official complained that they were violating their parole by a sudden alteration in countenance, "arrogant looks," and whispers of a general insurrection that would free Charleston by the first of September. Another officer declared that such insolent prisoners must be shown "that double dealing will not escape with impunity." The British had hanged a few rebels at Camden, Augusta, and Ninety-Six, and they were not above making examples at Charleston. The British were so afraid of an insurrection in Charleston that they abruptly decided to move the rebel leaders to a "place where it will be out of their power to continue mischievous and treasonable practices."[29]

Before dawn on August 27, 1780, armed redcoats moved stealthily through the quiet streets of the city. At the house on the corner of Washington and Front streets, they demanded that Lieutenant Governor Gadsden arise from his bed and submit himself to their custody. The women in the house must have been frightened and bewildered as they watched their husband or father led away into the darkness. Gadsden was taken to the arcade beneath the Exchange Building where the British had brought twenty-eight other political prisoners. Above them was the great hall, empty now, where six years earlier a tumultuous crowd of citizens had first voted to send Gadsden to the Continental Congress. In the basement below was a prison where the British kept both men and women whom they did not trust to stay at home on parole.

The twenty-nine confused, frightened men stayed only briefly beneath the Exchange. The British soldiers herded them into boats and rowed them out to the armed prison ship, *Sandwich*, that was resting at anchor in the harbor. Life on a prison ship was particularly dreaded, because the patriots knew that they would be overcrowded and would have only what food and supplies their families and friends could send to the ship. On board *Sandwich*, Gadsden gathered the twenty-eight others into a huddle and drew up a memorial demanding to know why they had been brought from their homes to the ship. The British officer to whom Gadsden gave the memorial said not a word in reply; he simply handed the lieutenant governor a paper that had been drawn up in advance and which stated that Lord Cornwallis was "highly incensed at the late perfidious revolt," that he had been informed that the people on parole in Charleston planned "to promote and ferment their spirit of rebellion," and therefore he found "himself under the necessity . . . to change their place of residence on parole from Charlestown to St. Augustine."[30]

Gadsden made a mental note that the order had come from Cornwallis himself. Cornwallis became the focus of his hatred, but Gadsden was powerless to do anything to save himself or his friends. The news that they were to be taken to St. Augustine was not welcome, but at least they were relieved to know that they would not be kept indefinitely on a prison ship. Later in the first day of their captivity, a British officer informed Gadsden and the others that they were being removed as a matter of policy rather than punishment. His carefully worded explanation indicated that he had no concrete evidence that the rebels were planning an insurrection. Nevertheless, Gadsden himself would probably be safer in St. Augustine than in Charleston. Commandant Balfour, who had gladly ordered prisoners hanged in his presence at Ninety-Six, probably would have been happy to dispatch Gadsden upon the slightest excuse.

For a week the twenty-nine prisoners lived aboard *Sandwich*. Then, on September 3, the conquerors transferred them to a smaller ship, *Fidelity*, for the voyage to Florida. Ten more prisoners were already on board *Fidelity*, and in November the British sent out twenty-five others. As lieutenant governor, Gadsden was their highest ranking prisoner, but the British also held Thomas Ferguson, John Edwards, and David Ramsay, the three members of the Privy Council who had not fled to the High Hills. Edward Rutledge and Thomas Heyward, junior, signers of the Declaration of Independence, were also among the captives. Gadsden looked around him to find officers Robert Cochran and Charles Cotesworth Pinckney, and mechanics George Flagg, William Johnson, and John Neufville. Dr. John Budd, who had led the radical democrats against Gadsden in the summer riots of 1778, was himself held upon the same ship with Gadsden. The most distinguished leaders of the patriots in Charleston, save those who had fled with John Rutledge, were all present. The British listed their more important prisoners coldly as one lieutenant governor, three privy councilors, and fifteen other civil officers.[31]

During the week that the prisoners remained on board *Sandwich* and *Fidelity* in the harbor, their families and friends went out to visit and to give them food and other necessities for their confinement. The British demanded that they provide the essential items for their own upkeep as well as make a money payment to cover the cost of the voyage and lodging once they arrived in St. Augustine. Gadsden refused to pay. According to David Ramsay, he "drew from a pocket half a dollar, and turning to his associates with a cheerful countenance assured them that was all the money he had at his command."[32] The others, however, paid and hastened to make themselves as comfortable as possible. Collectively they took with them twenty-six servants and a large quantity of livestock. The livestock, which would provide their food in Florida, were crowded with the 106 people into the hot, steamy *Fidelity* for the four-day voyage.

On Monday, September 4, shortly after *Fidelity* lifted anchor, her captain read the Carolinians the following statement: "Will the gentlemen bound for St. Augustine accept their paroles? I consider the word parole to mean that the gentlemen while on board and at St. Augustine are not to do anything whatever prejudicial to his Majesty's service. If the gentlemen are not retaken, it is not expected that they are to return to any part of America under the British government, but are to consider themselves on parole." The British routinely extracted a promise from political prisoners that they would not run away. Although the captives had given their parole when they were first taken in Charleston on May 12, the British distrusted them so much that they demanded the reassurance of a second parole. Except for Gadsden, all complied. He was insulted to be asked to give his parole a second time. The word that he had given on May 12 was still good, he said. The officer in charge tolerated the lieutenant governor's stubbornness for the remainder of the voyage, but Gadsden was now identified as a man who should be carefully watched.[33]

On September 8, the prisoners were led into the courtyard of the Castillo de San Marcos, a spacious fortress at St. Augustine. Governor Patrick Tonyn was present to receive them. The British officer in charge announced that "expedience" and "a series of political occurrences" had made it necessary to bring them here, "but, gentlemen, we have no wish to increase your sufferings; to all, therefore, who are willing to give their paroles, not to go beyond the limits prescribed to them, the liberty of the town will be allowed; a dungeon will be the destiny of such as refuse to accept the indulgence." The officer then demanded that each man, as his name was called, must appear before Governor Tonyn and again give his parole.

"Lieutenant Governor Christopher Gadsden," the officer probably called first.

Gadsden stepped forward, perhaps cast a glance about to his fellows, then looked at the officer and indignantly exclaimed, "With men who have once deceived me, I can enter into no new contract. Had the British commanders regarded the terms of the capitulation of Charlestown, I might now, although a prisoner, under my own roof, have enjoyed the smiles and consolations of my surrounding family; but even without a shadow of accusation proffered against me, for any act inconsistent with my plighted faith, I am torn from them, and here, in a distant land, invited to enter into new agreements. I will give no parole."

"A dungeon will be your fate," snapped the officer.

"Prepare it then," Gadsden snapped back. "I will give no parole, so help me God"[34]

Gadsden was led away. He was naturally stubborn; he thought

Castillo de San Marcos, St. Augustine, Florida, where Gadsden was held prisoner from September 8, 1780, through July 17, 1781. Courtesy of the National Park Service.

Carcel, or dungeon, in the Castillo de San Marcos. Here Gadsden spent forty-two weeks in solitary confinement. Courtesy of the National Park Service.

he was proving a point of honor and was attempting to set an example for the others. Perhaps he thought that the news of his resistance would get back to Charleston and give hope to the thousands left behind. He may even have hoped that the British would break and leave him alone without giving his parole again. He was aware of the seriousness of his action and was willing to die if necessary to prove his point. Maybe he was foolhardy, or slyly hoped that word of his bravery would filter back to his old adversary John Rutledge. Rutledge had judiciously taken safety in the High Hills, but Gadsden stood recklessly in the face of death. Rutledge could continue to serve by operating a patriot government in exile; Gadsden could serve only through his example of stubborn resistance.

The other prisoners at St. Augustine did not imitate Gadsden's example. When their names were called, they marched obediently before Tonyn, gave their parole, and accepted the privilege to move freely through the fort and the town. They had to answer roll call twice a day, were forbidden to socialize with the soldiers, and were required to remain relatively close to the fort. They were among more than 2,000 prisoners whom the British held at the fort, which made it almost impossible for the officers to keep close watch upon every man. When the officers learned that the Charlestonians who were not Anglicans were holding "private meeting for purpose of performing Divine Service, agreeable to their Rebellious principles," they ordered them to attend the parish church. Tonyn himself instructed them to "behave with decency" and to pray for His Majesty George III.[35] They attended the Anglican church as ordered, but they refused to pray for the king.

With the passing of weeks and months, life for the Carolinians at St. Augustine became more difficult. They were allowed to send letters back home requesting supplies, but anything derogatory they might say about the prison was censored. They sent requests home for casks of Jamaica rum, bottles of Port wine, dozens of chickens, gallons of French brandy, fishhooks, and playing cards in such quantity as to guarantee an almost luxurious existence. At first their requests were fulfilled, but by the spring of 1781 their relatives were unable to get additional supplies to them. The British in Charleston had sequestered their estates and claimed the produce thereon for themselves. In the spring, the men in St. Augustine began to go hungry. The British granted them permission to go out in groups of ten to fish in the river from sunrise until four o'clock in the afternoon. Thus they passed the eleven long months of their imprisonment.[36]

Gadsden suffered more than the others. For forty-two weeks he was kept in solitary confinement in the *carcel*, a dungeon behind the guardroom. His quarters were spacious, perhaps the size of his living room at home, but very uncomfortable. The dirt floor, thick stone walls with no windows or slits to let in light, and arched, solid stone ceiling gave the place the appearance of an oversized tomb. Gadsden was not ever let out into the courtyard for exercise. British soldiers brought him food and tended to his needs at regular intervals. They refused to give him any news of what was happening outside. They did allow him to have a candle and his Hebrew books, but once an angry guard took away his candle for several days. Gadsden passed his time studying Hebrew when he had a light, sleeping, and probably doing calisthenics. He was not allowed to send or to receive letters.[37]

Those who awaited anxiously in Charleston for news about Gadsden's fate were harassed by wild rumors. The British themselves possibly circulated false stories to discourage an uprising in Gadsden's behalf. John Rutledge heard on one occasion that Gadsden had died in prison.[38] Ann Gadsden waited at their home in Charleston. She knew that her husband had been tossed into a dungeon and that he had his Hebrew books with him, but beyond that she knew nothing. And Gadsden himself was not given any comforting information about his family. His guards did tell Gadsden about British victories but never about defeats. They told him that they had sequestered his estate and taken over his wharf. Gadsden knew that his wife and daughters were still in the home, but he could only guess what suffering they might have to endure.[39]

In a different way, Ann Wragg Gadsden suffered humiliation, too. She apparently stayed at home and was given enough of the produce from Gadsden's estate to survive, but she must have been often in fear for her livelihood. As the wife of a prominent political prisoner, she was watched by patriots and British officials alike. One young British soldier taunted her unmercifully. He "consumed of the midnight oil," he said, composing a satirical note to the wife of the imprisoned rebel lieutenant governor. He found in her "warm principles" and "glowing zeal," qualities which she drew "from the veteran and rooted honors of that exalted character, the general." He continued, "A character allied to you *by all the warm*, as well as tender ties; it is with pleasure I ever view the *wharf and bridge*, those works of his hands, which stand like the boasted independence of your country, the crumbling monuments to his august reputations. With what rapture do I behold him in the obscure recesses of St. Augustine, planting deep in Hebrew ground the roots of everlasting fame." Captain Harry Barry, the author of this epistle, said that a celebrated off-color poem then being circulated in the city ought to have been dedicated to Mrs. Gadsden.[40] The manner in which she bore this insult is unrecorded, but it could only have added to her suffering.

No records have survived to tell what damage was actually done to Gadsden's house or precisely how the women inside fared during the long ordeal. But one can imagine that the house was damaged and the women taunted. Henry Laurens's house, which was just across the street from Ann Gadsden's, was "rudely handled by the Enemy's shot," the mansion rendered uninhabitable, and the garden fence and garden "shared the fate of everything of the kind in that neighborhood." Enemy soldiers occupied the servants' dwellings.[41] John Rutledge reported that the conquerors "have burnt a great number of houses and turned many women, formerly of good fortune, with their children (whom their husbands and parents, from an unwillingness to join the enemy, had left), almost naked, into the woods."[42] Charles Cotesworth Pinckney's family was turned out of his house; Pinckney had commanded Fort Moultrie at the time of the surrender and was now a prisoner at St. Augustine. "In short," wrote Rutledge, "the enemy seem determined, if they can, to break every man's spirit, and if they can't, to ruin him."[43]

To escape such horrors, many people in Charleston, including some who had been prominent patriots, declared their loyalty to Great Britain. Daniel Huger, who had been among the members of Rutledge's exiled Council, was among them. The elderly Charles Pinckney, also a member of Rutledge's exiled Council, felt certain that the Continental Congress would abandon the Carolinas and Georgia to the British. Therefore, he came back into the city, declared his loyalty to the king, and asked for protection. Commandant Balfour kept a list of 163 men who repented for taking up arms against the mother country. The list contained the names of Elias Horry, a planter from Prince George Winyah Parish who had previously served the rebel government faithfully; Gabriel Manigault, the wealthiest merchant and private banker in the province who had loaned hundreds of thousands of pounds to the rebel government with no inconvenience to himself; and Rawlins Lowndes.[44]

The state and Continental officials, however, did not intend to abandon Charleston or the men at St. Augustine. Governor John Rutledge urged Congress to retaliate by burning towns and houses in Great Britain.[45] Edmund Pendleton of Virginia demanded from James Madison, then a member of Congress, some information about the course Congress would pursue. "How do Congress bear the horrid confinement of Gov.ʳ Gasdsden & Co?" he asked. "Do they mean to retaliate," or leave "our friends" to stifle and suffocate "with the stench of a prison ship or a dungeon in St. Augustine?" Madison replied promptly that Congress felt "a becoming resentment of the barbarous treatment of the gentlemen in captivity" and had directed General Washington to demand an explanation from General Clinton. When Clinton told Washington that he had not yet been officially informed and that Cornwallis could be trusted to be humane, Madison continued, Washington had "handsomely communicated to Sir Henry" two of "the Earl's bloody proclamations."[46]

Clinton was simply putting Washington off; the British were not ready to discuss the exchange of important political prisoners. They were incensed by the hanging of their own Major John André on October 2, 1780. André had been captured while attempting to buy West Point from Benedict Arnold, and the British had tried in vain to persuade the Americans to exchange him for one of their American prisoners. During André's trial, Clinton offered to exchange Gadsden for André. Benedict Arnold, who had safely escaped into British custody, sent a letter to Washington hinting that if André were hanged, retaliation might be exacted against the South Carolina prisoners. Within the Castillo de San Marcos a British officer advised Gadsden to prepare for the worst; if André were executed, he intimated, then Gadsden could expect the same fate. Gadsden replied that he had always been willing to die for his country, would not shrink from the sacrifice, and would rather ascend the scaffold than purchase with his life the dishonor of his country. The threat was not carried out. André was hanged, and Gadsden languished in his dungeon with his Hebrew books, unaware of the military and political maneuverings that months later would finally procure his release.[47]

Despite their secure base in Charleston, the war in South Carolina went badly for the British. They were unable to establish a viable tory government in the city. Their harsh treatment of the prisoners probably discouraged many from returning their loyalty to the king. The success of the guerrilla fighters in the backcountry had practically rearmed the state as quickly as the British passed through. Washington had sent General Nathanael Greene, a capable Rhode Islander, to command the Continental troops in the Southern Department. After several American victories, Lord Cornwallis and Nathanael Greene signed a cartel on May 3, 1781, for the exchange of prisoners in the Southern Department.

When the news arrived in St. Augustine, the suffering Carolinians rejoiced at the thought of being returned to their homes. They expected to be returned to Charleston promptly, but they were to be disappointed. Charleston remained in the hands of the British. Commandant Balfour was determined not to allow the troublemakers back into the city. He declared that they might go to Virginia or Philadelphia as they wished, but by no means were they to be allowed to stop at Charleston. Balfour ordered that their relatives, totaling 841 persons, be removed from his domain and sent to Philadelphia to greet the returning exiles. Balfour was not acting out of kindness; he wanted to be rid of the responsibility of caring for the kin, and he wanted to offer the exiles an incentive to remain in Philadelphia once they got there.

The British officers at St. Augustine were displeased with their orders to release the prisoners. They decided to make it as difficult for them as possible. On July 5, 1781, one officer ordered them to march the 25 miles to the St. Johns River and embark for

Savannah. Such a march in the summer heat would pose a major challenge of survival to a healthy man, and many of them were old and infirm. They begged their tormentors to reconsider and provide adequate transportation from St. Augustine.

On July 7 the guards at the Castillo de San Marcos received new instructions from Balfour. He directed that one schooner, so small that it would not hold even their baggage, be provided for them in St. Augustine. The commander of the fort realized the impracticality of the order; he therefore decided that he would allow them to use a larger schooner, *East Florida*, provided they would pay £100 sterling for her hire. They could not raise so much money and begged the commander to relent. He finally agreed to give them *East Florida* and a four-weeks' supply of provisions at government expense. At their own expense of 200 guineas, the former prisoners hired the brigantine *Nancy* to accommodate those who could not fit into *East Florida*. They divided themselves into two groups of thirty and thirty-one and cast lots for the vessels. Gadsden was the leader of the group of thirty-one; they won the draw for *Nancy*. All of the men spent another week happily scurrying about in the heat to get themselves and their possessions loaded and ready to depart. On July 17, 1781, with white flags of truce blowing in a gentle Florida breeze, *East Florida* and *Nancy* glided down the St. Johns River into the freedom of the open sea.[48]

CHAPTER TWELVE

The Trials of Victory

Christopher Gadsden lived aboard *Nancy* for seventeen days before he arrived in Philadelphia on August 2, 1781. It must have been a bittersweet voyage. The sweetness of liberation from St. Augustine was tempered by the pain of sailing so near Charleston and not being able to go directly home. He faced numerous readjustment problems after spending forty-two weeks in a dungeon. He wrote George Washington that he arrived at Philadelphia in "good Health and Spirits,"[1] but a year later he confessed that his health had been wrecked at St. Augustine. He began to suffer from dizzy spells and lapses of memory that occasionally disoriented him completely. He was almost fifty-nine years old. He was determined to pursue the war to a successful conclusion, wreak vengeance upon Cornwallis if possible, and return to private life as a factor. Such determination drove him to deny the realities of his age and declining health. Not until the war was over would he be willing to admit that he no longer had the physical strength upon which he had prided himself for so many years.

If Gadsden's anxious eyes strained for a glimpse of his wife, Ann, in the crowd that gathered to welcome *East Florida* and *Nancy*, he was disappointed. She was delayed in leaving Charleston and did not arrive in Philadelphia until after August 10, more than a week later than her husband. What conversation transpired between them when they finally met can only be imagined. Presumably Mary and some servants had come to Philadelphia with her. Ann Lord's husband died that year, and perhaps she, too, a seventeen-year-old widow, went to Philadelphia with her sister and stepmother. The family decided that the women would remain in Philadelphia until the British had evacuated Charleston. Gadsden no doubt inquired diligently of Ann and others about the fate of his beloved sons Thomas and Philip. Both had been taken by the British; both were released by the same cartel that gave their father his freedom. Perhaps they, too, came to Philadelphia and the entire family was joyously, although briefly, reunited.[2]

Gadsden still felt like an exile in Philadelphia. Leading military and civil officers in the continental capital paid high tributes to him and the others who had been released from St. Augustine, but Gadsden could not relax until Charleston was free, Cornwallis captured, and American independence certain. Gadsden and his fellow exiles wrote the president of the Continental Congress that they were eager to hurry home "to chastise a merciless and perfidious Enemy and to rescue their Country from their Tyrannical domination." They requested supplies for their trip. Congress gladly honored their petition. It gave Gadsden, Thomas Ferguson, Richard Hutson, Benjamin Cattell, and David Ramsay each $266.66 and wagons for their journey. John Edwards did not make the trip; he died of apoplexy in Philadelphia.[3] The others waited in Philadelphia for cooler weather before undertaking an arduous expedition through territory in which Cornwallis's army still roamed.

During the six weeks that Gadsden spent in Philadelphia, he wrestled with a severe conflict between his religious principles and his hatred for the man who had sent him to a dungeon in St. Augustine. "Vengeance belongeth to the Almighty," Gadsden wrote one fellow ex-prisoner; "however, a just retaliation, upon an abandoned and cruel enemy, may be sometime absolutely necessary and unavoidable." Retaliation should not take the form of "bayoneting poor soldiers"; but if "a few heads" of their officers could be hanged "on the lines, in the presence of the soldiers," this punishment would be just and honest. It would also be consistent with the will of God, Gadsden rationalized, because the cause of the patriots could be "justly called the cause of God also." And if the head and body of "Even Lord Cornwallis himself" could be separated, "it would be the highest justice."[4] Since Lord Francis Hastings-Rawdon, a prisoner of the French since 1781, had been especially brutal during his campaigns in South Carolina, Gadsden urged the delegates from his state to use their "utmost influence with Congress . . . to obtain him for the purpose of retaliation."[5]

In September, Gadsden and the other Charlestonians left Philadelphia by wagon, bound for Governor Rutledge's headquarters at the High Hills of Santee.[6] Rutledge himself had spent five months in Philadelphia, but he had returned to his rural capital about the first of August when General Greene's army had been able to give him protection. Gadsden was in transit when Lord Cornwallis surrendered at Yorktown on October 17, 1781, but apparently he did not witness it. Gadsden's entourage must have stopped often to rest and perhaps took an unusually circuitous route to avoid enemy soldiers. The journey took two months; not until early November did the tired heroes present themselves to Governor Rutledge.

Rutledge had been waiting for them before he called for new elections. On November 23 he issued writs for elections to be held in all areas of the state that were in patriot hands. He disfranchised anyone who had not borne arms for the state prior to September 27, 1781. The result was a legislature filled with revengeful patriots, including most of the ex-prisoners and a large number of officers. Gadsden himself was chosen to represent Prince George Winyah Parish, where his plantation was located. The continuing British occupation of Charleston that prevented voting there and the bravery of many men from the backcountry who had fought in the war resulted in the election of the first Assembly in the history of the state that was not dominated by the tidewater elite. On January 18, 1782, Gadsden sat proudly among the eighty-three other members in its opening session at Jacksonborough, a village on the west bank of the Edisto River about 35 miles southwest of Charleston.[7]

On the very first day of its meeting, the Jacksonborough Assembly elected Christopher Gadsden to be the new governor of South Carolina. It was a highly emotional moment in Gadsden's life. A hero returning from a long imprisonment, he had perhaps suffered greater hardships for his patriotism than any other survivor. Some members of the legislature had voted for him as a reward for his heroism, but probably he savored the commendation more because it came from the most democratic and patriotic legislature yet assembled. From the time of the Stamp Act and especially during the nonimportation crisis of 1769, Gadsden had fought to protect the rights of the lower and middle classes, especially the mechanics and people in the backcountry. The composition of the Jacksonborough Assembly itself represented for him a victory more important than the governorship.

But Gadsden remembered very well the severe problems he had confronted as vice president and as lieutenant governor; as quickly as the governorship was offered to him, he declined to accept it. He gave a short speech on January 18, 1782, laced with the melancholy tones of a tired, but still spirited man for whom the vindication of his principles was reward enough. These were his words:

> My sentiments of the American cause, from the Stamp Act downwards, have never changed. I am still of opinion that it is the cause of liberty and of human nature. . . . The present times require the vigour and activity of the prime of life; but I feel the increasing infirmities of old age to such a degree, that I am conscious I cannot serve you to advantage. I therefore beg, for your sakes, and for the sake of the publick, that you would indulge me with the liberty of declining the arduous task.[8]

Gadsden was a few months short of fifty-nine, weary and debilitated from his ordeal of the previous year. He could not have been unaware of the energy it would require to restore his wharf and other properties after the British evacuated them. He realized that partisan rivalry was as real in 1782 as it had been during his vice presidency in the riot-torn summer of 1778. The glory of his imprisonment would soon wear away, and being governor would be a very difficult task. Perhaps he suspected that many had voted for him not so much because they wanted him to be governor, but as an unreasoned emotional response to his heroism. The Assembly did not try to persuade him to change his mind; it elected thirty-eight-year-old John Mathews, a moderate patriot who belonged to Rutledge's faction.

One member of the Assembly was glad that Gadsden did not accept. Aedanus Burke, an eccentric Irishman with a fiery temper, believed in liberty, democracy, and justice. He and Gadsden often agreed with each other, but Burke did not trust ex-military officers and apparently feared that Gadsden was too sympathetic with the elite. Burke thought that Gadsden's declining the offer and his manner of doing it was "the most illustrious action of his Life." Burke was glad that Gadsden had been given the compliment, "but more so he did not accept it."[9] The Assembly did, however, pay Gadsden other compliments. It reelected him to the Privy Council and to the Continental Congress. Gadsden accepted the position on the Privy Council, but he declined to return to Philadelphia because of his age and health.[10]

Governor John Mathews, the members of the Privy Council, and other officers assumed their duties in a chaotic time. Charleston was still occupied, the countryside and city abounded with tories, the courts were virtually inoperative, and maintenance of numbers and discipline in the Continental and state troops was almost impossible. The government had to take strong action to encourage recruits to join the militia and to discourage civilians from seeking protection from the British. Therefore, on February 26, 1782, the Jacksonborough Assembly passed a severe confiscation act. It listed six categories of people who should have all of their property taken away for aiding or congratulating the enemy. The Assembly passed a second act to amerce, or fine, those who had taken British protection 12 percent of the value of their estates. The confiscation and amercement acts were partly the work of bitter, angry patriots who themselves had fought so recently and had learned to hate traitors. Still exiled from Charleston, they particularly disliked those men who had at first supported the Revolution and then taken British protection. The laws were also considered a practical measure to encourage men to join the militia. The confiscated property was to be sold at auction, and the slaves, wagons, and horses thereon turned over to the army. The Assembly then listed the names of 239 people who were to have their property confiscated and 47 more who were to be amerced.[11]

In the debate over confiscation and amercement, the old fire came back into Gadsden. Recalling ten months later what he had said at Jacksonborough, he wrote that he had spoken out passionately against both laws. He feared that they would divide the patriots, punish innocent men who had sought British protection only under duress, and retard the final expulsion of the enemy from Charleston. When he saw that he could not win, he begged the Assembly *"only to defer it"* until the Carolinians had taken possession of Charleston. He "reminded them of the proverb not to sell the bear-skin before they had catched the bear." Holding out both of his hands, he said he would suffer them to be cut off before he would vote for such a bill. The acts "haunted" him, he said, before they were ever passed. Even in his dungeon at St. Augustine, he had feared that a "vindictive spirit . . . would increase and spread the resentment of citizens one against another."[12]

But Gadsden himself was not entirely free of vindictiveness. Nor was he absolutely opposed to confiscation and amercement. If his memory of the session is to be trusted after a lapse of ten months, he must have been inconsistent, confusing, and perhaps a bit amusing to his colleagues as he harangued them with his opinions. The very same man who said he would allow his hands to be cut off before he would vote for the laws had used one of those very hands to write the clause in the confiscation act that condemned to death all those who had congratulated Lord Cornwallis upon his victory at Camden.[13]

In December 1781, the month after his return to South Carolina, Gadsden had chanced to meet with Elias and Thomas Horry, sons of Elias Horry, who had congratulated Cornwallis upon his victory at Camden. They offered their hands in greeting. Gadsden became very angry and told them that he did not shake hands with rascals. They said they had come to give themselves up and asked what would be done with them. "Why hang'd to be sure," Gadsden growled. The terrified Horry brothers climbed upon their horses and fled.[14] Gadsden's memories of that experience and of his dungeon were still fresh when he wrote the law condemning those who congratulated Cornwallis. The Horry brothers did not come under it, but their names were eventually added to the amercement list.

Gadsden also actively participated in drawing up the lists of those to be punished. One of the more difficult cases was that of the elderly Colonel Charles Pinckney, a member of the Privy Council who had gone into exile with Governor Rutledge but later returned and sought British protection. Some members of the legislature now wanted to confiscate his property, but the many virtues of the Pinckney family saved him from that more severe fate. According to Edward Rutledge, no one would say anything in favor of the old colonel, and "Gadsden said a great deal against him."[15] Pinckney was amerced 12 percent of the value of his estate. He died the following September with the humiliation still upon him.

The Pinckney case is a good illustration of the anguish that the amercement and confiscation acts caused both to those punished and to their tormentors. The desire for revenge against intestine enemies temporarily blinded the Jacksonborough legislators to the need for rational consideration of ways to restore domestic harmony. But the gentlemen on both sides of the question were men of reason, and they often acted to negate their votes on the laws themselves. Those who had favored the laws as a means of raising money for the army often worked to make them inoperable. And those who had opposed them, such as Gadsden, were sometimes willing to use them for the security of the state or personal revenge. The confiscation and amercement laws were no more than emergency legislation that could not survive the departure of the British. Once the patriots regained their capital almost a year later, they would raise anew the problem of punishment for former loyalists. It was perhaps the most divisive issue in state politics throughout America in the 1780s.

After the adjournment of the Jacksonborough Assembly on February 26, 1782, civil government consisted of executive action by Governor Mathews and his Privy Council. As a member of the Privy Council, Gadsden passed the year near the governor's headquarters at Jacksonborough. By August 1782 the British knew that they would soon have to evacuate Charleston, and their merchants applied to Governor Mathews for permission to stay long enough to complete their mercantile affairs. On October 10 Mathews agreed that they could sell their goods without fear of confiscation of their property and could open the courts in Charleston to collect their debts. In return, he demanded that they not take slaves belonging to the natives with them when they evacuated. Mathews did not consult the Privy Council or the legislature before making the agreement.

Gadsden, an unconsulted member of the Privy Council, was quick to question the constitutionality of Mathews's action. He wrote Mathews a respectful but wordy letter complaining that the governor's agreement with the British made it appear that the Privy Council had been consulted, which was not true. He feared that the governor's implication that the Privy Council was not a part of the executive branch would "reduce this Government to a kind of Principality." Regardless of what learned lawyers might say, Gadsden continued, the South Carolina Constitution was clear; executive actions without the advice and consent of the Privy Council were illegal. Furthermore, Mathews's agreement insulted natives of the province, was unfriendly toward the other states, and encouraged the enemy to linger in Charleston. It encouraged tories to join the British and guaranteed that the British would be well supplied while the natives were running out of rice and beef. But worst of all, Gadsden argued, it "seems so particularly careful of the great negro owners, that I wish the country at large may not think their honor and safety sacrificed to that particular species of property."[16]

Gadsden was attacking the antidemocratic nature of Mathews's decree, not the institution of slavery. At the time of the Stamp Act, Gadsden, like other leaders of the Revolution, had seen the inconsistency of slaveowners' demanding that Mother England not treat them like slaves. But Gadsden had accepted the ownership of slaves as a natural part of the life of a wealthy South Carolinian; he may have disliked the institution, but he did nothing to end it. The census of 1790 showed that he owned 128 slaves, 38 of whom he kept in Charleston and the rest at his plantation near Georgetown. No one else in the city had more than 30 slaves, and in the entire state only two men owned more than 200. In 1790 Gabriel Manigault owned 210 slaves, John Huger had 207, Theodore Gourdin kept 150, and Gadsden ranked fourth with 128.[17]

What separated Gadsden from other large slaveowners was his peculiar sympathy for those people who owned few or no slaves. For all of his career Gadsden had worked to promote the political and economic interests of his friends the mechanics and the people in the backcountry. He had sponsored the circuit court bill for the backcountry in 1768 and had worked to get farmers to sign the nonimportation agreement of the following year. He knew, too, that many middling and poor men had fought and were still fighting in the Revolution. He suspected that the majority of loyalists within the city were large slaveowners; this was certainly true of Gabriel Manigault, who had taken British protection after the fall of Charleston. Gadsden was simply infuriated that Governor Mathews would make an agreement with the British that would favor the very people who had done the least for the patriot cause. He understood that the cause and success of the Revolution rested in part upon the rise of democracy in South Carolina, and he did not want to see any gains that had been made by the poorer classes sacrificed for the good of a few rich slaveowners.

Gadsden's anger with Governor Mathews gradually intensified during the trying year of 1782. His confidant became Francis Marion. Where and how Gadsden had first met Marion is unknown, but the chances are that the two men had known each other since the Cherokee wars. Marion was eight years younger than Gadsden; he had fought in the Cherokee wars, served in the First Provincial Congress in 1775, been a member of Moultrie's Second Regiment during the Battle of Sullivan's Island in 1776, and finally won fame as the Swamp Fox during his guerrilla attacks against Cornwallis's men. From Philadelphia, Gadsden sent his compliments to Marion "for his friendship at my plantation on Black River."[18] What service Marion rendered at Gadsden's plantation is unknown, but perhaps their friendship blossomed from that moment. Marion's men were protecting the government at Jacksonborough, and Marion himself had been a member of the Jacksonborough Senate. Marion had joined Gadsden in opposition to the confiscation and amercement acts. In 1782 the two men apparently had become close friends, and Gadsden freely poured out his thoughts in private letters to Marion.

The first theme that dominates Gadsden's correspondence with Marion is his abhorrence of South Carolinians who traded with the British while they occupied Charleston. "Trade is the greatest band that ever existed," Gadsden wrote; "if there is anything deserves the name of the Great Whore of Babylon, it is certainly her ladyship." Although Gadsden did not "reckon" himself "a severe man in [his] politics," he did strive to get those who sold provisions to the town tried under the sedition law. If a poor man selling out of necessity were caught and convicted, Gadsden's "bowels might yearn . . . to endeavor to procure his pardon, but if a rich fellow, if I had ten thousand notes they should all go for a halter for him, and nothing else." Referring to the wrecked health of the St. Augustine prisoners and to the hundreds of others who had been unable to procure the minimum necessities, Gadsden wrote Marion, "I have told my friends if I die now I lay my death to the charge of those wretches, as much as if they had shot me." These "life traders" were the ones who ought to be punished, not those who had done nothing more serious than take British protection to save their own necks.[19]

Gadsden's distrust of lawyers is the second theme that emerges from his letters to Marion. That attitude was a whig characteristic. When the whig politician Sir Anthony Ashley Cooper and his secretary John Locke had first written a constitution for Carolina in 1669, they had specified that no lawyers be allowed in the province. After South Carolina had become a royal province, however, lawyers abounded. Gadsden feared that lawyers would interpret the state constitution to suit their own purposes and trample upon the rights of the poorer classes. Mathews himself was a lawyer and had attempted to justify his agreement with the British. "We must lose no time to join shoulder to shoulder to check the rapaciousness, tyranny and insolence of too many of our lawyers," Gadsden wrote Marion. Gadsden feared that the governor would always be chosen from among lawyers and that "our posterity will . . . be more abjectly at the feet of lawyers, than ever our forefathers were at those of the Priesthood." He predicted that lawyers would become secret aristocrats who would want to outdo His Holiness and "insist that their *wished for* Chancellor the Pope of the Law pageantry should have perhaps his — — —kissed."[20]

Gadsden also hoped that the national congress would never be taken over by rapacious lawyers who might destroy the democratic gains of the Revolution. Nevertheless, he was convinced that as the successor to his beloved Stamp Act Congress, the Continental Congress was "as honest and respectable as any in the world." Although some "rascals" could occasionally be found among its members, he wrote, it was basically a noble body. He did suggest, however, that delegates should be rotated to keep them honest. A fair and objective Congress would allow even the poorest man to "enjoy every social right and comfort under a good government that I wish for myself," he told Marion. He agreed with Marion that "we can not be too watchful and jealous of men in power."[21] Gadsden wanted a regulated, strong central government that could prevent social inequities from being perpetuated by local partisan rivalries.

Even as Gadsden spilled his thoughts about a future American government to his friend Marion, an American delegation in Paris was taking the last steps to rid Charleston and the rest of the thirteen states of the redcoats. On November 30, 1782, Great Britain signed a preliminary treaty by which she promised to withdraw her troops from her former provinces. In Charleston, the long-awaited and wildly celebrated moment of evacuation occurred at three o'clock in the afternoon of December 14, 1782. General Nathanael Greene triumphantly escorted Governor Mathews, Christopher Gadsden, the other members of the Privy Council, and dozens of leading citizens into the city. Thirty members of Light Horse Harry Lee's dragoons served as an advance guard, but the militia was banned for fear it would attack the tories. Protected by a rear guard of about 200 American cavalrymen under the command of General Anthony Wayne, this entourage followed only 200 yards behind the British soldiers, who by the thousands were making their way to their departure point on Gadsden's Wharf. Almost 4,000 tories and more than 5,000 confiscated slaves went with them. Gadsden kept his thoughts upon the occasion to himself. But he must have felt profound satisfaction upon seeing the enemy's fleet, "upwards of three hundred sails," resting at anchor in a curved line across the harbor, waiting for the tide that would take it across the bar.[22] After twenty-eight long months of exile, almost eleven of which he had spent in a dungeon, Gadsden had at last returned home.

CHAPTER THIRTEEN

Keeper of the Revolution

For two decades after the Revolution, Gadsden used his influence as a private citizen and as a hero of the war to preserve the victory. The departure of the last British ship in December 1782 marked the end of the Revolution in South Carolina but not the genesis of domestic tranquility. Those who had taken protection during the occupation were now at the mercy of the victorious patriots, many of whom were bent upon revenge. The struggle for economic stability in the aftermath of war complicated the discussion of proper treatment for tories and threatened to ignite a class war between debtors and creditors. The absence of the common enemy raised anew the question of the status of the states in relationship to each other. The Articles of Confederation had been ratified in 1781; whether or not they would be viable for a strong new nation was unknown. Independence created a need for new constitutions at both the state and federal levels. The transition of the confederacy into a strong nation, the emergence of national political parties, and the threatening French menace in the 1790s posed enormous problems. In resolving some of these problems at the state level, Gadsden played an active role, and about the others he had a strong opinion.

In November 1782, Gadsden was elected by Prince George's Parish Winyah to his last two-year term in the South Carolina House of Representatives. On February 4, 1783, this House elected Benjamin Guerard governor. Probably in his late thirties, Guerard was a lawyer and planter who had been incarcerated by the British on a prison ship during the war. The large number of ex-prisoners in the legislature probably accounts for his election;

he belonged to the moderate political faction of John Rutledge and outgoing Governor John Mathews. Gadsden did not oppose his election, but Guerard was inclined to exercise greater executive power than Gadsden thought legal.

Under Guerard's leadership, the legislature voted to extend the time Mathews had given the British merchants, who still lingered in the city, to complete their business. The law, passed on March 3, 1783, instructed the British not to add any goods to their stocks and to conclude their mercantile affairs within a year. Gadsden voted against it.[1] He wanted the British completely out of town as soon as possible so that the native merchants, such as himself, could take charge of all trade. Gadsden had resumed business at his wharf immediately upon his return to the city, and he did not want to have to compete with the British. The law itself was another irritant to the archpatriots who had learned to hate anything British and to resist any official attempt to deal realistically with the other side.

Gadsden attended every session of the legislature. He served on numerous committees, conveyed House bills to the Senate, introduced a number of petitions, and attempted to influence the session significantly. He favored legislation that would recognize the supremacy of the Continental Congress over the state legislature, repeatedly introduced a motion to call a new state constitutional convention, and worked for a property tax that would be heavier upon the rich than the poor. He succeeded in getting legislation passed that recognized the right of the Continental Congress to tax foreign trade in South Carolina, but the South Carolina Senate persistently rejected the House bill calling for a state constitutional convention. On February 25, 1783, he proposed a tax of $2.00 per head on slaves, but he had to settle for a compromise of $1.50. He also proposed a tax of $2.00 per 100 acres on all land owned by one individual in excess of 20,000 acres, but that motion was defeated soundly.[2]

The question of punishment for natives who had taken British protection during the war became the most troublesome issue for Gadsden and the other members of the General Assembly of 1783 and 1784. The confiscation and amercement laws of 1782 were one year old, haphazardly enforced, and just as controversial as when they were first passed. Gadsden, Marion, and Burke continued to argue for leniency. More and more other members were coming to agree with them; no longer could they justify the laws as necessary to raise recruits for the army, and many of them had themselves at some time been reticent in their support of the Revolution. Of 381 persons who the British publicly announced had taken protection, only 47 were punished. Each new session of the legislature revised the lists of 1782 by adding and subtracting names. More names were subtracted than added; the lists were gradually shortened until 1784, when the state either returned or paid for most of the confiscated property. Tory merchants, planters, and lawyers were welcomed back into the upper levels of Charleston society.[3]

Gadsden took a leading role in scaling down the lists. He had opposed the laws in 1782, despite his willingness to use them occasionally for personal revenge, and he welcomed the chance to render them ineffective. His motives were complex. He wanted to restore harmony as quickly as possible, and he was genuinely sympathetic with those who had taken protection to save their skins. A number of the old mechanics who had followed Gadsden in 1766 were in that group, and Gadsden seemed eager to help them if possible.

Gadsden also had a number of tory in-laws. His wife Ann came from one of the most famous loyalist families in the province; her brother, John Wragg, age sixty, was on the confiscation list. Gadsden's daughter Ann was the widow of tory merchant Andrew Lord; seventy-five slaves, twenty-two horses, and hundreds of head of cattle and sheep that she had inherited from him had been confiscated. Gadsden's son Thomas had married Martha Fenwicke of another prominent loyalist family. She and Thomas petitioned for payment for confiscated property that she had inherited. Alexander Gillon accused Gadsden of taking pains to remove from the confiscation list the names of his relatives. He said Gadsden bullied other members of the House and Senate into voting to remove the names of his friends and relatives by threatening to place the names of their relatives on the list if they did not.

The journal shows that Gillon was correct. Gadsden personally introduced petitions for redress by his daughter Ann and his brother-in-law John Wragg. In both cases he was successful; Ann

Lord was paid £6,160 sterling for her losses, and the name of John Wragg was moved from the confiscation list to the less severe amercement list. Gadsden did not present Thomas and Martha's petition to the House; it included the names of many other relatives of Martha and apparently was rejected. Gadsden had sound idealistic and political reasons for wanting to rescind the confiscation and amercement laws, but the fact remains that if the lists had not been revised, a great deal of wealth in Gadsden's immediate family would have been lost.[4]

The question of how to treat former loyalists divided the city into two hostile political factions similar, but not identical, to those that had existed before and during the Revolution. The moderates included the wealthy elite, many of whom had favored the war for independence and who now promoted a stable government in which they would exercise power. John Rutledge, the Pinckneys, John Mathews, and Benjamin Guerard were in this group. The second group was the radical democrats, including many of the same people who had rioted against the loyalty oath in the summer of 1778. Most were men of little property or money who wanted to punish the former tories and were willing to use mob action to promote their own ends. Their principal leader was Alexander Gillon, a man who had grown wealthy speculating in confiscated property. The moderates dominated the state legislature, and the radical democrats formed vigilante groups who rioted sporadically throughout 1783 and 1784. They belonged to two organizations, the Marine Anti-Britannic Society led by Gillon and the Whig Club of Six Hundred. They sometimes dominated the town meetings in Charleston, but they were unable to gain control of the legislature.[5]

The radical democrats were accused of setting fire to a warehouse on Gadsden's Wharf on the night of September 20, 1783. It destroyed 200 hogsheads of sugar and 94 puncheons of rum; the losses were insured, but the damage to the wharf, estimated at £1,000, was borne by Gadsden. The authorities assumed that the fire was deliberately set, and they held the second mate of an unnamed vessel for questioning. Governor Guerard offered a reward of 100 guineas for the capture of the "evil minded persons" responsible, but apparently no arrest or conviction was ever made.[6]

The disturbances abated during the winter months, and on March 26, 1784, the General Assembly adjourned, marking the end of Gadsden's service in nineteen consecutive legislative bodies in South Carolina since 1757. Gadsden was sixty years old, sometimes forgetful, and occasionally suffering from attacks of dizziness. He was ready to retire from public life, but he was generally pleased with the political progress that had been made in his lifetime and characteristically optimistic about the future. Six weeks before his retirement, he wrote General Henry W. Harrington of North Carolina: "Nothing I think but our own Faults, our Indolence & Inattention to publick Business can prevent our being as happy a People as any that were ever under the Sun, & Securing that Happiness to our Posterity. The Cup is in our Hands & if we prove so lazy as not to bear it up to our Lips, we must deservedly be ruined, & so far from meriting any Pity cannot but expect the highest Degree of Laughter & Contempt."[7] But retirement from government did not quiet Gadsden's voice in the events that marked the emergence of a new nation. Age increased his pride in being present at what he judged to be the dawn of the republic in 1765; only his death, and that was yet far away, could end his defense of what he considered to be in part his personal creation.

Gadsden's attention was soon turned sharply back to raucous activities in the streets of Charleston. In April 1784 trouble broke out anew. The radicals set fire to several wharf storehouses which contained property belonging to tories, but apparently none of the damage took place at Gadsden's Wharf. Captain William Thompson, an advocate of "social equality" for all except propertied tories, exchanged harsh words with John Rutledge, a member of the House and a special target of the tory-baiters, that led to Thompson's brief imprisonment for contempt of the legislature. He was punished, he complained, simply because "*the great John Rutledge* was individually offended by a *plebeian*." In the same month "a few sons of Liberty" chased loyalist William Rees to the roof of his house, "stripped off his shirt, and laid on his bare back, the juice of hickory, to the amount of fifty stripes." Governor Guerard issued a proclamation warning the radicals not to insult citizens of the state and offering a reward of $1,000 for the conviction of persons who were maliciously forcing citizens to leave. The city council passed a riot ordinance that eventually helped to turn the tide against the radicals.[8]

Gadsden remained aloof until May 6, 1784, when he entered the fray with a letter to the public printed in the *Gazette of the State of South Carolina*, the organ of the radical faction. He found himself about halfway in each camp. He had opposed both extended privileges for British merchants and mistreatment of former loyalists. He favored a republican form of government that would guarantee the natural rights of man as delineated by John Locke, including the right to own property. He was particularly anxious to protect the trade of the state. Whether he was democrat or republican, radical or conservative, depended upon the particular event in which he was involved at the moment. When rallying the Sons of Liberty against the Stamp Act in 1766 or criticizing the lawyers in 1781 who approved of trade with the enemy, he appeared to be a democrat and a radical. When defending the Constitution of 1778 against the mob and writing against the excesses of the Marine Anti-Britannic Society in 1784, he seemed to be a republican and a conservative. But in every case he was squarely on the side of law, order, the authority of a strong government, and respect for the constitution in effect at the time. His participation in the events that led to independence was intended to preserve the virtues of the British constitution, not to destroy them. His radicalism in the decade before independence was made in London, not in Charleston. And his opposition to mob action against the rights of tories in 1784 was commensurate with the principles he had cherished since the beginning of his public life.

Signing himself "A Steady and Open Republican," Gadsden was remarkably restrained in his letter to the public in the spring of 1784. Mistreatment of foreigners and tories by the mob, he argued, had greatly injured the trade and credit of the state. Foreigners would not likely want to deal "with such mad-men" as had laid the "juice of the hickory" upon the back of William Rees. The function of the government should be to make an example "of three or four of the most notorious Delinquents of rank," after a *"fair and candid trial,"* and then offer amnesty to the rest. Mob action against tories merely undercut a "respectable and fatherly" government's duty to show itself "ready to protect the poorest citizen, and not afraid of the highest." The formation of an anti-Britannic society, or any other antiforeign society, was self-defeating, he said. South Carolina should seek active trade with all foreigners, including the British, and treat all equally.

Gadsden also attacked Alexander Gillon and his Marine Anti-Britannic Society. In these unsettled years, Gadsden said, the state did not need *"overcareful reformers and self created censors"* who undermined the new government by leading mobs. He regretted to see "any worthy man tarnish his former conduct by contrary behaviour." Referring to Gillon's Dutch birth and ancestry and to his extensive purchases of tory estates, Gadsden said he liked a "Stadtholder" no better than he liked a king; mobbing might lead once again to a monarchy. Gadsden found the use of the word "marine" laughable; less than twenty Carolinians were at sea, and the private raising of a navy was contrary to the laws of the Confederation. Gadsden implied that the Marine Society was nothing more than the personal vehicle of its president, Alexander Gillon, who in "the *bare hire* of one single frigate" had embroiled the state in a financial and political embarrassment.

Gadsden was referring to the Luxembourg claims, a major financial and diplomatic crisis that lingered from the Revolution. During the war, Gillon had acquired the frigate *South Carolina* from the French Chevalier Luxembourg for 300,000 livres. For that amount Gillon pledged his personal fortune and the credit of the state of South Carolina. One-fourth of the proceeds from prizes captured were to go to Luxembourg, one-fourth to South Carolina, and half to the crew and officers. The ship was to be returned at the end of the war, but if it were captured, Gillon and the state were supposed to pay the 300,000 livres. The British captured the vessel in 1782, and Luxembourg demanded payment. Gadsden condemned the episode as a wild project, *"a mere Pandora's Box,"* that had laid a heavy burden upon the state. Gillon was in truth an economic opportunist, but Gadsden was unfair to him. The state had authorized the purchase and took so long to make the payment because it could not decide whether the money was owed to Luxembourg or to the French government. Before the ship was captured, South Carolina collected about $115,000 in prize money from her operations; the amount South Carolina finally paid many years later was only $65,000. Gillon himself attempted to honor his part of the bargain and died impoverished in 1794. The affair was not finally settled until seventy-three years later, when South Carolina made the final payment.⁹

In quick reply to Gadsden's attack, Gillon's comrade, brewer William Hornsby, signing himself "Democratic Gentle-Touch," asked Gadsden and "the other Nabobs and their creatures" if they had given the "opprobrious epithet of MOBS" to the leaders of the Stamp Act rebels. Gadsden, he feared, now wished to lead an aristocratic few who desired to dominate the government. The fate of the frigate *South Carolina* was not unlike that of other frigates, and it had served the colonies well, which was to the credit of her commander. "Of how much more use, or what less expence than the Carolina Frigate, was the well constructed, and useful zigzag bridge, which united the continent to Sullivan's Island?" Hornsby asked sarcastically.¹⁰

Gadsden ignored Hornsby and attacked Gillon himself. On July 17, again using the signature "A Steady and Open Republican," he angrily leveled public charges against Gillon which many gentlemen might have considered grounds for a duel.¹¹ In his quaint, disorganized, turgid, and lengthy prose, sprinkled with quotations in Latin and from Alexander Pope, Gadsden reverted to his old rashness. He alleged that Gillon was among those "indefatigable sons of *Cunning*, who wish to set us by the ears for *their own* purposes," and he was "the principal ring leader of our late public disturbances." The peace, good order, and prosperity of the state demanded that he desist immediately from "the mobbing and bullying business." Gadsden laughed at any accusation that he, Christopher Gadsden, had "Aristrocratical designs," for every man in America who had known him for thirty years could testify to the "active, steady, uniform, open unequivocal, . . . *disinterested* part" he had taken in every matter. Not so with Gillon. Certainly Gillon, whom Gadsden referred to in print only as "his honor Mr. Dupe-Master General," had been willing to acquire the frigate on his own credit. Everything Gillon did was to his own credit! "This *important* man condescends to let us know, *with the gravity of a professor* . . . that 'patriotism has been the pretense of traitors and malcontents in all ages.' "

Gillon was a candidate for intendant, or mayor, of Charleston in the fall elections, and part of Gadsden's attack was motivated by his desire to block Gillon's election. Gadsden urged the public to vote against Gillon. The hostility between Gadsden and Gillon went back to January 1770, when Gadsden presided at the meeting that forced Gillon not to sell some wine he had imported before the nonimportation crisis. Gadsden remembered also that in the summer of 1778 Gillon had been the real leader of the radical democrats who rioted against the loyalty oath that Gadsden as vice president was bound to enforce. Gadsden contended that Gillon was a patriot only because he saw an opportunity to enrich himself. Gadsden concluded his letter by saying that the only reason he had undertaken "a work almost as offensive as *raking* into a common jakes" was to end the mob's activities by exposing its leader.

In his description of Gillon, Gadsden had characteristically blended the truth with exaggeration. Although he was Dutch born, Gillon was unquestionably loyal to South Carolina and America. He was certainly an economic opportunist, but he broke no law. His purchase of thousands of acres of confiscated tory property was strictly legal. His role in the *South Carolina* affair showed neither bad judgment nor any dishonesty on his part; in fact, Gillon never collected his own share of the prize money and did make an honest effort to pay his part of the debt.[12]

Gadsden had started the public quarrel in 1784, and Gillon was equal to the contest. He responded with a brief public note "To Christopher Gadsden, Esq.," explaining that since no ideas were too gross for Gadsden, it would be futile to respond to him with moderation. "Composed as your language is, of the coarsest importations from Bilingsgate, the hair stroke of decorum and delicacy . . . would rouse your sensibility with as little effect as they would that of a *gut-eating Hottentot*." Gillon suspected that Hornsby's letter had zigzagged Gadsden's brains; he denied that he had influenced that letter or the antitory mobs. Although Gillon had once conjectured that Gadsden was "a good citizen, an honest man, a brave man, a very disinterested man, a man destitute of hypocrisy, one that had never swerved from facts, no slanderer, and no back-biter," he now wished "to make some apology to the public" for having entertained such an opinion. He dismissed Gadsden's insulting letter as "*a Bag of Feathers ript open in a gale*."[13]

After one more public letter from Gadsden and two from Hornsby, Gillon finally on September 9, 1784, lost all patience and launched the most critical account of Gadsden's career that has survived.[14] In more than 3,000 words, he painted every episode in Gadsden's life in the darkest tones. He said that Gadsden was dumb, jealous, and a liar. He accused Gadsden of placing on the confiscation and amercement lists, that "*Doomsday record* for the future historian," the names of many persons who had committed no more serious crime than "offending your little Majesty." He said that Gadsden had always been a disturber of the peace, "a petulant factioneer, and a quarrelling tumultuary against [his] neighbors, friends, and even betters." He had led the mob against Henry Laurens's house in 1765, fanned the quarrel between Middleton and Grant during the Cherokee uprising, and quarreled with Major General Howe and "nearly received the proper chastisement."

"Having run over" Gadsden's "riotous and hypocritical character," Gillon then turned to his "interested one." He was tired of hearing Gadsden "continually bellow forth" that he had never received any payment for his thirty years of public service. He presumed that as "a politician, a superintendent of mechanical works, or a Brigadier General," Gadsden had been paid, and he trusted that Gadsden would be likewise punished for any disservices he was plotting against the public. For every year that Gadsden had attended the House of Representatives, he had "put the state to an expence of 9000 dollars," besides "tiring out at every session, the aggregate body" with his "drawling, endless, and disgusting debates and motions." There were many who believed that Gadsden's "famous Zig-zag bridge" had cost the state more than her entire navy, and now the state would have to spend at least that much again "to have the remnant of that curious edifice removed." Gadsden had plunged the state into needless expense by demanding that Boundary Street be extended to his wharf; he had worked for a law requiring the inspection of tobacco because he wanted the inspection warehouses to be on his wharf. Gadsden himself was the son of a foreign-born "passage bird" and had borrowed large sums of money to build and repair his wharf but had repaid it in depreciated paper currency.

Gadsden would injure an entire society for his personal gain, Gillon continued; his character had always been "revengeful, suspicious, jealous, and designing." In the first stage of his life, he had been intemperate; in the second, corrupt; and in the third, seditious. Gillon was reminded of the story of the mad pig hanged by the hind legs and whipped until he frothed at the mouth. The froth was then given to all whom the operator wished to drive mad. Gadsden must have received a double portion because he acted like a madman. "And should pigs grow scarce," Gillon continued, "and the old custom be again renewed, I would recommend your being hung by the heels to save trouble: as I presume you will not need much whipping to make you foam and produce froth sufficient to set the whole world in a fit of madness."

Gadsden no doubt frothed sufficiently when he read Gillon's public letter, but the attack had been primarily personal and he did not reply. Gadsden may or may not have known about a threat against his life the day before Gillon's letter appeared. One Herbert Hodson informed Justice John Logan that Benjamin Harvey had told him that Thomas Ferguson, Gadsden, Thomas Pinckney, Richard Hutson, and several others "should soon be put to death, but did not mention for what reason." When Hodson told Thomas Ferguson of the plan, Ferguson replied that both Harvey and Hodson might "kiss his Backside," the same response which Gadsden himself no doubt would have made.[15] Apparently an idle threat from the camp of the radical democrats, this report probably had little to do with Gadsden's decision not to answer Gillon.

Gillon had exaggerated to make his point, but his charges against Gadsden could not be lightly dismissed as complete falsehoods. Gadsden would have found it difficult to deny that he had favored legislation which served his wharfage business well, and in the 1780s everyone practiced paying debts with depreciated paper money. There is no proof that Gadsden had any outstanding debts in the 1780s; in fact, there is no record that he was ever heavily in debt. The gradual manner in which he built his wharf probably enabled him to pay his expenses as he went. To disclaim being a debtor in an era when almost everyone in Charleston was one would have made Gadsden very unpopular, and he wisely remained silent. Gillon did claim that his countrymen the Dutch had "dared to refuse the loan of a cool thousand to Christopher Gadsden," but they generously offered it to others of inferior fortune.

The major reasons for the end of the public debate between Gadsden and Gillon were Gadsden's fear of another duel and Gillon's defeat in the fall elections. Gillon did not become mayor, and his party won very few seats in the legislature. In February 1784, however, the General Assembly had named Gillon as a delegate to the Continental Congress. But he did not attend a single session and seems to have been so consumed with interest in his private financial affairs that he became a liability to the state. In 1786 Gillon was elected to the House of Representatives, where he succeeded in getting passed legislation that would help the debtor class. In 1792 he was elected to the Congress of the United States, a position that he held at the time of his death two years later. In their public fight in 1784, neither Gillon nor Gadsden was quite so wicked as the other said, and perhaps both were glad to end their quarrel.

Gadsden's colorful newspaper battle with Gillon and his condemnation of the tactics of the radical democrats tended to obscure his ideas about republican government and the nature of representation. Gadsden believed that the franchise should be extended as broadly as practical, but once the election was over the people should drop back into their nonpolitical pursuits and defer to the wisdom of their elected officials. If those officials proved to be incompetent or corrupt, then the people should vote against them in the next election, not riot in the streets and destroy private property. Mob violence had sometimes been necessary to bring about change within and later independence from the British system of government, because in that system great power resided with an hereditary monarchy and nobility, but in the new American system of republicanism no rulers could win or retain their positions without ultimate approval by the electorate.

Gadsden's criticism of Gillon and his followers did not extend to a general condemnation of the middle and lower classes. In fact, in the very last session of the General Assembly in which he served, he had supported tax legislation that would have hurt the rich and helped the poor. His basic sympathy with the mechanics and the people in the backcountry remained unchanged, and some of them continued to count themselves among his friends. In matters relative to the strength of the central government, foreign policy, trade, and the rise of political parties, he was largely in agreement with the federalist ideas of Alexander Hamilton, but his opinion about democracy was more akin to the thinking of Thomas Jefferson.

Nevertheless, it was business, not politics, that occupied most of the aging Gadsden's attention during the 1780s and 1790s. A severe two-year depression hit South Carolina in 1785, but in time there was a good recovery. Although many of the tidewater planters were still burdened with prewar debts, their ability to retain ownership of their lands and slaves would guarantee them success within a few years. Henry Laurens lived comfortably, although he could not raise as much as one dollar in cash. Still he was able to contribute food to help Edward Rutledge feed his slaves. South Carolina increased her production of agricultural exports. The growing of tobacco had spread into the backcountry during the war. The indigo industry revived so rapidly that much more in quantity and in value was being exported after the war than before. The cotton industry was on the threshold of a gigantic growth that would bring a new source of great wealth to the state. Corn and wheat, produced largely in Virginia and to a lesser degree in South Carolina, were very much in demand in the West Indies, England, and France.[16]

Gadsden fared quite well financially during the 1780s and 1790s. In addition to his realty in Charleston and his wharf, he owned about 1,000 acres on the Pee Dee River near Georgetown. Sometime before 1784 he bought 200 more acres on the Black River, which flows into the Pee Dee above Georgetown. And in 1801 he bought the 144-acre Beneventum Plantation because it would merge his lands on the Pee Dee with those on the Black River.[17] Few records have survived that would reveal the details of his planting operations, but he probably grew indigo and corn before the Revolution and added cotton and tobacco in the 1790s. In 1790 he had ninety slaves on the plantation and probably more than one hundred in 1800. Since he did not live there himself, he must have employed an overseer and probably made regular trips from Charleston to Georgetown himself to check upon the operation. He no doubt enjoyed a good share of the agricultural boom of the 1780s and 1790s.

Gadsden was never enthusiastic about the institution of slavery, but he owned slaves all of his adult life. He inherited several from his father and later purchased others to work on his plantation. In dealing with them, he seems to have been a kind master. The newspapers contain no record of his advertising for runaways. Nanny and Elsy were his favorite house servants. By the end of the eighteenth century he owned five generations of the descendants of Nanny and was particularly proud that he had never sold any of her offspring. Conversely, the implication is that he did sell the children of other slaves whom he owned. Two elderly men, "helpless Strephon" and "old Ned," the latter of whom was the son of "old Betty," seem also to have been among his favorites. In 1781 he manumitted "old Betty" and "old Billy." In 1789 he freed Abram, who had been with him for many years, but who he learned was the son of free blacks in Virginia. A court inventory of Gadsden's estate in 1805 listed more than fifty slaves by name ranging from George, who was worth $500, to Friday, who was "deaf and dumb, worth nothing." References were made to numerous unnamed wenches and children, the majority of whom no doubt lived on his Black River plantation. Of the thirty-eight slaves he kept in Charleston in 1790, twenty-four staffed his town house and the rest worked at his wharf.[18]

Gadsden's wharf and factorage business in Charleston occupied most of his attention after the war. He had no substantial prewar debts, and although his property had been damaged heavily during the war, he was in a good position to take advantage of the trade that flourished in Charleston. The third largest port in the colonies in terms of tonnage, Charleston suffered more damage than any other port with the possible exception of New York. Recovery, however, was rapid. An average of 31,000 tons cleared the port in 1772; 50,961 tons cleared between November 1783 and November 1784. Since there was no great reduction in price levels after the war, it would be safe to assume that merchants and wharfowners did not suffer severely.[19]

As the owner of the largest wharf in the harbor, Gadsden certainly received a generous share of this trade. The only warehouses officially designated for the inspection of tobacco destined for exportation were on his wharf. Although the wharf was damaged during the war, it was never completely inoperable; ships could arrive and depart from certain sections while other sections were being repaired. He and his sons, Thomas and Philip, organized a factorage business in 1783 under the name "Christopher Gadsden & Sons," and within a year they announced that planters who used their wharf would never be obliged to sell their rice for want of storage space.[20]

Gadsden made a public announcement that because of "his advanced time of life" he would retire on October 31, 1791, and leave the business entirely in the hands of Thomas and Philip. He was sixty-seven, but he appeared to be much older. He had lost his teeth and his mouth had sunken in. All that remained of his hair was a few long, yellowish strands flowing from the perimeter of his skull. But his eyes were bright and his mind still alert.

Despite his age, Gadsden's plan to retire was interrupted when Thomas died suddenly in Philadelphia on November 4, 1791, at the age of thirty-five. Thomas had been Gadsden's eldest living son, had enjoyed a brief political career as lieutenant governor of the state from 1787 through 1789, and had been the son upon whom Gadsden had based his dreams for the future political and economic status of the family. Thomas's death in 1791 must have struck him even harder than the death of Christopher, junior, twenty-five years earlier.

The death of Thomas apparently created a temporary financial crisis for the business. Gadsden pledged to sacrifice his plantation and slaves on the Black River if necessary to pay Thomas's obligations. But such drastic action was not necessary. Instead, Gadsden reorganized the business with Philip and his son-in-law Thomas Morris as partners. Morris was a merchant from Philadelphia who had moved to Charleston after the war and married Gadsden's daughter Mary. Notices in the local press and sporadic correspondence with merchants and bankers in Philadelphia suggest a thriving enterprise. One or more of the partners bought land at sheriffs' sales and resold it, leased numerous lots and released them at a profit, and occasionally served as agent to sell the property of someone who was deceased. On October 10, 1795, Gadsden and Company advertised to purchase a gang of seventy

Portrait of Christopher Gadsden in 1797. Rembrandt Peale, artist. Independence National Historical Park Collection, Philadelphia.

or eighty slaves. Whether they actually made the purchase is unknown, but the slave trade increased sharply after the invention of the cotton gin in 1793 and no doubt some sales took place at Gadsden's Wharf. Gadsden himself never fully retired, but after 1795 he seems to have relinquished most of the responsibility for the business to the younger men.[21]

Gadsden's role in state and national politics after 1784 was that of observer and critic. He was not a delegate to the Constitutional Convention in 1787, but he did send advice to George Washington and John Adams. To Washington, he suggested that Congress be given greater power than the states, the importation of slaves be restricted, and paper money be tightly controlled. Writing to John Adams in more detail, Gadsden drew upon his own experience in framing the South Carolina Constitution of 1778. He said that the three branches of government ought to be distinctive and that the president should be given veto power. The peace and security of the nation, Gadsden contended, could be maintained only by balancing the "various and contradictory" economic groups against each other.[22]

Satisfied with the completed Constitution, Gadsden wrote Thomas Jefferson that he expected a "new and important Epocha" to arise in which "our Trade wou'd soon be on a safe, proper and respectable Footing." He added with his characteristic enthusiasm that he thanked God to "have lived to see this important Point in so fair a Way to be accomplish'd, and if I live to see it compleatly so, I shall be apt to cry out with old Simeon: Now may thy Servant depart in Peace for mine Eyes have seen thy Salvation."[23]

The South Carolina General Assembly called a ratifying convention to meet in Charleston on May 12, 1788. Before it met, Gadsden, on May 5, published an open letter to the public urging adoption of the Constitution. He believed that "nothing less than that superintending hand of providence" could have produced a document that so perfectly reconciled "so many jarring interests and prejudices." He reminded the public that the Constitution "takes its rise, where it ought, from the people; its president, senate, and house of representatives, are sufficient and wholesome checks on each other, and at proper periods are dissolved again into the common mass of the people; longer periods would probably have produced danger; shorter, tumult, instability, and inefficiency, every article of these and other essentials to a republican government, are, in my opinion, well secured."[24]

Gadsden was among the Charleston representatives to the ratifying convention. The convention voted 149 to 73 in favor of ratification. Gadsden voted against one motion that would have postponed consideration until Virginia had made her decision and against another motion that would have weakened the power of the presidency. On January 7, 1789, the state legislature named Gadsden, Henry Laurens, Arthur Simkins, Edward Rutledge, Charles Cotesworth Pinckney, Thomas Heyward, and John Faucheraud Grimké to be the state's first electors. On February 4, all seven voted for George Washington.[25]

Gadsden took a slightly more important part in the writing of a new state constitution for South Carolina in 1790. As early as January 1783 he had suggested that the Constitution of 1778 should be revised, but the wealthy men in the lowcountry were so fearful of losing power to the growing population in the upcountry that they had resisted any effort to change the constitution.[26] In 1786 the General Assembly had voted to move the state capital from Charleston to Columbia, a new town in the upcountry at the confluence of the Congaree and Broad rivers. The first streets were named for South Carolina's heroes of the Revolution, including one in honor of Gadsden. Perhaps Gadsden himself had helped to select the name Columbia for the capital city. Writing more than a dozen years later and indulging himself in the digressive reveries of old age, he lamented that the nation had not been called Columbia. Every time he heard the word American, he wrote, "methinks I hear the shade of the great Columbus reproaching us for abetting and continuing the cheat upon him."[27]

The Charleston aristocrats felt cheated themselves when the capital was moved to Columbia; they wanted to bring it back home to the confluence of the Ashley, the Cooper, and the Atlantic Ocean. Some even acted as if the new capital did not exist. Nevertheless, the General Assembly called for the state constitutional convention to meet in Columbia on May 10, 1790. At the opening session, Gadsden, a delegate from Charleston, was chosen to preside. He presided that day only and probably did not influence the convention in a major way, although he was satisfied with the completed document.

The first issue that brought forth a heated debate in the convention was the question of a permanent location of the state's capital. The representatives from the upcountry wanted it to stay at Columbia; the others hoped to move it back to Charleston. On a day when a large number of delegates from the lowcountry were absent, the convention voted 109 to 105 to retain Columbia as the capital. Gadsden would have preferred that it be moved back to Charleston. He promoted Charleston as a matter of convenience only, he said, not as a way of favoring tidewater aristocrats. Gadsden recommended, and the majority approved a clause prohibiting the capital from being moved except by a two-thirds majority vote, and only then after the members of the legislature were given sufficient advance warning to get to the new location.[28] Perhaps Gadsden remembered how a royal governor long ago had moved the Commons House of Assembly to Beaufort to attempt to stop the rising power of the natives. He was determined that no such trick should ever again be played upon the people of South Carolina.

The second major issue debated in the convention concerned the matter of representation in the legislature. Many, including Gadsden, had already accepted the fact that the upcountry was going to have a greater voice in the state's affairs. It had contributed many heroes to the Revolution, was growing rapidly, and was demanding political change. Eighty percent of the state's 140,000 white citizens lived in the upcountry. The minority of rich planters and merchants along the coast, however, did not want to surrender their control. After the fashion of a good English whig, Gadsden wanted to give the upcountry seats in the legislature but not a majority. From the Stamp Act onward he had attempted to protect the rights of the middle and lower classes, but he was not ready to give them control.

After a long and heated debate, the convention finally worked out a compromise. The lowcountry won 70 of the 124 seats in the House and 20 of the 37 seats in the Senate. Although this compromise represented a victory for the lowcountry, the delegates from the upcountry accepted it because they knew that their region was growing more rapidly and that within a few years they could reasonably expect to control the House of Representatives. Gadsden thought the compromise was fair; the aristocratic stability of the lowcountry would dominate the government for the present, and gradual change favoring a maturing backcountry could take place within the system.

The balance of the constitution also represented a compromise between the upcountry and the lowcountry, the rich and the poor, but the lowcountry and the rich retained greater power. Religious qualifications for officeholding and rights of primogeniture were abolished, but significant property qualifications to vote or be eligible for office were kept. The legislature elected the governor, United States senators, presidential electors, and many local officers down to county tax collectors. The governor had no veto power and could not succeed himself after a four-year term. Gadsden did not mind that the state constitution was more conservative than the federal document; he thought both were practical and honest. Although he was more democratic than the typical Charleston aristocrat, he was never in favor of an absolute democracy that would undermine his whiggish principles.[29]

Insofar as active political involvement was concerned, Gadsden's role in the state constitutional convention of 1790 was his swan song. But his interest in politics did not wane. In the remaining fifteen years of his life he addressed thousands of words to the public, giving his opinion on the major events of the Federalist era, defending the Constitution, reflecting upon his career, and attempting to justify himself. He expounded upon the whig interpretation of history and government, attacked the French, and promoted the presidential candidacy of his friend John Adams. His writings were filled with his usual appeals to antiquity, colorful illustrations, flashes of optimism, and disorganized, impassioned jargon. The burden of more than seventy years did not improve his writing style, and he became so repetitious that his readers must have found it a tedious business to labor through his works. Yet his arguments were the product of a clear head and a generous spirit. He usually succeeded in making his point, and he was as sincerely concerned about the future of his posterity as he had been about his own future when he was a young man.

In the fluid political climate after the first national elections, Gadsden associated with the Federalists. The Federalists divided loosely into two general groups. The first group was the old-school Federalists, most of whom had been born between 1720 and 1760 and had fought in the Revolution. Many of them had been radicals in the decades before the war; all had been whigs and they tended to remain individualists rather than become party men. The younger Federalists, with a few exceptions, were born after 1760. Some had fought in the war, but many had not. They were strong party men who often became professional politicians and fought valiantly to maintain the power of their party against the rise of Thomas Jefferson's Democratic Republicans.

Gadsden associated with the old-school Federalists. Like them, he deplored partisan bitterness and regretted the rise of national parties. He had a sharp sense of duty to perform public service. He advocated political and economic independence under a sound constitution, national unity above state rights, and an economic environment that would promote free domestic and foreign trade. He believed firmly in a constitution that could transcend the whims of leaders and the passage of time in order to preserve the basic rights of man. When he thought that such a constitution was under attack, he was quick to come out of retirement to defend it. The federalism of Gadsden and the old school was a natural extension of the whig principles that had led them to demand reform within the empire and then independence. Yet, Gadsden was not blindly loyal to the old school; he analyzed each new development on its own merits and retained a peculiar sympathy with the people that was unbecoming for a Federalist of any school.

The old-school Federalists were often men whom Gadsden had known in the Stamp Act Congress or the first two sessions of the Continental Congress. They included George Washington, Patrick Henry, and Richard Henry Lee of Virginia; John Adams, Benjamin Lincoln, and Henry Knox of Massachusetts; William Samuel Johnson of Connecticut; John Jay of New York; and William Tilghman of Maryland and Pennsylvania. In South Carolina the old-school Federalists included Gadsden, Thomas Bee, John Barnwell, Ralph Izard, Charles Cotesworth Pinckney, Thomas Pinckney, and Jacob Read. All except Barnwell and Bee had studied in England. Barnwell, Bee, and Izard were wealthy planters who had served the patriot government before and during the war. The Pinckney brothers were lawyers, planters, and military men who absorbed the prevalent English whig ideas of their environment and became Federalists without considering any other possibility. Jacob Read, a pompous elitist who had been one of Gadsden's fellow prisoners at St. Augustine, was a London-trained lawyer who periodically served the state and national governments from 1781 through 1800. Despite their general agreement upon the course of American politics in the 1790s, there were wide individual variations among the old-school Federalists.[30]

The loyalty of the South Carolina Federalists was put to a severe test when John Jay negotiated a highly controversial treaty with Great Britain, the terms of which were known in Charleston on July 11, 1795. The treaty seemed to make major concessions to Great Britain while procuring few gains for the United States. The British did promise to withdraw their troops from the northwestern forts and to pay damages to American shippers whose goods they had seized, although the details for accomplishing these aims made them almost impossible to enforce. On the other hand, the Americans were committed to pay debts they owed to British creditors, abandon their trade with France, and cease the exportation of cotton and all trade with the British West Indies. No mention was made of compensating southerners for the slaves the British had confiscated during the Revolution, nor did the British agree to stop impressing Americans into their navy. The Republican followers of Thomas Jefferson opposed the treaty, whereas the Federalists who rallied behind Washington and Alexander Hamilton favored it. The Senate approved the treaty by one vote.

The treaty revealed a significant dichotomy among South Carolina Federalists and brought Gadsden, now seventy-one, out of retirement with a vengeance. Senator Pierce Butler of South Carolina voted against it; Senator Jacob Read voted for it. William Loughton Smith, a young Federalist congressman from South Carolina whose candidacy for reelection in 1793 Gadsden had publicly supported, was a leading advocate of the treaty. Fifteen Republicans wrote Smith an anonymous letter promising to murder him and mangle his body for supporting the treaty. Thomas Pinckney, United States minister to Great Britain, inevitably favored the treaty.[31]

One day in late July 1795, a group of Federalists gathered at the Exchange Building in Charleston to discuss the crisis. Gadsden presided with as much spirit as he had had when he rallied the Liberty Boys against the Stamp Act thirty years earlier. He declared that he would "as soon send a favourite virgin to a Brothel, as a man to England to make a treaty."[32] Refusing to be a staunch party man, he perhaps thought that the Treaty of Paris of 1783 contained the only agreement with Great Britain that the United States should make; he was as stubbornly opposed to a new treaty as he had been to giving his parole a second time when the British hauled him away to St. Augustine more than a dozen years earlier.

Later the same day, a more responsible group gathered in St. Michael's Church to denounce the treaty. Federalists from the old and new schools were present, including Gadsden, John Rutledge, David Ramsay, Edward Rutledge, Charles Cotesworth Pinckney, and Aedanus Burke. All expressed their indignation over the Jay Treaty. These six gentlemen and nine others were elected to a committee charged with the responsibility to convey the sentiments of the meeting to President Washington. Gadsden and John Rutledge received 792 votes each, more than any other members of the committee. Their efforts were in vain, however, for Washington signed the treaty into law, thus preventing a potential war with England.[33]

Gadsden disliked the treaty, but once it had become law, he thought that it should be obeyed. Although it had been ratified by the Senate and signed by the president, there were many members of Congress who still wanted to change it. This move would create a constitutional crisis which Gadsden hoped to avoid. Writing in 1797, he eloquently defended the constitutional system that had enacted into law a treaty which he disapproved. "Let the President and the Senate *make* a treaty as *directed*," he wrote, "without the congress interfering. Let the congress, when a treaty is *made*, provide for it, if they think it not contrary to the welfare of the United States." Although "no favourer of the British treaty while pending," Gadsden "never at any time thought that treaty of such moment, that it should be refused to be provided for by our representatives."[34] He was ever on the side of law, order, and the Constitution.

Unshaken in his federalism by the debacle over the Jay Treaty, Gadsden moved even deeper into the camp of the old-school Federalists in response to the French threat to American security in the late 1790s. After 1795 France began to seize American merchant vessels and to impress American sailors into her navy. The French minister to the United States, Pierre August Adet, campaigned for Thomas Jefferson and against John Adams in the presidential election of 1796, an interference in American politics that infuriated Gadsden. This turn of events was "but a romantic giddiness of a restless power, setting itself *no bounds*," he wrote; clearly, the French had become jealous of American commerce, and Americans would be deceiving themselves if they did not expect others to follow the French example. The preservation of the nation depended upon maintaining a unified stand against the French and any other like-minded nation, he said. Although Americans did owe gratitude to the French for their help during the war, he continued, "we must have eyes surely that see not, if their *very great love and friendship* do not appear to us . . . craftily intended to make us merely their puppets."[35]

The xyz Affair, which marked the final disruption of goodwill between the United States and France, soon proved Gadsden to be correct. President John Adams sent a special mission to negotiate an end to the French interference with American commerce. The French foreign minister, Charles Maurice de Talleyrand, demanded through his agents a bribe before he would confer with the American delegation. Rather than raise the money, Congress began to prepare for war with France after President Adams revealed the complete details of the aborted negotiations. In South Carolina, Adams's old friend Christopher Gadsden supported the president. In an open letter of April 21, 1798, he wrote, "My fellow Citizens of South Carolina, . . . come forward, and demonstrate whether your independence, be now as dear to you, as at the time you struggled to gain it. Give to the French for their Motto of, 'Divide and Conquer,' United we are and we will stand."[36]

Two weeks later an open meeting in Charleston elected Gadsden to a committee charged with informing Senator Jacob Read of the Carolinians' determination to support the federal government. On July 16, 1798, Gadsden wrote him that he hoped the American delegation to Paris would soon be "done with the monsieurs[;] I am still afraid of some delusive diplomatic Slobberings and Patchings on their Side, to gain time to repair their shattered perfidious dividing Scheme against us." But France was torn by more divisive forces than the United States. The turn of events there shortly ended the undeclared war between the two nations. In 1799 Napoleon Bonaparte took control of the French government, and the next year he signed a treaty with John Adams to end the hostilities.[37]

Gadsden was just as happy to see the matter settled as John Adams was. The two men had enjoyed a close friendship and mutual respect for each other's politics since they first had met at the Continental Congress in 1774. Gadsden's early political thought and career fitted Adams's belief that the Revolution had been accomplished in the hearts and minds of the people long before independence was actually declared. Gasden's loyalty to Adams as president ran deeper than the ties of friendship; theirs was an intellectual unity that found a mutually rewarding companionship in the common struggle for liberty. They had similar personalities. Both men struggled with an inner conflict between their enormous egos and deep belief that they should render disinterested public service, and both were forced to live within the shadow of more powerful and prominent leaders. Adams's successes as president Gadsden accepted as his own, and he was grieved over Adams's failures. "A better and firmer piece of live Oak [than Adams] was not to be found in the United States," he wrote.[38]

When the hope for John Adams's reelection in 1800 seemed irrevocably lost, Gadsden wrote three public appeals to the people of Charleston to vote for legislators who would support the president.[39] He argued that since George Washington had served two terms, Adams ought to have the same honor. He was irritated by the maneuverings of the Jeffersonian Republicans from Virginia and New York to influence the voters and electors in South Carolina and feared that Virginia might become as much a tyrant as England had been. He warned that "violent parties" in American politics would undercut the simplicity of the Constitution and destroy the gains of the Revolution. He urged the mechanics, who had once followed him, to support President

Adams. The city did vote for Adams, but the rest of the state went for Jefferson. The democratic and egalitarian forces that Gadsden had welcomed in the 1760s elevated Jefferson to the presidency.[40]

A week after the inauguration, Gadsden, a sad but not bitter old man, wrote John Adams expressing his sincere disappointment that Adams had not been reelected. "God grant that the recollection of your ungrateful treatment may not deter truly firm, virtuous men from venturing their names to be held up to the public on such elections!" Gadsden did not fully understand or appreciate the changes brought by the rise of political parties. He was apprehensive that such changes might destroy rather than secure the type of government he had spent his life trying to establish. "Long have I been led to think our planet a mere bedlam, and the uncommonly extravagant ravings of our own times, . . . have greatly increased and confirmed that opinion." Nevertheless, Gadsden said that he was confident that "Our all knowing, unerring Physician" would interfere to release all "miserable captives" from their distress.[41] His forlorn letter to John Adams contains less political comment than genuine despair over Adams's defeat, simply because Adams was his friend.

Adams was touched by his friend's devotion. "Gadsden was almost the only stanch old companion, who was faithful found," he replied. "[I] perceive that your friendly sentiments for me are as kind and indulgent as they were six-and-twenty years ago, . . . and with a tenderness which was almost too much for my sensibility." As the political mantle passed to other shoulders, the two old patriots were drawn closer, and each welcomed the compliments of the other. In June, Gadsden again wrote Adams that he was "endeavouring to be resign'd with Regard to Politics and 'tis Time I shou'd." Nevertheless, he hoped that a Caesar or Brutus would never "shake to the foundation all our promising Hopes and Expectations" and destroy "the Blessings, we with the favor of the Almighty, have so dearly earn'd, to our latest Posterity."[42]

Gadsden outlived almost every other South Carolinian of his generation. In his old age, perhaps the result of his religion, he became embarrassed over his reputation as a troublemaker. He was eager to forgive his enemies and have them forgive him. He did not hold personal grudges and was remarkably unvindictive. "In short, he that forgets and forgives most," he wrote in 1782, "is the best citizen." Before former Lieutenant Governor William Bull died in 1791, he named Gadsden as one of the executors of his will, which suggests a friendship that survived their differences of opinion before the Revolution. After John Rutledge died in 1800, Gadsden referred to him as "our worthy deceased friend." Rutledge had opposed the Jay Treaty along with Gadsden, but otherwise their political differences continued until Rutledge's death.[43]

What relationship Gadsden had with Henry Laurens after the war can only be guessed, but their lives had paralleled each other so doggedly that Gadsden must have been saddened by Laurens's death in 1792. Born only eight days apart, they had grown up together, then argued with each other from the time of the Cherokee wars until both were taken prisoner by the British in 1780. At the very time Gadsden was in a dungeon at St. Augustine, Laurens, who had been captured on the high seas as he sailed upon a mission to the Netherlands, was incarcerated in the Tower of London. Released at the same time Gadsden was, Laurens rested in England, then went to the Peace Conference in Paris, returned to Philadelphia, and finally made his way home to South Carolina in 1785. His health was wrecked by his imprisonment. Except for service in the South Carolina ratifying convention of 1788, he lived in seclusion at Mepkin, his plantation on the Cooper River. Both men had lost beloved sons. Gadsden's Christopher, junior, had died in 1766 and Thomas in 1791; Laurens's son John had been killed in 1782 while his father was in Europe. Gadsden probably saw very little of Laurens after he returned in 1785, but the loss of the man who had been both his closest friend and his bitterest enemy must have left an empty place in his own life.

A man of devout Christian faith, Gadsden faced his own death with quiet courage, resignation, relief, and the optimistic expectation that he would go to heaven. "More and more happy, I bless God, do I every day feel myself to find that my passage over this life's Atlantic is almost gained, having been in the soundings for some time, not far from my wished-for port, waiting for a favorable breeze from our kind Savior to waft me to that pleasing and expected land for which I cheerfully and humbly hope," he wrote when he was seventy-seven years old in 1801.[44] But that favorable breeze did not waft him away for four more years, and he had time to make peace with his fellow man. Three days before his eighty-first birthday he wrote to his friend Daniel Horry that he did not wish anything disagreeable to transpire from his published letters now that the crises which had elicited them were over. He shunned the public eye. "Of Mrs. Gadsden and her old gentleman I have heard nothing lately," wrote one of their friends. Two weeks later, the same friend informed Mrs. Ralph Izard that "Old Gen. Gadsden too desired me to assure you of his warmest regard and attachment—those were his words."[45]

Gadsden put his affairs in order; on June 5, 1804, he wrote the final draft of his will. His estate was worth more than a quarter of a million dollars, which placed him among the wealthiest men in Charleston. Upon his death, he wanted his plantation on the Black River, slaves thereon, and a lot in Georgetown to be sold to pay his debts. He forgave the debts which Philip owed him. The remainder of his property was not to be divided in any manner until seven years after his death. He left his wife Ann £400 sterling annually for her lifetime, their house on Front Street, the furniture, liquor, cows, his grey horse, and favorite chair. For their lifetimes, he provided an annual income of at least £250 sterling for his daughter Mary and daughters-in-law Martha and Catharine. Martha was the widow of Thomas, Catharine was the wife of Philip, and Mary was married to Thomas Morris. Since he did not mention his youngest daughter, Ann, she had probably died in England where she had moved with her husband in the late 1790s. To his grandsons, Christopher Edwards, James, and John, he left his Greek, Latin, and Hebrew books and pamphlets. He reminded his children "not to forget the faithful services of the descendants of old Nanny and Elsy." He also asked them to place his body in a plain coffin and bury it in an unmarked grave.[46]

Except for the forgetfulness and dizzy spells Gadsden had experienced since his imprisonment, he had rarely suffered from any illness during his eighty-one years. "Of Physicians he thought very little," wrote his physician-friend David Ramsay. "He considered temperance and exercise superior to all their prescriptions, and that in most cases they rendered them altogether unnecessary."⁴⁷ For exercise he took long walks around his property. Every day he crossed a narrow plank that had been placed over a ditch. Philip urged him to walk a few extra yards and go around the ditch, but the old man stubbornly refused to change his habit. Late in August 1805 he slipped from the plank, hit his head, and suffered a cut lip and other injuries that confined him to his room for a few days. On August 28, while briefly unattended by a servant, he arose from his bed and attempted to dress himself. He fell, injuring himself more, and lay bleeding and unconscious on his bedroom floor. Alarmed by the noise of his fall, members of the family in the room below rushed to his aid. There was nothing they could do; within a few hours he was dead. But he had gotten one of his wishes; he had desired to be spared a long illness and had even declined using the prayer in the Litany for deliverance from "sudden death."⁴⁸

The next day, August 29, Charleston gave him a hero's burial. The governor decreed thirty days of mourning, and the commandant of Fort Johnson ordered a gun fired every ten minutes from dawn until the hour of Gadsden's interment at one o'clock in the afternoon. The Artillery Company which Gadsden himself had founded in 1755 and other military groups escorted his body from his home to St. Philip's Church. The procession consisted of sixty coaches containing the members of his family, the governor, all federal and state officers in the city, and many of his former friends. After brief services in the church and in the churchyard, they watched the simple coffin containing his body descend into an unmarked grave near that of his parents.⁴⁹

Several years after Christopher Gadsden's death, David Ramsay wrote a fitting eulogy. "His passions were strong and required all his religion and philosophy to curb them. His patriotism was both disinterested and ardent. . . . His character was impressed with the hardihood of antiquity; and he possessed an erect, firm, intrepid mind, which was well calculated for buffetting with revolutionary storms."⁵⁰ Ramsay said nothing about the temper, the fervid language, and the drive for social status and economic success that had also buttressed his patriotism. The complex factors that had formed Gadsden's character, the ideas of English whigs and Enlightenment philosophers, the emerging nation's experiment with a new form of republican government, and the innumerable events of chance had dragged him into the tide of the eighteenth century until he became a part of its force. The idiosyncracies of his personality were buried with him, but the continuing success of the American Revolution snatched from him forever the prize of anonymity.

Abbreviations

Am.	American
Assoc.	Association
Biog.	Biography
Coll.	Collections
Council Journal	Council Journal, 1765–1766, S.C. Archives
DAB	*Dictionary of American Biography*
Eng.	England
Gadsden Writings	Richard Walsh, ed., *The Writings of Christopher Gadsden, 1746–1805* (Columbia, S.C., 1966)
Gen.	Genealogical
Hist.	Historical
J.	Journal
JCHA	Journal of the Commons House of Assembly, S.C. Archives
LC	Library of Congress
Laurens Papers	Philip M. Hamer, George C. Rogers, Jr., and David R. Chesnutt, eds., *The Papers of Henry Laurens*, 9 vols. to date (Columbia, S.C., 1968–)
Mag.	Magazine
MCO	Mesne Conveyance Office, Charleston, S.C.
MS, MSS	Manuscript(s)
N.C.	North Carolina
NYHS	New York Historical Society

NYPL	New York Public Library
Pa.	Pennsylvania
PRO CO	British Public Record Office, Colonial Office Papers
PRSC	Transcripts of Records in the British Public Record Office Relating to South Carolina, located in S.C. Archives
Pub.	Publications
Quart.	Quarterly
Rev.	Review
S.C.	South Carolina
S.C. Archives	South Carolina Department of Archives and History, Columbia
S.C. Hist. Soc.	South Carolina Historical Society, Charleston
Soc.	Society
SCHGM, later *SCHM*	*South Carolina Historical and Genealogical Magazine*
trans.	transcript

Notes

NOTES TO CHAPTER ONE

1. This portrait, still privately owned, was probably the work of the Charleston artist Jeremiah Theus. Perhaps it is the one that was commissioned by the South Carolina Commons House of Assembly in 1766 to honor the province's delegates to the Stamp Act Congress, but that cannot be proved. For generations it has been handed down among Christopher Gadsden's descendants. An old tradition that it was painted by Sir Joshua Reynolds is apparently incorrect.

2. Information received in 1932 from Mrs. Van Smith, Summerville, S. C., and Miss Jeanne Gadsden, Charleston, S. C. See also Thomas Fuller, *The History of the Worthies of England*, ed. John Freeman (London, 1952 [1840]), 233; "Extracts from the Parish Register of Ardeley, Co. Hertford, England," *New Eng. Hist. and Gen. Register* 40 (July 1886): 276.

3. Information on Thomas Gadsden's early career, some of which is contradictory, is found in the following sources: E. I. Renick, "Christopher Gadsden," *Pub. of the Southern Hist. Assoc.* 2 (Jan. 1898): 244; Oliver R. Johnson, Vice and Deputy Consul General, London, to Mr. Wharton, an antiquarian of Hertfordshire, Sept. 12, 1890, U. S. Archives, Dept. of State MSS; Elizabeth Donnan, ed., *Documents Illustrative of the History of the Slave Trade to America*, 4 vols. (Washington, D. C., 1931), II, 242; *S. C. Gazette*, Aug. 15, 1741 (obit.); PRSC, XI, 78; Francis Nicholson to the Board of Trade, Jan. 1725, in *Coll. of the S. C. Hist. Soc.* 1: 288; records in the Bible of Alice Mighells, in the *SCHGM* 32: 312; Book F, pp. 90, 92, MCO.

4. Information in the possession of Mrs. Van Smith, 1932.

5. *A Few Observations on Some Late Public Transactions*, in *Gadsden Writings*, 278.

6. A. S. Salley, Jr., ed., *Register of St. Philip's Parish, Charles Town, South Carolina, 1720–1758* (Charleston, S.C., 1904), 58, 61, 158, 228, 237. See also the family record in the Bible of Alice Mighells, *SCHGM* 32: 312–13.

7. John Charnock, *Biographia Navalis* (London, 1795), III, 74–81.

8. *S. C. Gazette*, May 8, 1736; PRSC, XVIII, 162–65. For the schedule of the collector's fees, 1739, see Commissions and Instructions, 1732–1742,

pp. 269–70, S. C. Archives. For other casual references to Thomas Gadsden's performance of his duties, see Walter B. Edgar, ed., *The Letterbook of Robert Pringle, April 2, 1739–April 29, 1745*, 2 vols. (Columbia, S. C., 1972), I, 29, 169, 194.

9. The figures are doubtless not exact. Fifteen years might elapse between the date of the grant and its recording, which often caused confusion. Records of these transactions, which are often contradictory, are in the following sources: Memorial Book VII, 328; Index to Plats, I, 190; Index to Memorials, Vol. AAL to Myrick, p. 351, under the date of May 25, 1733; Charleston County Will Book, 1740–1747, p. 42—all in S. C. Archives; Book H, pp. 301, 304, Book GG, p. 344, Book V, p. 63, MCO; *SCHGM* 9:95.

10. *S. C. Gazette*, Dec. 2, 1732; Mar. 1, 1734; Aug. 9, Sept. 6, 1735; June 25, 1737; Feb. 1, Aug. 11, 1739.

11. Book F, pp. 90, 92, MCO; *S. C. Gazette*, June 9, 1739; Walter Vernon Anson, *The Life of Admiral Lord Anson* (London, 1912), 3–5; John Barrow, *The Life of George, Lord Anson* (London, 1839), 13–15; Joseph Johnson, *Traditions and Reminiscences Chiefly of the American Revolution in the South* (Charleston, S. C., 1851), 38; David D. Wallace, *The Life of Henry Laurens* (New York, 1915), 30. For a description of Charleston and boundaries, 1710–1770, see *Year Book, City of Charleston, 1881*, 379.

12. Bernard Bailyn, *The Ideological Origins of the American Revolution* (Cambridge, Mass., 1967), 41–42, 123.

13. James was born Apr. 13, 1734; Thomas was born Oct. 30, 1737; *SCHGM* 32: 313. An Eleanor Gadsden was buried in St. Philip's Churchyard July 4, 1740, and may have been an infant sister of James and Thomas; *Register of St. Philip's, 1720–1758*, 267. The later reference, p. 79, gives the date of Thomas's birth as Oct. 11, 1737. For a speculative essay on the chaotic family structure in colonial South Carolina as a possible cause of the development of rebellious personalities, see Robert M. Weir, "Rebelliousness: Personality Development and the American Revolution in the Southern Colonies," in Jeffrey J. Crow and Larry E. Tise, eds., *The Southern Experience in the American Revolution* (Chapel Hill, N. C., 1978), 25–54.

14. Edward McCrady, *The History of South Carolina under Royal Government, 1719–1776* (New York, 1899), 373. Johnson, *Traditions*, 37, adds algebra. See also David Ramsay, *History of South Carolina from Its Earliest Settlement in 1670 to the Year 1808*, 2 vols. (Charleston, S. C., 1809), II, 253.

15. R. Alonzo Block, ed., "Journal of William Black, 1744," *Pa. Mag. of Hist. and Biog.* 1 (1877): 404n; Charles I. Landis, "The Juliana Library Company in Lancaster," *ibid.* 43 (1919): 241; "Journal of William Logan," Oct. 24, 1745, *ibid.* 36: 165; Ramsay, *History of S. C.*, II, 253; Johnson, *Traditions*, 38.

16. *S. C. Gazette*, Aug. 15, 1741; *Register of St. Philip's, 1720–1758*, 268; *SCHGM* 32: 313.

17. James became a merchant in London and outlived his two brothers. Thomas eventually returned to South Carolina as a merchant and was

there during the Stamp Act and later troubles. In a note to his will as an afterthought, Thomas Gadsden said, "I give to my two Sisters in England, Twenty five pounds each," which is the only reference to brothers and sisters. The will, dated July 20, 1741, is in Charleston County Will Book, 1740–1747, p. 42; see also Inventories, 1741–1743, pp. 83–92, both in S. C. Archives.

18. [Sept. 1746], *Laurens Papers*, I, 2. See also *S. C. Gazette*, Aug. 4, 1746; *Register of St. Philip's 1720–1758*, 183.

19. Ramsay, *History of S. C.*, II, 253; see also Wallace, *Life of Laurens*, 14.

20. Gadsden to Laurens, Sept. 1746; Laurens to Thomas Savage, Nov. 11, 1747; Laurens to Gadsden, Dec. 28, 1747, all in *Laurens Papers*, I, 1, 82, 93–95, 97–98. See also *Gadsden Writings*, 3–4; *S. C. Gazette*, Dec. 8, 1746; *SCHGM* 30: 96.

21. Laurens to Gadsden, Dec. 28, 1747, *Laurens Papers*, I, 97–98; *Register of St. Philip's 1720–1758*, 100.

22. Mar. 3, 1748, *Laurens Papers*, I, 115–16.

23. *S. C. Gazette*, Jan. 9, 1742, supplement.

24. Sept. 11, 1746, *Gadsden Writings*, 3–4; *Laurens Papers*, I, 2.

25. *S. C. Gazette*, Sept. 25, 1749, Apr. 16, 1750.

26. George C. Rogers, Jr., *The History of Georgetown County, South Carolina* (Columbia, S. C., 1970), 47, 50.

27. *S. C. Gazette*, July 15, 1756, Jan. 24, 1761; see also Alexander Gregg, *History of the Old Cheraws* (New York, 1867), 62.

28. *S. C. Gazette*, Mar. 26, Sept. 24, Oct. 3, 1753; July 18, 1754; Nov. 11, 1756; July 8, 1757.

29. See MS volume, Cash Dr. to General Duty, Sept. 20–29, 1765, S. C. Archives. The date of this volume is misleading; it ranges from Mar. 25, 1750, to Sept. 29, 1760. The last entry under Gadsden's name is for the Mar.–Sept. 1760 period, when he paid a duty of £15.10.6 on imports from Antigua.

30. Leila Sellers, *Charleston Business on the Eve of the American Revolution* (Chapel Hill, N. C., 1934), 84.

31. Nov. 13, 1760, Mortgages YY, pp. 287–88, S. C. Archives.

32. *S. C. Gazette*, Jan. 24, 31, Sept. 26, 1761; Feb. 6, 1762.

33. Records in the Office of the Clerk of Court, Charleston, 1758–1762. Some of the individuals whom Gadsden sued were George Rowe, William Bonneau, Thomas Ralph, John Dunlop, Daniel McGinney, William Ferrel, Hardey Counsel, and George Pawley, Jr.

34. *S. C. Gazette*, Feb. 12, 1750; Jan. 28, 1751; Dec. 18, 1752; Sept. 24, 1753; May 17, 1760.

35. July 6, 21, Feb. 15, 1753, *Gadsden Writings*, 5–7.

36. *S. C. Gazette*, Aug. 8, 1754; Nov. 4, Dec. 25, 1756.

37. Journal of the Commissioners of Fortification, Feb. 23, 1758, S. C. Hist. Soc.

38. *S. C. Gazette*, Nov. 20, 1755; Apr. 15, 1756.

39. Book QQ, p. 609, Book S #3, pp. 139, 273, Book TT, p. 85, Book D #3, p. 472, Book VV, p. 320, MCO. Index to Memorials, VII, 24; Index to

Grants, Book 2S, p. 45 (under date of Aug. 2, 1757), S. C. Archives. The ratio of current money to sterling in 1756 and in 1771 was approximately seven to one. For a discussion of current or lawful money, which was the paper currency printed in the colony, see David D. Wallace, *The History of South Carolina*, 4 vols. (New York, 1934), I, 314–15. For a comprehensive study of the relationship of colonial currency to that of the mother country and tables to use in making the conversion, see John J. McCusker, *Money and Exchange in Europe and America, 1600–1775: A Handbook* (Chapel Hill, N. C., 1978).

40. Apr. 19, 1758, Book TT, p. 80, MCO.

41. For a good, brief description of Charleston in the eighteenth century, see George C. Rogers, Jr., *Charleston in the Age of the Pinckneys* (Norman, Okla., 1969).

42. McCrady, *S. C. under Royal Government*, 487; Wallace, *History of S. C.*, I, 405; *S. C. Gazette*, Jan. 30, 1755; Rogers, *Georgetown County*, 87–88.

43. *Rules of the South Carolina Society*, 11th ed. (Charleston, S. C., 1870), 32, 33.

44. McCrady, *S. C. under Royal Government*, 510–12, 539; *S. C. Gazette*, Apr. 16, 1750; *SCHGM* 23: 170.

45. *S. C. Gazette*, Apr. 3, 1755.

46. To Thomas Lawrence, Feb. 15, 1753, *Gadsden Writings*, 6.

47. In 1761 he wrote letters to the newspaper from the Farm. The dwelling built by Lord Anson on his property stood in the center of a farm, and this place was probably called the Farm before it was known as Gadsdenboro. See Charles Fraser, *Reminiscences of Charleston* (Charleston, S. C., 1854), 25–26; Johnson, *Traditions*, 38.

48. D. E. Huger Smith and A. S. Salley, Jr., eds., *Register of St. Philip's Parish, Charles Town, South Carolina, 1754–1810* (Charleston, S. C., 1927), 278. She was buried in St. Philip's Churchyard on May 26, 1755. On Sept. 10, 1754, a child, Jane, preceded her. Other children who died were Philip, May 19, 1752, and John, May 16, 1753; *Register of St. Philip's, 1720–1758*, 101, 220, 222.

49. *S. C. Gazette*, Dec. 29, 1755, Dec. 25, 1756; "Extracts from the Journal of Mrs. Ann Manigault, 1754–1781," ed. Mabel L. Webber, *SCHGM* 20: 61.

50. *Register of St. Philip's, 1754–1810*, 6, 40, 48, 55.

51. PRSC, XXVII, 336–37; XXVIII, 7.

NOTES TO CHAPTER TWO

1. Except where otherwise noted, the account that follows is dependent upon Philip M. Hamer, "Anglo-French Rivalry in the Cherokee Country, 1754–1757," *N. C. Hist. Rev.* 2 (1925): 303–22; Hamer, "Fort Loudoun in the Cherokee War, 1758–1761," *ibid.*, 442–58; Robert L. Meriwether, *The Expansion of South Carolina* (Kingsport, Tenn., 1940), 213–40; Wallace, *History of S. C.*, II, chs. 41 and 42.

2. M. Eugene Sirmans, *Colonial South Carolina: A Political History, 1663-1763* (Chapel Hill, N. C., 1966), 194–95. For different evaluations of Glen, see Hayes Baker-Carothers, *Virginia and the French and Indian War* (Chicago, 1928), 44–45, 63–64; Chapman J. Milling, *Red Carolinians* (Columbia, S. C., 1969 [1940]), 238–43; Wallace, *History of S. C.*, II, 1.

3. Alan Calmes, "The Lyttleton Expedition of 1759: Military Failures and Financial Successes," *SCHM* 77 (Jan. 1976): 20.

4. *S. C. Gazette*, Oct. 14, 21, Dec. 9, 1756, Feb. 17, 1757.

5. JCHA, XXXII, 23, 24, 40, 54.

6. Lyttelton to the Lords of Trade, Dec. 22, 1757, PRSC, XXVII, 347.

7. David H. Corkran, *The Cherokee Frontier: Conflict and Survival, 1740-1762* (Norman, Okla., 1962), 157–59, 164–66, 170–71, 178–79, 181; Hamer, "Fort Loudoun," 447; Meriwether, *Expansion of S. C.*, 218–20; Sirmans, *Colonial S. C.*, 332–33.

8. Lyttelton to Board of Trade, Dec. 10, 1959, PRSC, XXVIII, 280–82; cited in Meriwether, *Expansion of S. C.*, 219.

9. *S. C. Gazette*, Jan. 8, 1760; Eliza Lucas Pinckney to Mrs. King, Feb. 1760, in Elise Pinckney, ed., *The Letterbook of Eliza Lucas Pinckney* (Chapel Hill, N. C., 1972), 138–39.

10. Lyttelton to Amherst, Dec. 28, 1759, PRO CO 5.57, LC trans.

11. *S. C. Gazette*, Jan. 26, Apr. 9, 26, 1760.

12. *Some Observations against the Cherokee Indians in 1760 and 1761 in a Second Letter from Philopatrios* (Charles Town, 1762), 17–18; see also PRSC, XXVIII, 313–15.

13. Meriwether, *Expansion of S. C.*, 225–26.

14. William Bull, Jr., to Lords of Trade, May 28, 1761, PRSC, XXIX, 109–10; Corkran, *Cherokee Frontier*, 207–25; Meriwether, *Expansion of S. C.*, 232–33; Sirmans, *Colonial S. C.*, 335; Duane H. King and E. Raymond Evans, eds., "Memoirs of the Grant Expedition Against the Cherokees in 1761," *J. of Cherokee Studies* 2 (Summer 1977): 271–337.

15. JCHA, XXXIII, 253, 307, 316, 367.

16. Ramsay, *History of S. C.*, II, 253. Johnson, *Traditions*, 207, says Gadsden was elected captain, but Ramsay is the better source.

17. Aug. 5, 6, 1761, JCHA, XXXIV, 232, 234.

18. Gadsden to Peter Timothy, Mar. 12, 1763, *Gadsden Writings*, 55. This letter, published in the *S. C. Gazette* on March 12, was in reply to Laurens's letter in Wells's *S. C. Weekly Gazette* on Feb. 28, 1763; *Laurens Papers*, III, 270–72.

19. Quoted in Wallace, *Life of Laurens*, 104.

20. Corkran, *Cherokee Frontier*, 258–61; Meriwether, *Expansion of S. C.*, 239–40.

21. First letter of Philopatrios, *S. C. Gazette*, Dec. 18, 1761.

22. Meriwether, *Expansion of S. C.*, 239; Wallace, *Life of Laurens*, 104–5.

23. Calmes, "The Lyttelton Expedition of 1759," 19, 27, 28. Calmes disproves the speculation by earlier scholars that Gadsden was the supplier for Lyttelton's campaign. That supplier was Joseph Nutt, whose accounts were carefully inspected by the House in an effort to hold down costs.

24. The second letter was published as a pamphlet entitled *Some Obser-*
vations of the Two Campaigns against the Cherokee Indians in 1760 and 1761 in a
Second Letter from Philopatrios (Charles Town, 1762).

25. John Dunnett to James Grant, Dec. 4, 1762, Ballindalloch Castle
Muniments for the Papers of General James Grant, Bundle 520.
Hereinafter cited as James Grant Papers.

26. *Laurens Papers*, III, 275–355.

27. In the *S. C. Gazette*, Feb. 19, 1763, Gadsden announced that he was
the author of the Philopatrios letters, an advertisement signed
Auditor-Tantum, and two letters signed with his own name. One of the
signed letters was to the Gentlemen Electors of the Parish of St. Paul,
Stono, Feb. 5, 1763; the second one has not been found. Laurens published his answer to that letter in Robert Wells's *S. C. Weekly Gazette* on
Feb. 28, 1763, but that issue of the newspaper is not extant.

28. *S. C. Gazette*, Dec. 26, 1761, Jan. 2, 9, 23, Feb. 6, 27, Mar. 6, 1762;
JCHA, XXXIV, 271; McCrady, *S. C. under Royal Government*, 353–55.
Thomas Pownall, appointed governor after Lyttelton, resigned before
coming to South Carolina.

29. JCHA, XXXV, pt. 1, p. 41.

30. Jack P. Greene, "The Gadsden Election Controversy and the Revolutionary Movement in South Carolina," *Mississippi Valley Hist. Rev.* 46
(Dec. 1959): 472–73.

31. *A Full State of the Dispute Betwixt the Governor and the Commons House*
of Assembly of His Majesty's Province of South Carolina, in America. With The
Proper Vouchers and Reasons in support of the Proceedings of the House of
Assembly, As transmitted to their Agent in Great Britain (London, 1763), 45.

32. *Ibid.*, 6–8; JCHA, XXXV, 158–59.

33. Hardwicke Papers, Add. MSS 25910, pp. 437–67, LC trans.

34. JCHA, XXXV, pt. 2, pp. 1, 2; *A Full State of the Dispute*, 27; Hardwicke
Papers, Add. MSS 25910, pp. 437–67, LC trans.

35. *A Full State of the Dispute*, 9.

36. *Ibid.*, 9–16; this pamphlet quotes verbatim from the JCHA.

37. *Ibid.*, 16–25.

38. Greene, "Gadsden Election Controversy," 479.

39. Ella Lonn, *The Colonial Agents of the Southern Colonies* (Chapel Hill,
N. C., 1945), 292–93. Garth was elected to fill his father's vacated seat in
Parliament in 1765, and he continued to serve as the colonial agent for
South Carolina.

40. Letter dated Dec. 13, 1762, reprinted in *S. C. Gazette*, Feb. 5, 1763;
see also *A Full State of the Dispute*, 26–27.

41. Pauline Maier, *From Resistance to Revolution: Colonial Radicals and the*
Development of Opposition to Great Britain, 1765–1776 (New York, 1972),
288.

42. Simpson's letter, dated Feb. 9, 1763, was reprinted at Gadsden's
request in the *S. C. Gazette*, Mar. 12, 1763. Laurens's letter, dated Feb. 28,
1763, is not extant.

43. To Christopher Rowe, Feb. 8, 1764, *Laurens Papers*, IV, 164–65.

44. *S. C. Gazette*, Apr. 20, July 9, 1763; the letter from "Man in the Moon" was published in the *S. C. Weekly Gazette* and is not extant.

45. Greene, "Gadsden Election Controversy," 483–84.

46. PRSC, XXIX, 275, 277–80, 296, 310–11, 321.

47. *Ibid.*, XXX, 145, 149–51, 173.

48. There were two similar cases in Massachusetts and one in New Jersey; Leonard Woods Labaree, *Royal Government in America* (New Haven, Conn., 1930), 330–31, 335–36, 343.

49. JCHA, XXXVI, 250–51.

50. To Joseph Brown, Aug. 30, 1764, *Laurens Papers*, IV, 389–90.

51. W. Roy Smith, *South Carolina as a Royal Province, 1719–1776* (New York, 1903), 167–68, 296–97; a copy of the thirty-fifth instruction is appended to *A Full State of the Dispute*.

52. The clause reads: "11. And be it further enacted, by the authority aforesaid, that all and every member and members of the Commons House of Assembly of this province, chosen by virtue of this act, shall have as much power and privilege, to all intents and purposes, as any member or members of the Commons House of Assembly of this province heretofore of right had, might, could, or ought to have in the said province; provided the same are, such as are according to his majesty's thirty-fifth instruction." *A Full State of the Dispute*, 74–75.

53. The issues of the *S. C. Weekly Gazette* containing these letters have not survived.

54. Nov. 25, 1765, quoted in Greene, "Gadsden Election Controversy," 489.

55. Jan. 24, 1766, *Coll. S. C. Hist. Soc.*, II, 189.

56. Leonard Woods Labaree, ed., *Royal Instructions to British Governors, 1670–1760* (New York, 1935), 387.

57. To Committee of Correspondence, Jan. 19, 1766, Garth trans., LC; see also Smith, *S. C. as Royal Province*, 348–49.

58. MS, Journal of the Proceedings of the Charles Town Library Society, 1759-[1790], Charleston Library Society; see esp. 33, 38, 42, 44, 49, 52, 53, 54, 208.

59. Quoted in Bailyn, *Ideological Origins*, 26. For a thorough discussion of the impact of the classics on American thought, see *ibid.*, 23–26; H. Trevor Colbourn, *The Lamp of Experience: Whig History and the Intellectual Origins of the American Revolution* (Chapel Hill, N. C., 1965), 21–39; Gordon S. Wood, *The Creation of the American Republic, 1776–1787* (Chapel Hill, N. C., 1969), 48–53. The list that Gadsden drew up for the society is not extant.

NOTES TO CHAPTER THREE

1. To William Henry Drayton, June 1, 1778, *Gadsden Writings*, 128.

2. Quoted in George Bancroft, *History of the United States*, 6 vols. (Boston, 1882–1886), III, 121; Bancroft's source is apparently lost.

3. P. D. G. Thomas, *British Politics and the Stamp Act Crisis* (Oxford, 1975), 49–50.

4. Joseph Albert Ernst, *Money and Politics in America, 1755–1775* (Chapel Hill, N. C., 1973), 77–81, 215–20.

5. Sept. 4, 1764, in Robert Wilson Gibbes, *Documentary History of the American Revolution, 1764–1776* (New York, 1855), 1–6. See also Edmund S. Morgan and Helen M. Morgan, *The Stamp Act Crisis: Prologue to Revolution* (Chapel Hill, N. C., 1953), 64.

6. Lonn, *Southern Colonial Agents*, 292–93; Morgan and Morgan, *Stamp Act Crisis*, 53–70; Thomas, *British Politics and the Stamp Act Crisis*, 85–100; C. A. Weslager, *The Stamp Act Congress* (Newark, Del., 1976), 31–41.

7. Wallace, *History of S. C.*, II, 253; see also David Ramsay, *The History of the Revolution of South-Carolina from a British Province to an Independent State*, 2 vols. (Trenton, N. J., 1785), I, 13–14; Weslager, *Stamp Act Congress*, 91–93.

8. JCHA, XXXVII, 94–98. See also John Drayton, *Memoirs of the American Revolution*, 2 vols (Charleston, S. C., 1821), I, 39–41; McCrady, *S. C. under Royal Government*, 561–63; Morgan and Morgan, *Stamp Act Crisis*, 89–102; *S. C. Gazette and Country Journal*, Dec. 17, 1765.

9. *S. C. Gazette*, Aug. 31, Sept. 28, 1765.

10. Journal of the Stamp Act Congress, in Hezekiah Niles, ed., *Principles and Acts of the Revolution in America* (New York, 1876), 163–64; James Truslow Adams, *Revolutionary New England 1691–1776* (Boston, 1923), 330; Morgan and Morgan, *Stamp Act Crisis*, 103–4; Weslager, *Stamp Act Congress*, 70.

11. *Gadsden Writings*, 68, n. 6. Walsh suggests other possible pamphlets also, but the date, place of publication, and content of the Dulany work make it a more likely choice. See also Weslager, *Stamp Act Congress*, 74, 110.

12. Quoted in Morgan and Morgan, *Stamp Act Crisis*, 106–7.

13. To William Johnson and Charles Garth, Dec. 2, 1765, *Gadsden Writings*, 64–68; see also Weslager, *Stamp Act Congress*, 129–34.

14. To Morton Wilkinson, Sept. 1782, *Gadsden Writings*, 174–75.

15. To Johnson and Garth, Dec. 2, 1765, *ibid.*, 66–67.

16. *Ibid.*, 65.

17. Richard Walsh, *Charleston's Sons of Liberty: A Study of the Artisans, 1763–1789* (Columbia, S. C., 1959), 3–25.

18. Johnson, *Traditions*, 41.

19. Walsh, *Charleston's Sons of Liberty*, 28–31, 35; see also Maier, *Resistance to Revolution*, 81–82, 85, 298.

20. To Lord Commissioners, Nov. 3, 1765, PRSC, XXX, 281–82; see also Richard Hutson to Joel Benedict, Oct. 30, 1765, in Charleston *Yearbook, 1895*, 313.

21. *S. C. Gazette*, Oct. 19, 1765. This was the last issue of the *S. C. Gazette* until the repeal of the Stamp Act; extracts from it have been reprinted in the Charleston *Yearbook, 1885*, 331–37.

22. To Lords Commissioners, Nov. 3, 1765, PRSC, XXX, 286.

23. To Joseph Brown, Oct. 28, 1765, *Laurens Papers*, V, 29–31. James Grant had been appointed governor of East Florida. See also *S. C. Gazette*, Oct. 19, 1765.

24. Henry Laurens, *Appendix to Extracts from the Proceedings of the High Court of Vice-Admiralty, in Charlestown, South Carolina* (Charles Town, 1769), 59–60.

25. Gadsden to Johnson and Garth, Dec. 2, 1765, *Gadsden Writings*, 65–66.

26. *Ibid.*; JCHA, XXXVII, 1, 3, 16–18; *S. C. Gazette*, Oct. 5, 1765. The South Carolina delegates had already dispatched copies of the minutes to Georgia and North Carolina; see also Delegates to Garth, New York, Oct. 26, 1765, Garth trans., LC.

27. Robert M. Weir, " 'Liberty and Property, and No Stamps': South Carolina and the Stamp Act Crisis" (Ph.D. diss., Western Reserve Univ., 1966), 200.

28. Gadsden to Johnson and Garth, Dec. 2, 1765, *Gadsden Writings*, 66; see also JCHA, XXXVII, pt. 2, pp. 15, 26–31.

29. Committee of Correspondence to Garth, Dec. 16, 1765, Garth trans., LC.

30. Weslager, *Stamp Act Congress*, 141–42. For a provocative discussion of the subtle understanding of virtual representation in South Carolina, see Kenneth S. Greenberg, "Representation and the Isolation of South Carolina, 1776–1860," *J. Am. Hist.* 64 (Dec. 1977): 723–43.

31. To Capt. Burden, Feb. 20, 1766, Dartmouth Papers D. 1778-2-169, Staffordshire County Record Office, Eng. See also Gadsden to James Pearson, Feb. 20, 1766, Dartmouth Papers; Gadsden to James Pearson, Feb. 20, 1766, Dartmouth Papers; Gadsden to William S. Johnson, Apr. 16, 1766, *Gadsden Writings*, 72–73; William Bull to Henry Seymour Conway, Dec. 17, 1765, PRSC, XXX, 277–78, and Feb. 6, 1766, PRSC, XXXI, 22–23; John Richard Alden, *The South in the Revolution, 1763–1789* (Baton Rouge, La., 1957), 76; Pauline Maier, "The Charleston Mob and the Evolution of Popular Politics in Revolutionary South Carolina, 1765–1784," *Perspectives in Am. Hist.* 4 (1970): 176. In October 1768, Gadsden and his associate Roger Smith, addressing a committee of Boston merchants, said, "with regard to ourselves we have both . . . been entirely out of trade several years." *New Eng. Hist. and Gen. Register* 29: 246. No records have survived that would reveal the amount of Gadsden's income from other sources during this time, but he probably enjoyed a comfortable livelihood from his property in Ansonborough and his plantation near Georgetown.

32. John Stuart to James Grant, Feb. 20, 1766, identifies Gadsden as "Homespun Free-man," James Grant Papers, Bundle 261. See also *Laurens Papers*, V, 110–11, n. 6.

33. For the impact of the Stamp Act crisis on Georgia, see W. W. Abbot, *The Royal Governors of Georgia, 1754–1775* (Chapel Hill, N. C, 1959), 103–25; Kenneth Coleman, *The American Revolution in Georgia, 1763–1789* (Athens, Ga., 1958), 20–24; Charles A. Risher, Jr., "Propaganda, Dissen-

sion, and Defeat: Loyalist Sentiment in Georgia, 1763-1783" (Ph.D. diss., Mississippi State Univ., 1976), 19-33.

34. Feb. 17, 1766, James Grant Papers, Bundle 261.

35. To James Pearson, Feb. 20, 1766, Dartmouth Papers.

36. To John L. Gervais, Jan. 29, 1766, *Laurens Papers*, V, 52-53.

37. Council Journal, 1765-1766, p. 706, S. C. Archives; *S. C. Gazette and Country Journal*, Feb. 18, 1766.

38. Gadsden to William S. Johnson, Apr. 16, 1766, *Gadsden Writings*, 70-72; Drayton, *Memoirs*, I, 86-91; Council Journal, XXXII, 739-50; JCHA, XXXVII, 73, 79; PRSC, XXXI, 86-230; Wallace, *History of S. C.*, II, 71-72.

39. Gadsden to William S. Johnson, Apr. 16, 1766, *Gadsden Writings*, 70.

40. "Journal of Mrs. Ann Manigault," *SCHGM* 20: 209.

41. To John L. Gervais, Jan. 29, 1766, *Laurens Papers*, V, 53-54. See also Herbert Aptheker, *American Negro Slave Revolts* (New York, 1943), 197-98; Maier, "Charleston Mob," 176; Rogers, *Charleston in the Age of the Pinckneys*, 41-42.

42. To William S. Johnson, Apr. 16, 1766, *Gadsden Writings*, 72.

43. Wallace, *History of S. C.*, II, 38-56; Richard Maxwell Brown, *The South Carolina Regulators* (Cambridge, Mass., 1963), 13-37.

44. Charles Martyn to the Bishop of London, Charleston, Dec. 20, 1765, Fulham MSS, no. 90, LC. For the career of Woodmason, see Richard J. Hooker, ed., *The Carolina Backcountry on the Eve of the American Revolution* (Chapel Hill, N. C., 1953), xi-xxxix.

45. Woodmason to Bishop of London, Oct. 19, 1766, in Hooker, ed., *Carolina Backcountry*, 86; see also Woodmason Notes, Fulham MSS, N. C., S. C., Ga., no. 72, undated, LC.

46. "Sylvanus" [Woodmason] in *S. C. Gazette*, Mar. 28, 1769, quoted in Hooker, ed., *Carolina Backcountry*, 262.

47. JCHA, XXXVII, 35, 62; Gadsden to William S. Johnson, Apr. 16, 1766, *Gadsden Writings*, 72.

48. Woodmason to the Bishop of London, Oct. 19, 1766, in Hooker, ed., *Carolina Backcountry*, 86.

49. Quoted in Claude H. Van Tyne, *The Causes of the War of Independence* (New York, 1922), 187-88.

50. Two letters of Richard Champion to John and Caleb Lloyd, Feb. 15 and 23, 1766, in George Herbert Guttridge, ed., *The American Correspondence of a Bristol Merchant, 1766-1776* (Berkeley, Cal., 1934), 10, 13, 14.

51. Peter Manigault to Thomas Gadsden, May 14, 1766, quoted in Harriott Horry Ravenel, *Charleston, The Place and the People* (New York, 1907), 163.

52. To John L. Gervais, May 12, 1766, *Laurens Papers*, V, 129.

53. JCHA, XXXVII, 120; *S. C. Gazette*, June 2, 1766. The surviving portrait of Gadsden at middle age, attributed by its owner and some art experts to artist Jeremiah Theus, was probably painted at this time. There are no records to prove that it is the one officially commissioned by the Commons.

54. JCHA, XXXVII, 142, 164.

55. June 29, 1766, PRSC, XXXI, 72. See also JCHA, XXXVII, 154–55; *S. C. Gazette*, June 2, 1766; *S. C. Gazette and Country Journal*, June 17, 1766; McCrady, *S. C. under Royal Government*, 588–89.

56. Johnson, *Traditions*, 27, 30–34; Drayton, *Memoirs*, II, 315. There is no certainty of the date of this meeting, but it is usually referred to as having taken place in the fall of 1766.

57. Johnson, *Traditions*, 28–29.

58. A sketch of Gadsden signed "P. G." (probably Philip Gadsden, a grandson) appeared in the Charleston *Courier* on July 17, 1857. It said that during the debate on the Articles of Association, probably during the Frist Continental Congress, Samuel Adams paused and "with a stentorian voice, exclaimed: 'Mr. President, from this hour I renounce all allegiance to Parliament and King.' " Whereupon Gadsden, also a member of the Congress, "as animated on his legs as he was intemperate in speech, quickly rose from his chair. 'Mr. President,' he exclaimed, 'I did that in '63.' "

Johnson, *Traditions*, 41, says Gadsden spoke out for independence in 1764. David Ramsay, *Revolution of S. C.,* I, 164, says that the "decisive genius" of Gadsden "at a much earlier day" than 1776 "might have desired the complete separation," but that until 1776 reconciliation "was the unanimous wish of almost every American."

59. Dec. 2, 1765, *Gadsden Writings*, 68.

60. To William S. Johnson, Apr. 16, 1766, *ibid.*, 74. For an account of the actions and attitudes in other colonies, see Maier, *Resistance to Revolution*, 77–112.

61. Joseph Ernst, " 'Ideology' and an Economic Interpretation of the Revolution," in Alfred F. Young, ed., *The American Revolution: Explorations in the History of American Radicalism* (DeKalb, Ill., 1976), 177–78.

62. Adams to Gadsden, Dec. 11, 1766, in Harry Alonzo Cushing, ed., *The Writings of Samuel Adams*, 4 vols. (New York, 1904–1908), I, 108–11.

NOTES TO CHAPTER FOUR

1. To Joseph Brown, Aug. 21, 1766, *Laurens Papers*, V, 131; see also Laurens to John Lewis Gervais, Sept. 1, 1766, *ibid.*, 184.

2. *S. C. Gazette*, May 21, 1772; *Register of St. Philip's, 1754–1810*, 210.

3. Gadsden to Samuel Adams, May 23, 1774, *Gadsden Writings*, 92.

4. *S. C. Gazette*, Jan. 12, 1767; Apr. 19, June 7, 1770; July 4, Aug. 22, Oct. 17, 1771; *S. C. Gazette and Country Journal*, Feb. 23, 1768.

5. *S. C. Gazette*, Nov. 23, Dec. 7, 1767; Jan. 18, 1770; July 16, Aug. 23, Oct. 1, 1772; Mar. 8, Oct. 11, Nov. 1, 1773.

6. This statement was a reminiscence of John Couper, age eighty-three, in a letter dated St. Simon's, Apr. 16, 1842, George White, ed., *Historical Collections of Georgia* (New York, 1854), 472; see also McCrady, *S. C. under Royal Government*, 411.

7. *S. C. Gazette*, June 22, 1769.

8. Laurens, *Appendix to Extracts . . .* , 19–21; see also McCrady, *S. C. under Royal Government*, 279–81.

9. For details and widely varying interpretations of the case, see Robert M. Calhoon and Robert M. Weir, "The Scandalous History of Sir Egerton Leigh," *William and Mary Quart.* 26 (Jan. 1969): 47–74; *Laurens Papers*, V, 283, 286–87; McCrady, *S. C. under Royal Government*, 471–72; Sellers, *Charleston Business*, 178–202; Carl Ubbelohde, *The Vice-Admiralty Court and the American Revolution* (Chapel Hill, N. C., 1961), 26, 100–14; Wallace, *Life of Laurens*, 103, 116–22, 147.

10. Thomas, *British Politics and the Stamp Act Crisis*, 337–63.

11. Ernst, *Money and Politics*, 81–86, 106, 120–21, 133, 215–20; see also Thomas, *British Politics and the Stamp Act Crisis*, 350–51.

12. Laurens to James Grant, Oct. 1, 1768, and Laurens to Lachlan McIntosh, Oct. 15, 1768, both quoted in Wallace, *Life of Laurens*, 152–53; see also *S. C. Gazette*, Oct. 3, 10, 1768.

13. *S. C. Gazette and Country Journal*, Oct. 4, 1768; *S. C. Gazette*, Oct. 3, 1768.

14. *New Eng. Hist. and Gen. Register* 29 (1875): 246.

15. Quoted in Wallace, *Hist. of S. C.*, II, 83; see also Smith, *S. C. as Royal Province*, 362; *S. C. Gazette and Country Journal*, Nov. 22, 1768; *S. C. Gazette Extraordinary*, Nov. 24, 1768.

16. Smith, *S. C. as Royal Province*, 363–64; see also Wallace, *History of S. C.*, II, 83.

17. JCHA, XXXVIII, 1–7, 16–17.

18. *Ibid.*, 91–92. See also McCrady, *S. C. under Royal Government*, 617–20; Smith, *S. C. as Royal Province*, 258–59; Wallace, *History of S. C .*, II, 80.

19. *S. C. Gazette*, Feb. 2, 1769; see also "Journal of Mrs. Ann Manigault," *SCHGM* 21: 12.

20. Quoted in Arthur M. Schlesinger, *The Colonial Merchants and the American Revolution, 1763–1776* (New York, 1939 [1918]), 140.

21. Hooker, ed., *Carolina Backcountry*, 213–14.

22. *Ibid.*, 267–78.

23. *S. C. Gazette*, July 27, 1769; McCrady, *S. C. under Royal Government*, 651, lists the names of the members of the committees. See also Sellers, *Charleston Business*, 208–10.

24. A copy of the resolutions and a list of the places where the subscription papers could be signed appeared in the *S. C. Gazette*, Aug. 3, 1769. William Henry Drayton, who played an important role in the nonimportation debate, later collected the relevant letters from the *S. C. Gazette* and published them as a pamphlet entitled *The Letters of Freeman, Etc.* (London, 1771). A published edition of the pamphlet, edited with an introduction and notes by Robert M. Weir (Columbia, S.C., 1977), contains useful sketches of the lives of the disputants and summaries of their arguments.

25. PRSC, XXXII, 415–16.

26. William M. Dabney and Marion Dargan, *William Henry Drayton and*

the American Revolution (Albuquerque, N. M., 1962), 25-29; McCrady, *S. C. under Royal Government*, 651-52.

27. Weir, ed., *Letters of Freeman*, 7-9, 125 (n. 5), 146 (n. 4).

28. *Ibid.*, 11-12.

29. *Ibid.*, 14-18.

30. *Ibid.*, 19-26.

31. James Grant Papers, Bundle 272.

32. *S. C. Gazette*, Apr. 5, 1770; McCrady, *S. C. under Royal Government*, 654.

33. Weir, ed., *Letters of Freeman*, 26-29.

34. *Ibid.*, 29-33.

35. *Ibid.*, 33-42.

36. *Ibid.*, 111-14.

37. *Ibid.*, 53-57.

38. *Ibid.*, 57-86; see also *S. C. Gazette*, Oct. 26, Nov. 9, 1769; Walsh, *Charleston's Sons of Liberty*, 53-54.

39. Weir, ed., *Letters of Freeman*, 86-95.

40. *Ibid.*, 95-114; see also JCHA, XXXVIII, pt. 1, p. 9.

41. *S. C. Gazette*, Aug. 17, 24, Sept. 7, Nov. 9, 23, Dec. 14, 1769; *S. C. Gazette and Country Journal*, Aug. 27, Sept. 5, 1769. The names of non-subscribers were not published in the newspapers but in handbills.

42. *S. C. Gazette*, Jan. 25, Feb. 1, 1770; *S. C. Gazette and Country Journal*, Feb. 6, 1770.

43. Bull to Lord Hillsborough, Dec. 13, 1770, PRSC, XXXII, 434. See also Bull to Hillsborough, July 16, 1770, *ibid.*, 298-99; *S. C. Gazette*, May 17 (supplement), July 5, Nov. 8, and Dec. 13, 1770; McCrady, *S. C. under Royal Government*, 674-75.

44. For a discussion of the political consensus in South Carolina before the Revolution, see Robert M. Weir, "The Harmony We Were Famous For: An Interpretation of Pre-Revolutionary South Carolina Politics," *William and Mary Quart.* 26 (Oct. 1969): 473-501. A good account of nonimportation debates in all of the colonies may be found in Maier, *Resistance to Revolution*, 113-38.

45. For a general discussion of whig political philosophy in America, see Colbourn, *Lamp of Experience*; for an analysis of the terminology of American protesters, see Bailyn, *Ideological Origins*, 230-319; for a discussion of the royal government's understanding of its own motivations, see John Derry, *English Politics and the American Revolution* (New York, 1977), 1-38.

NOTES TO CHAPTER FIVE

1. For a brief sketch of the life and character of Wilkes, see Louis Kronenberger, *The Extraordinary Mr. Wilkes* (New York, 1974). On the Wilkite movement in London, see Goerge Rudé, *Wilkes and Liberty: A Social Study of 1763 to 1774* (Oxford, 1962).

2. A map of Charleston and Gadsden's subdivision of Middlesex is reproduced in the Charleston *Yearbook, 1880*, opp. 257. See also Maier, *Resistance to Revolution*, 162–69, 201; Wallace, *Life of Laurens*, 163; Walsh, *Charleston's Sons of Libeerty*, 31.

3. JCHA, XXXVIII, 215.

4. The definitive account of the Wilkes Fund dispute is Jack P. Greene, "Bridge to Revolution: The Wilkes Fund Controversy in South Carolina, 1769–1775," *J. of Southern Hist.* 29 (Feb. 1963): 19–52. Other useful accounts may be found in Ernst, *Money and Politics*, 334–50; Wallace, *Life of Laurens*, 159–76. For an account of the impact of Wilkes upon the American colonies in general, see Pauline Maier, "John Wilkes and American Disillusionment with Britain," *William and Mary Quart.* 20 (July 1963): 373–95.

5. Gadsden's arguments were published in the *S. C. Gazette*, Dec. 3 and 24, 1764; they are discussed at length in ch. 2.

6. PRSC, XXXII, 132.

7. Greene, "Bridge to Revolution," 26; *S. C. Gazette*, Apr. 12, 1770; David D. Wallace, *Constitutional History of South Carolina from 1725 to 1775* (Abbeville, S. C., 1899), 64–68.

8. JCHA, XXXVIII, 382, 387–92; see also Greene, "Bridge to Revolution," 26–27.

9. *S. C. Gazette*, Apr. 19, July 5, 1770; *S. C. Gazette and Country Journal* Apr. 24, 1770.

10. JCHA, XXXVIII, 430–33; see also Ernst, *Money and Politics*, 338–39; Greene, "Bridge to Revolution," 28–30.

11. JCHA, XXXIX, 11–12, 18, 20; see also Greene, "Bridge to Revolution," 38–39.

12. JCHA, XXXIX, 2, 16–18, 25–29; see also McCrady, *S. C. under Royal Government*, 701. For the career of Rawlins Lowndes, see Carl J. Vipperman, *The Rise of Rawlins Lowndes, 1721–1800* (Columbia, S. C., 1978).

13. Committee to Garth, Oct. 30, 1772; Garth to Committee, Nov. 30, 1772, Force trans., LC.

14. Greene, "Bridge to Revolution," 41–42; McCrady, *S. C. under Royal Government*, 704; Smith, *S. C. as Royal Province*, 385.

15. Sept. 18, 1773, PRSC, XXXIII, 309. For Gadsden's reports, see JCHA, XXXIX, 38, 48–49, 53, 90. A thorough discussion of the decline of the Council may be found in M. Eugene Sirmans, "The South Carolina Royal Council, 1720–1763," *William and Mary Quart.* Ser. 3, 18 (July 1961): 373–92. See also Jackson Turner Main, *The Upper House in Revolutionary America, 1763–1788* (Madison, Wis., 1967), 18–19; Wallace, *History of S. C.*, II, 97–98.

16. For a discussion of the subtle nature of colonial constitutions, see the introduction in Jack P. Greene, ed., *The Nature of Colony Constitutions: Two Pamphlets on the Wilkes Fund Controversy in South Carolina By Sir Egerton Leigh and Arthur Lee* (Columbia, S. C., 1970), 42–55. On the question of the colonial suspicion of a ministerial conspiracy, see Bailyn, *Ideological Origins*, 94–159.

17. Quoted in Josiah Quincy, *Memoir of the Life of Josiah Quincy, junior* (Boston, 1825), Mar. 19, 1773, pp. 84–85.

18. *S. C. Gazette*, Dec. 6, 1773; see also *S. C. Gazette*, Nov. 22 and 29, 1773.

19. On the importance of the Dec. 3 meeting, see George C. Rogers, Jr., "The Charleston Tea Party: The Significance of December 3, 1773," *SCHM* 75 (1974): 153–68; Wallace, *History of S. C.*, II, 109–10.

20. James Laurens to Henry Laurens, Dec. 2, with postscript dated Dec. 4, 1773, Henry Laurens Papers, S. C. Hist. Soc.; quoted in Rogers, "The Charleston Tea Party," 159.

21. This statement is the thesis of Rogers, "The Charleston Tea Party"; see esp. 161.

22. *S. C. Gazette*, Dec. 6, 1773; Schlesinger, *Colonial Merchants*, 295.

23. Rogers, "Charleston Tea Party," 162–63; *S. C. Gazette*, Dec. 20, 1773.

24. *S. C. Gazette*, Jan. 17, Feb. 7, 14, Mar. 21, 1774. For a complete list of members of the General Committee, see Gadsden to Samuel Adams, June 14, 1774, *Gadsden Writings*, 98–99, including n. 2.

25. Drayton, *Memoirs*, I, 112; see also William Moultrie, *Memoirs of the American Revolution, so far as it related to the States of North and South Carolina and Georgia*, 2 vols. (New York, 1902), I, 10.

26. Timothy to Samuel Adams, June 13, 1774, and June 27, 1774, Samuel Adams Papers (Committee of Correspondence, S. C.), NYPL.

27. Gadsden to Adams, May 23 and June 5, 1774, *Gadsden Writings*, 92–96. All quotations are from the second letter. See also Schlesinger, *Colonial Merchants*, 373.

28. *Gadsden Writings*, 99.

29. Samuel Adams to Gadsden, July 18, 1774, Cushing, ed., *Writings of Samuel Adams*, III, 141–43.

30. Gadsden and Secretary Clarkson to Boston Committee of Correspondence, June 28, 1774, *Gadsden Writings*, 101; see also *S. C. Gazette*, June 27, 1774.

NOTES TO CHAPTER SIX

1. Gadsen's appeal to the backcountry is implied in his letter to Samuel Adams, May 23, 1774, *Gadsden Writings*, 92–94. On the significance of the July meeting, see Drayton, *Memoirs*, I, 126; McCrady, *South Carolina under Royal Government* 735–42; Allan Nevins, *The American States During and After the Revolution, 1775–1789* (New York, 1924), 61; Rogers, "Charleston Tea Party," 165–66.

2. For the career of Powell, see Walter B. Edgar, N. Louise Bailey, and Elizabeth Ivey Cooper, eds., *Biographical Directory of the South Carolina House of Representatives*, 3 vols. to date (Columbia, S. C., 1977), II, 538–39.

3. For implications of the rivalry between Boston and Charleston, see Gadsden to Samuel Adams, June 5, 1774, *Gadsden Writings*, 94, including

n. 3; *S. C. Gazette*, Jan. 17, 1774; Greene, "Bridge to Revolution," 22.

4. Edward Rutledge to Ralph Izard, July 21, 1774, in Anne Izard Deas, ed., *Correspondence of Mr. Ralph Izard of South Carolina from the year 1774 to 1804* (New York, 1844), 2; see also Drayton, *Memoirs*, I, 129, 131.

5. Moultrie, *Memoirs*, I, 11. See also McCrady, *S. C. under Royal Government*, 738–40; Van Tyne, *Causes of the War of Independence*, 430; Wallace, *History of S. C.*, II, 113–14.

6. JCHA, XXXIX, 172–73; Letter from Charles Town, Aug. 3., 1774, and Bull to Dartmouth, Aug. 3., 1774, both in Force, *American Archives* (4th ser.), I, 672.

7. *S. C. Gazette and Country Journal*, Aug. 2, 16, 30, 1774; *S. C. Gazette*, Sept. 19, 1774; William Duane, ed., *Extracts from the Diary of Christopher Marshall, Kept in Philadelphia and Lancaster, During the American Revolution, 1774–1781* (Albany, N. Y., 1887), Aug. 22, 1774, p. 9; Wallace, *History of S. C.*, II, 114.

8. On Philadelphia in the eighteenth century, see Carl and Jessica Bridenbaugh, *Rebels and Gentlemen: Philadelphia in the Age of Franklin* (New York, 1965).

9. Silas Deane to Elizabeth Deane [Aug. 31–Sept. 5, 1774], in Paul H. Smith, ed., *Letters of Delegates to Congress, 1774–1789*, 4 vols. to date (Washington, D.C., 1976–), I, 15.

10. Silas Deane to Elizabeth Deane, Aug. 29, 1774, Deane Papers, *Coll. NYHS*, XIX, 5–6. John Adams's description of his arrival is in his diary, Aug. 29, 1774, in Smith, ed., *Letters of Delegates*, I, 3; for the complete Adams diary, see L. H. Butterfield, ed., *Diary and Autobiography of John Adams*, 4 vols. (Cambridge, Mass., 1961). See also Edmund C. Burnett, ed., *The Letters of Members of the Continental Congress*, 8 vols (Washington, D. C., 1921–1936), I, 1; John C. Miller, *Sam Adams: Pioneer in Propaganda* (Boston, 1936), 314.

11. On the importance of Samuel Adams's career and for a survey of the major biographies of him, see Pauline Maier, "Coming to Terms with Samuel Adams," *Am. Hist. Rev.* 81 (Feb. 1976): 12–37.

12. For an analysis of John Adams's personality, see Peter Shaw, *The Character of John Adams* (Chapel Hill, N. C., 1976).

13. Edmund C. Burnett, *The Continental Congress* (New York, 1941), 33; see also List of Delegates to Congress and Robert Treat Paine's Diary [Sept. 30, 1774], both in Smith, ed., *Letters of Delegates*, I, 29.

14. Caesar Rodney to Thomas Rodney, Sept. 9, 1774, George Herbert Ryden, ed., *Letters to and from Caesar Rodney, 1756–1784* (Philadelphia, 1933), 45–46.

15. Burnett, *Cont. Cong.*, 36.

16. John Adams's diary, Sept. 6, 1774, in Smith, ed., *Letters of Delegates*, I, 29.

17. To Mrs. Elizabeth Deane, Sept. 6 and 7, 1774, in Smith, ed., *Letters of Delegates*, I, 29, 34–35.

18. Quoted in Burnett, *Cont. Cong.*, 39.

19. *Ibid.*, 41; W. C. Ford, *et al.*, eds., *Journals of the Continental Congress*, 34 vols. (Washington, D. C., 1904–1937), I, 25n, 29.

20. Bancroft, *History of the U. S.*, IV, 71; Burnett, *Cont. Cong.*, 42–45, 47.

21. Drayton, *Memoirs*, I, 165.

22. Quoted in Burnett, *Cont. Cong.*, 43.

23. Butterfield, ed., *Diary and Autobiography of John Adams*, II, 139.

24. Edmund Pendleton quotes Gadsden to James Madison, Jan. 28, 1782, in Mass. Hist. Soc. *Proceedings* (2nd ser.), XIX, 146–47.

25. Charles Francis Adams, ed., *The Works of John Adams*, 10 vols. (Boston, 1850–1856), II, 383; Moultrie, *Memoirs*, I, 28–33; David Ammerman, *In the Common Cause: American Response to the Coercive Acts of 1774* (Charlottesville, Va., 1974), 35–51, 82–84.

26. Butterfield, ed., *Diary and Autobiography of John Adams*, II, 133–34.

27. Adams, ed., *Works of John Adams*, I, 157.

28. To Judge Bee, Oct. 1774, quoted in John Sanderson, *Sanderson's Biography of the Signers of the Declaration of Independence*, ed. Robert T. Conrad (Philadelphia, 1847), 16–17.

29. To Ralph Izard, Oct. 29, 1774, Deas, ed., *Correspondence of Ralph Izard*, 22.

30. Quoted in Adams, ed., *Works of John Adams*, II, 384, 393; see also Burnett, *Letters*, I, 49–50.

31. Quoted in William Wirt Henry, ed., *Patrick Henry, L:ife, Correspondence, and Speeches*, 3 vols. (New York, 1891), I, 229.

32. Ammerman, *In the Common Cause*, 58–61.

33. *S. C. Gazette*, Nov. 21, 1774; *S. C. Gazette and Country Journal*, Nov. 8, 1774; see also Alden, *South in the Revolution*, 178.

34. Dec. 19, 1774, PRSC, XXXIV, 230.

35. *S. C. Gazette*, Dec. 12, 1774.

36. William E. Hemphill and Wylma A. Wates, eds., *Extracts from the Journals of the Provincial Congresses of South Carolina, 1775–1776* (Columbia, S. C., 1960), xvii, 3–7. See also Jack P. Greene, Review of *Extracts Prov. Cong. S. C.*, in *Mississippi Valley Hist. Rev.* 48 (June 1961): 101; Wallace, *History of S. C.*, II, 115–17; Walsh, *Charleston's Sons of Liberty*, 64–65.

37. To Thomas and William Bradford, Mar. 28, 1775, *Gadsden Writings*, 102.

38. Drayton, *Memoirs*, I, 169–71, 178.

39. *Ibid.*, 172, 174–75.

40. Laurens to John Laurens, Jan. 18, 1775, Laurens Papers, S. C. Hist. Soc.

41. Hemphill and Wates, eds., *Extracts Prov. Cong.*, 28–29.

42. To John Laurens, Jan. 22, 1775, Laurens Papers, S. C. Hist. Soc.

43. JCHA, XXXIX, 190–91.

44. Drayton, *Memoirs*, I, 167.

45. Gadsden to Thomas and William Bradford, June 28, 1774, *Gadsden Writings*, 101–4; Hennig Cohen, *The South Carolina Gazette, 1732–1775* (Columbia, S. C., 1953), 156.

46. Drayton, *Memoirs*, I, 182–85; Sellers, *Charleston Business*, 220; Wallace, *History of S. C*, II, 119.

47. For an example of how the wealthy were injured, see Ralph Izard to Thomas Lynch, June 7, 1775, Deas, ed., *Correspondence of Ralph Izard*, 83.

48. To Henry Laurens, Mar. 14, 1775, Henry Laurens Papers, LC.

49. To Lord Dartmouth, Mar. 28, 1775, PRSC, XXXV, 79–80.

50. The statements of Bull and the House are quoted in Johnson, *Traditions*, 52–53. See also Wallace, *History of S. C.*, II, 120. The members of the Secret Committee were William Henry Drayton, Arthur Middleton, Charles Cotesworth Pinckney, William Gibbes, and Edward Weyman.

NOTES TO CHAPTER SEVEN

1. For a chronology of the Congress and a list of delegates, see Smith, ed., *Letters of Delegates*, I, xxiv–xxxii.

2. B. D. Bargar, *Lord Dartmouth and the American Revolution* (Columbia, S. C., 1965), 156–57; T. C. Hansard, *Parliamentary History of England from the Earliest Period to 1803*, 36 vols. (London, 1813), XVIII, 696. A copy of the Olive Branch Petition is in Benjamin Franklin Stevens, *B. F. Stevens's Facsimiles of Manuscripts in European Archives Relating to America, 1773–1783*, 24 vols. (London, 1889–1898), vol. 5, no. 454.

3. Butterfield, ed., *Diary and Autobiography of John Adams*, III, 317, 357.

4. Duane, ed., *Diary of Christopher Marshall*, 32, 43.

5. Paul Ivar Chestnut, "The Universalist Movement in America, 1770–1803" (Ph.D. diss., Duke Univ., 1973), 74, 179.

6. Gadsden to Samuel Adams, Apr. 4, 1779, *Gadsden Writings*, 163–64; see also Butterfield, ed., *Diary and Autobiography of John Adams*, III, 317, 357.

7. Ford, ed., *Journals of the Cont. Cong.*, II, 106.

8. Gadsden, *et al.* to the S. C. Secret Committee, July 1, 1775, *Gadsden Writings*, 104–7. An Account of the Certificates Issued to the Creditors of the Public, Apr. 10, 1774–June 10, 1775, S. C. Archives; Gadsden's certificates were nos. 2204 through 2287. See also Burnett, *Cont. Cong.*, 74, 102.

9. Journal of the Council of Safety, July 19, 1775, in *Coll. S. C. Hist. Soc.*, II, 52; see also Edward McCrady, *The History of South Carolina in the Revolution, 1775–1780* (New York, 1901), 21.

10. Ford, ed., *Journals of the Cont. Cong.*, II, 191, 234, 262.

11. *Ibid.*, 177.

12. Gadsden to Thomas Jefferson, Oct. 29, 1787, *Gadsden Writings*, 245–47; see also Butterfield, ed., *Diary and Autobiography of John Adams*, II, 137–39.

13. Quoted in Butterfield, ed., *Diary and Autobiography of John Adams*, II, 192–93; see also William Bell Clark, ed., *Naval Documents of the American Revolution*, 8 vols. to date (Washington, D. C., 1964–), II, 309.

14. William M. Fowler, Jr., *Rebels under Sail: The American Navy during the Revolution* (New York, 1976), 42–43.

15. Quoted in Nathan Miller, *Sea of Glory: The Continental Navy Fights for Independence, 1775-1783* (New York, 1974), 40; see also John Adams to Elbridge Gerry, June [7], 1775, in Clark, ed., *Naval Documents*, I, 628; Fowler, *Rebels under Sail*, 43.

16. Fowler, *Rebels under Sail*, 44, 47–49, 54.

17. All quotations except that of Edward Rutledge are from Butterfield, ed., *Diary and Autobiography of John Adams*, II, 198–99, 201–2; the Edward Rutledge quotation is from Charles R. Smith, *Marines in the Revolution: A History of the Continental Marines in the American Revolution, 1775-1783* (Washington, D. C., 1975), 10.

18. Ford, ed., *Journals of the Cont. Cong.*, II, 294, 428; Butterfield, ed., *Diary and Autobiography of John Adams*, II, 201–2, 205, 220, 229–30, III, 345; James Warren to John Adams, July 11, 1775, in *Warren-Adams Letters, Being Chiefly a Correspondence Among John Adams, Samuel Adams, and James Warren, 1743-1814*, 2 vols., Massachusetts Hist. Soc. Coll. 72–73 (Boston, 1917–1925), I, 81; John Adams to James Warren, Apr. 6, 1777, *ibid.*, 311; Burnett, *Cont. Cong.*, 119–20; Miller, *Sea of Glory*, 49, 58; and Smith, *Marines in the Revolution*, 10–11.

19. Miller, *Sea of Glory*, 2; Smith, *Marines in the Revolution*, 11.

20. Naval Committee to Silas Deane, Nov. 7, 1775; Naval Committee to Dudley Saltonstall, Nov. 27, 1775; Naval Committee's Warrant to John Barriman, Dec. 23, 1775; Naval Committee to Esek Hopkins, Jan. 5, 1775; in Clark, ed., *Naval Documents*, II, 917–18, 1163; III, 216–18, 636–38. See also "Diary of Richard Smith," Jan. 6, 1776, *Am. Hist. Rev.* 1 (1895–96), 305; Miller, *Sea of Glory*, 53.

21. Butterfield, ed., *Diary and Autobiography of John Adams*, III, 350.

22. Smith, *Marines in the Revolution*, 14; for the Charleston opinion of the rattlesnake, see Alexander Hewat, *An Historical Account of the Rise and Progress of the Colonies of South Carolina and Georgia*, 2 vols. (London, 1779), I, 86–87.

23. Gilbert Grosvenor and William J. Showalter, "Flags of the World," *National Geographic* 66 (Sept. 1934): 340–42. Miller, *Sea of Glory*, 93, says Gadsden sent the flag to Hopkins, then stationed in the Chesapeake Bay, in mid-January 1776. See also Anna (Farwell) De Koven, *The Life and Letters of John Paul Jones*, 2 vols. (New York, 1913), I, 90–92; William James Morgan, *Captains to the Northward: The New England Captains in the Continental Navy* (Barre, Mass., 1959), 37; Hugh F. Rankin, "The Naval Flag of the American Revolution," *William and Mary Quart.* 11 (July 1954): 339–53; Smith, *Marines in the Revolution*, 14.

24. "Diary of Richard Smith," Jan. 8, 1776, *Am. Hist. Rev.* 1 (1895–96, 298, 305–6.

25. Butterfield, ed., *Diary and Autobiography of John Adams*, III, 317; see also Gadsden to Samuel Adams, Apr. 4, 1779, *Gadsden Writings*, 163.

26. Peter Timothy to Gadsden, Jan. 5, 1776, in Ford, ed., *Journals of the Cont. Cong.*, IV, 54; Gadsden to Esek Hopkins, Jan. 10, 1776, *Gadsden*

Writings, 111; "Diary of Richard Smith," *Am. Hist. Rev.* 1 (1895-96), 302, 309.

27. To Henry Ward, Philadelphia, Jan. 25, 1776, in Bernhard Knollenberg, ed., *Correspondence of Governor Samuel Ward, May 1775–March 1776* (Providence, R. I., 1952), 180.

28. Gadsden to Esek Hopkins, Jan. 10, 15, 1775, *Gadsden Writings*, 108-11; see also Morgan, *Captains to the Northward*, 37.

29. To P. Schuyler, Jan. 20, 1776, Burnett, *Letters*, I, 323.

30. Thomas Nelson, Jr., to Thomas Jefferson, Feb. 4, 1776, *ibid.*, 339.

31. R. H. Lee to Charles Lee, June 29, 1776, in J. C. Ballagh, ed., *The Letters of Richard Henry Lee*, 2 vols. (New York, 1911-1914), I, 205.

32. [Paul Wentworth], "Minutes respecting political Parties in America and Sketches of the leading Persons in each Province [1778]," in Stevens, *Facsimiles . . . Relating to America*, vol. 5, no. 487.

33. Extract of a letter of John Adams, Aug. 18, 1776, in Force, *American Archives* (5th ser.), I, 1025; Adams, ed., *Works of John Adams*, II, 408-9, 506; III, 20.

34. These notes have been translated by Paul A. Napier and transcribed by Richard Walsh; copies are on deposit with Gadsden's copy of the journal in the S. C Hist. Soc. (Charleston) and in the South Caroliniana Library, Columbia, S. C.. A summary of the notes and several long quotations from them are published in Richard Walsh, "The Gadsen [*sic*] 'Diary' Deciphered," *Manuscripts* 16 (1964): 17-23.

35. Dated June, 1775, John Adams's letter to Abigail is in Adams, ed., *Works of John Adams*, I, 178-79.

36. Campbell to Lord Dartmouth, Aug. 19, 1775, PRSC, XXXV, 186. See also Campbell to Dartmouth, July 2, 1775, PRSC, XXXV, 122-23; Campbell to Gen. Thomas Gage, July 1, 1775, PRSC, XXXVI, 15; Peter Timothy to William Henry Drayton, Aug. 13, 1775, in Gibbes, *Doc. Hist., 1764-1776*, 139; Alden, *South in the Revolution*, 199-201; Maier, "Charleston Mob," 185; McCrady, *S. C. in the Revolution, 1775-1780*, 3-8; Wallace, *History of S. C.*, II, 123, 127-28, 130-44; Marina Wikramanayake, *A World In Shadow: The Free Black in Antebellum South Carolina* (Columbia, S. C., 1973), 150.

NOTES TO CHAPTER EIGHT

1. Eric Foner, *Tom Paine and Revolutionary America* (New York, 1976), 1-17.

2. Gadsden's personal copy of *Common Sense* with his underlinings is in the College of Charleston Library. All quoted phrases in this paragraph and the next are among those Gadsden underlined. They may be found on pp. 13, 12, 20, 21, 22, 34, 36, 38 and 73, respectively, of Gadsden's copy.

3. *S. C. and American General Gazette*, Feb. 2, 1776; Henry Laurens to

John Laurens, Feb. 22, 1776, Laurens Papers, S. C. Hist. Soc.; Journal of H. M. S. *Tamar*, in Clark, ed., *Naval Documents*, IV, 16.

4. Hemphill and Wates, eds., *Extracts Prov. Cong.*, 182-83; see also Drayton, *Memoirs*, II, 172.

5. "Freeman [Drayton] to the Deputies of North America," Aug. 10, 1774, in Gibbes, *Doc. Hist.*, *1764-1776*, 12; Dabney and Dargan, *Drayton and the American Revolution*, 40-56; James Kirby Martin, *Men in Rebellion: Higher Governmental Leaders and the Coming of the American Revolution* (New Brunswick, N. J., 1973), 28-29, 115.

6. Drayton, *Memoirs*, II, 172-74; Johnson, *Traditions*, 41; Laurens to John Laurens, Feb. 22, 1776, Laurens Papers, S. C. Hist. Soc.; Ravenel, *Charleston*, 224; William Alexander Hyrne to William Tilghman, May 17, 1776, Mass. Hist. Soc. *Proceedings*, XI, 254.

7. Wallace, *History of S. C.*, II, 152; McCrady, *S. C. in the Revolution, 1775-1780*, 107, 112.

8. For a copy of the constitution, see Hemphill and Wates, eds., *Extracts Prov. Cong.*, 256-63; see also McCrady, *S. C. in the Revolution, 1775-1780*, 109-15; Wallace, *History of S. C.*, II, 150-54.

9. A. S. Salley, Jr., ed., *Journal of the General Assembly of South Carolina, March 26, 1776-April 11, 1776* (Columbia, S. C., 1906), 32.

10. Gadsden to Drayton, Aug. 15, 1778, *Gadsden Writings*, 146.

11. *S. C. and American General Gazette*, Apr. 10, 1776; McCrady, *S. C. in the Revolution, 1775-1780*, 117-22.

12. Charleston *Yearbook, 1896*, 345-46; see also Nevins, *American States*, 439.

13. Silas Deane to Elizabeth Deane, [Sept. 7, 1774], in Smith, ed., *Letters of Delegates*, I, 35. See also Gadsden's copy of *Common Sense* (College of Charleston Library), 73; Duane, ed., *Diary of Christopher Marshall*, May 9, 1775, pp. 24-25; Ramsay, *History of S. C.*, II, 255; Ravenel, *Charleston*, 123; George C. Rogers, Jr., *Evolution of a Federalist: William Loughton Smith of Charleston (1758-1812)* (Columbia, S. C., 1962), 32-33.

14. *S. C. and American General Gazette*, Apr. 10, 1776; *Register of St. Philip's, 1754-1810*, 221; "Journal of Mrs. Ann Manigault," Apr. 14, 1776, *SCHGM* 21: 113. For a chart of the Wragg family, see Henry A. M. Smith, "Wragg of South Carolina," *SCHGM* 19: 121-23.

15. It is not clear whether Ann owned the dwelling in Charleston or merely had the use of it. Marriage Settlements, I, 63; see also Charleston County Will Books 1742-1752 (p. 343) and 1761-1771 (p. 388), both in the S. C. Archives.

16. To Elias Ball, Apr. 15, 1776, Laurens Papers, S. C. Hist. Soc.

17. Don Higginbotham, *The War of American Independence: Military Attitudes, Policies, and Practice, 1763-1789* (New York, 1971), 136; Claude H. Van Tyne, *The War of Independence* (Boston and New York, 1929), 193n, 194n.

18. Diary of Captain Barnard Elliott, 1775-1778, Feb. 12, 13, 14, 20, 28, 1776, in Charleston *Yearbook, 1889*, 188-91; Drayton, *Memoirs*, II, 52, 53,

171–72, 174, 281, 290; Moultrie's Report of July 17, 1775, in *Coll. S. C. Hist. Soc.*, II, 47; Moultrie, *Memoirs*, I, 64–65, 75, 90, 182; extract from Captain Francis Marion's Orderly Book, 1775, In Gibbes, *Doc. Hist., 1764–1776*, 104; Letter from Charles Town to London, May 10, 1775, in Margaret Wheeler Willard, ed., *Letters on the American Revolution, 1774– 1776* (Boston and New York, 1925), 105; Charles M. Lefferts, *Uniforms of American, British, French, and German Armies in the War of the American Revolution, 1775–1783*, ed. Alexander J. Wall (New York, 1926), 58; McCrady, *S. C. in the Revolution, 1775–1780*, 10–14.

19. William Campbell to Lord Dartmouth, Aug. 19, 1775, PRSC, XXXV, 189; see also letter written by an English visitor to Charleston, ca. 1772– 1774, in *Southern Literary Messenger* 11 (March 1845): 139–40.

20. Walter J. Fraser, Jr., "Reflections of 'Democracy' in Revolutionary South Carolina?: The Composition of Military Organizations and the Attitudes and Relationships of the Officers and Men, 1775–1780," *SCHM* 78 (July 1977): 203–4, 208–11; see also Higginbotham, *War of American Independence*, 390–403.

21. Dr. Milligan's description of Fort Johnson in 1770, PRSC, XXV, 243; Bartholomew Rivers Carroll, ed., *Historical Collections of South Carolina*, 2 vols. (New York, 1836), II, 487–88; diary of Capt. Barnard Elliott, Nov. 2, 1775, Jan. 14, 1776, in Charleston *Yearbook, 1889*, 178–79, 183–84; Journal of Council of Safety, Jan. 11, 1776, in *Coll. S. C. Hist. Soc.*, III, 165; Campbell to Dartmouth, Jan. 1, 1776, PRSC, XXXVI, 2.

22. Henry Laurens to Provincial Congress of North Carolina, Feb. 14, 1776, in *SCHGM* 4:90; Hemphill and Wates, eds., *Extracts Prov. Cong.*, 186, 190, 206, 208, 210, 240, 241, 246; Charleston *Yearbook, 1889*, 191.

23. Henry Laurens to William Henry Drayton, Mar. 21, 1776, in Gibbes, *Doc. Hist., 1764–1776*, 271; R. Hutson to his brother, June 7, 1776, Charleston *Yearbook, 1895*, 216; Elliott's Diary, June 5, 7, 1776, Charleston *Yearbook, 1889*, 207–9; *S. C. and American General Gazette*, Apr. 17, 1776.

24. Elliott's Diary, Mar. 9, 1776, quoting instructions signed by Christopher Gadsden, in Clark, ed., *Naval Documents*, IV, 275, 277.

25. Moultrie, *Memoirs*, I, 14.

26. Ford, ed., *Journals of the Cont. Cong.*, V, 462.

27. For comprehensive secondary accounts of the Battle of Sullivan's Island, see Alden, *South in the Revolution*, 201–6; Higginbotham, *War of American Independence*, 136–37; McCrady, *S. C. in the Revolution, 1775– 1780*, 132–62; Edward M. Riley, "Historic Fort Moultrie in Charleston Harbor," *SCHGM* 51: 63–74; Wallace, *History of S. C.*, II, 154–59. For a sampling of primary accounts from both the American and British perspectives, see Charleston *Yearbook, 1883*, 474; *ibid., 1880*, 211; *ibid., 1895*, 317; Drayton, *Memoirs*, II, 280, 293–94, 306; Robert W. Gibbes, *Documentary History of the American Revolution, 1776–1782* (New York, 1857), 3, 5, 6, 10, 13, 17, 18; Charles Lee Papers, *Coll. NYHS*, II, 74, 140; Moultrie, *Memoirs*, II, 151, 156, 166–68, 174–82; James Murray-Puttenay, *Letters from America, 1773–1780, Being the Letters of a Scots Officer, Sir James Murray, to His Home during the War of American Independence*, ed. Eric

Robson (New York, n.d. [ca.1950]), 23–30; Robert Pringle to John Pringle, Esq., Aug. 13, 1776, in "Letters and Will of Robert Pringle (1702–1776)," ed. Mary Pringle Fenhagen, *SCHGM* 50: 147–49; Willard, ed., *Letters on the American Revolution*, 338–39.

28. July 1, 1776, *Gadsden Writings*, 114–15. See also Charles Cotesworth Pinckney to his mother, June 29, 1776, in Gibbes, *Doc. Hist., 1776–1782*, 7; R. Hutson to his brother, June 30, 1776, Charles Lee Papers, *Coll. NYHS*, V, 130; Gadsden to Charles Lee, Aug. 2, 1776, *Gadsden Writings*, 115–16.

29. On the South Carolina elite's struggle for power at home, see Robert M. Weir, "Who Shall Rule at Home: The American Revolution as a Crisis of Legitimacy for the Colonial Elite," *J. of Interdisciplinary Hist.* 6 (Spring 1976): 679–700; Martin, *Men in Rebellion*, 28–29, 102–3, 177, 190. On the problems faced by the Continental Congress in deciding when to declare independence and the assignment of guilt to England, see Jack N. Rakove, "The Decision for American Independence: A Reconstruction," *Perspectives in Am. His.* 10 (1976): 215–75.

30. Letter dated Feb., 1776, quoted in Wallace, *Life of Laurens*, 225; see also John Laurens to James Laurens, Oct. 24, 1776, *SCHGM* 10: 49–53.

31. On the tension of the parent-child relationship in South Carolina, see Weir, "A Crisis of Legitimacy," 686–88. For general discussions of the psychological trauma of separation, see Edwin G. Burrows and Michael Wallace, "The American Revolution: The Ideology and Psychology of National Liberation." *Perspectives in Am. Hist.* 6 (1972): 167–306; Winthrop D. Jordan, "Familial Politics: Thomas Paine and the Killing of the King, 1776," *J. of Am. Hist.* 60 (Sept. 1973): 294–308. For discussions of the broader social causes of separation, see Jack P. Greene, "Search for Identity: An Interpretation of the Meaning of Selected Patterns of Social Response in Eighteenth-Century America," *J. of Social Hist.* 3 (1969–1970): 189–224; Kenneth A. Lockridge, "Social Change and the Meaning of the American Revolution," *ibid.*, 6 (Summer 1973): 403–39.

32. John Laurens to James Laurens, Oct. 24, 1776, *SCHGM* 10: 51; see also McCrady, *S. C. in the Revolution*, 180–82.

NOTES TO CHAPTER NINE

1. Gadsden to John Rutledge, Dec. 14, 1776, Gadsden to Thomas Mumford, Feb. 19, 1777, *Gadsden Writings*, 117–21.

2. Ramsay, *History of S. C.*, II, 217.

3. Sept. 21, 1776, and Oct. 8, 1776, *Gadsden Writings*, 116, 117.

4. A letter apparently to John Rutledge published in the *Am. Autograph Journal* 4 (June 1940): 330.

5. To Thomas Mumford, Feb. 19, 1777, *Gadsden Writings*, 120; Letter from Charleston to the Hon. George Bryan, Vice President of Pa., in Johnson, *Traditions*, 156; *S. C. and American General Gazette*, Feb. 12, 1778.

6. For the legends that Gadsden paid for the bridge, see F. A. Porcher, *A Memoir of General Christopher Gadsden* (Charleston, S. C., 1878), 5;

Theophilus Fisk, *The Bulwark of Freedom* (Charleston, S. C., 1836), 11; Ramsay, *Revolution of S. C.*, I, 150. *The By-Laws of the South Carolina Society of the Sons of the Revolution* (Charleston, S. C., 1906), 17, says Gadsden paid one-third the cost. See also Gadsden to John Rutledge, Dec. 14, 1776, *Gadsden Writings*, 119; Account Book of the Commissioners of the Treasury, Jan.–Nov., 1778, pp. 9, 22, 29, 35, 38, 42, 49, 58, 68, 76, 86, 90, 106, 117, 138, 160, 198, 214, 229, 242, S. C. Archives; A. S. Salley, Jr., ed., *Journal of the Commissioners of the Navy of the South Carolina* (Columbia, S. C., 1912), 29, 30, 44, 79, 82, 86, 89.

7. Edward Rutledge to John Jay, June 29, 1776, in Henry P. Johnston, ed., *The Correspondence and Public Papers of John Jay*, 4 vols. (New York, 1890–1893), I, 67; see also Moultrie, *Memoirs*, I, 187; Arthur Middleton to William Henry Drayton, Sept. 18, 1776, *SCHGM* 27: 143.

8. A. S. Salley, Jr., ed., *Journal of the General Assembly of South Carolina, Sept.–Oct., 1776* (Columbia, S. C., 1909), 111. For sketches of Lowndes and Mathews, see Edgar, Bailey, and Cooper, eds., *Biographical Directory of the S. C. House of Representatives*.

9. To Robert Morris, Jan. 23, 1777, *The Confidential Correspondence of Robert Morris* (Philadelphia, 1917), 48.

10. Fletcher M. Green, "Democracy in the Old South," *J. of Southern Hist.* 12 (Feb. 1946): 8; McCrady, *S. C. in the Revolution, 1775–1780*, 211; Wallace, *History of S. C.*, II, 163, 168–70, 174.

11. Gadsden to John Adams, July 24, 1787, *Gadsden Writings*, 244.

12. Wallace, *History of S. C.*, II, 173–74; Nevins, *American States*, 173–75; D. Huger Bacot, "Constitutional Progress and the Struggle for Democracy in South Carolina Following the Revolution," *South Atlantic Quart.* 24 (Jan. 1925): 62.

13. Alden, *South in the Revolution*, 215–20; Wallace, *History of S. C.*, II, 173.

14. *The Speech of the Hon. William Henry Drayton . . . in the General Assembly . . . upon the Articles of Confederation . . .* (Charleston, S. C., 1778); see also Burnett, ed., *Letters*, III, lx–lxi; Wallace, *Life of Laurens*, 232–35.

15. Aug. 15, 1778, *Gadsden Writings*, 146.

16. Wallace, *History of S. C.*, II, 174–75; Nevins, *American States*, 370–72.

17. June 1, 1778, *Gadsden Writings*, 126.

18. To William Henry Drayton, June 15, 1778, *ibid.*, 132.

19. *Ibid.*

20. *Ibid.*, 132–33; see also Gadsden to Peter Timothy, June 8, 1778, *ibid.*, 130–31.

21. John Wells, Jr., to Henry Laurens, June 10, 1778, Henry P. Kendall Collection (microfilm, ed. Mass. Hist. Soc.), South Caroliniana Library, Columbia, S. C.

22. June 8, 1778, *Gadsden Writings*, 130–31.

23. Peter Timothy to Benjamin Franklin, June 12, 1777, *SCHGM* 35: 127–28.

24. *S. C. and American General Gazette*, June 11, 1778, italics added; John Wells, Jr., to Henry Laurens, June 10, 1778, Kendall Collection.

25. June 15, 1778, *Gadsden Writings*, 133.

26. Walsh, *Charleston's Sons of Liberty*, 85–87.

27. On the American conception of republican government, see Maier, *Resistance to Revolution*, 271–96.

28. Ramsay's oration is in Hezekiah Niles, ed., *Principles and Acts of the Revolution in America* (Baltimore, 1822), 375; see also *S. C. and American General Gazette*, July 9, 1778; John Wells, Jr., to Henry Laurens, Sept. 6, 1778, Kendall Collection.

29. To Thomas Bee, Oct. 5, 1778, *Gadsden Writings*, 155–56.

30. Gadsden to William Henry Drayton, Oct. 14, 1778, *ibid.*, 159. For secondary accounts of events during the summer of 1778 and diverse interpretations of them, see Jerome Joshua Nadelhaft, "The Revolutionary Era in South Carolina, 1775-1788" (Ph.D. diss., Univ. of Wisconsin, 1965), 44–45; Richard Walsh, "Christopher Gadsden: Radical or Conservative Revolutionary?" *SCHM* 63: 200–201.

NOTES TO CHAPTER TEN

1. For sketches of the life of Robert Howe, see J. G. deR. Hamilton, "Robert Howe," *DAB*, IX, 294–95; *Speech of the Hon. John D. Bellamy, of North Carolina, in the House of Representatives, February 14, 1903, on H. R. 17356* (Washington, D. C., 1903).

2. Quoted in [Janet Schaw], *Journal of a Lady of Quality*, ed. Evangeline Walker Andrews (New Haven, 1922), App. XI, p. 317.

3. *Ibid.*, 167.

4. Cornelius Harnett to Gov. Richard Caswell, Nov. 28, 1778, in Walter Clark, ed., *State Records of North Carolina*, 26 vols. (Goldsboro, N. C., 1886-1907), XIII, 305.

5. Moultrie, *Memoirs*, I, 191; see also General Orders by Gen. Howe, Nov. 26, 1776, and Feb. 14, 1777, in Gibbes, *Doc. Hist., 1776-1782*, 46, 54–55.

6. Gadsden to John Rutledge, June 7, 1977, *Am. Autograph J.* 4 (June 1940): 332.

7. Wallace, *History of S. C.*, II, 171–72; McCrady, *S. C. in the Revolution, 1775-1780*, 305–6.

8. Extract of a letter by Robert Howe to the Continental Congress, Aug. 28, 1777, *Hist. Mag.* 4 (Sept. 1860): 265–66.

9. Laurens to Howe, Oct. 20, 1777, Laurens to John Rutledge, Oct. 19, 1777, Laurens Papers, S. C. Hist. Soc.; Ford, ed., *Journals of the Cont. Cong.*, VIII, 757; Wallace, *Life of Laurens*, 300–301.

10. June 1, 1778, *Gadsden Writings*, 128–29.

11. *Ibid.*, 135–44.

12. Higginbotham, *War of American Independence*, 16, 26n.

13. July 29, 1778, Kendall Collection.

14. Laurens to Rawlins Lowndes, Aug. 5, 1778, Burnett, *Letters*, III, 361.

15. Gadsden to Drayton, Aug. 15, 1778, Gadsden to Heyward, Aug. 16, 1778, *Gadsden Writings*, 147–49.

16. John Wells, Jr., to Henry Laurens, Aug. 23, 1778, Kendall Collection.

17. Gadsden to William Henry Drayton, Sept. 9, 1778, *Gadsden Writings*, 151.

18. The following account of the duel is from the *South Carolina and American General Gazette*, Sept. 3, 1778, which reported it in minute detail. For Gadsden's account, see his letter to Drayton, Sept. 9, 1778, *Gadsden Writings*, 151.

19. The minor wound was not reported in the newspaper; references to it, with slight variations, may be found in Frank Moore, ed., *Songs and Ballads of the Revolution* (New York, 1856), 230; Charles Colcock Jones, ed., *Georgia (Colony) Laws, Statutes, etc.*, 2 vols (Philadelphia, 1881), II, 323–24; L. Van Loan Naisawald, "Major General Robert Howe's Activities in South Carolina and Georgia, 1776–1779," *Georgia Hist. Quart.* 35 (Mar. 1951): 29.

20. To William Henry Drayton, Sept. 9, 1778, and to William H. Drayton and John Neufville, Sept. 22, 1778, *Gadsden Writings*, 151, 152.

21. Petition to Pres. & other members of State Soc. of N. Y., MS, S. C. Archives.

22. Quoted in *Speech of the Hon. John D. Bellamy*, 11–12; Moore, ed., *Songs and Ballads*, 226–30.

23. Naisawald, "Major General Robert Howe's Activities," 8–30.

24. To William Henry Drayton, Sept. 9, 1778, *Gadsden Writings*, 150.

25. *Ibid.*, 152.

26. *S. C. and American General Gazette*, Oct. 29, 1778; see also sketch of Elliott in Edgar, Bailey, and Cooper, eds., *Biographical Directory of the S. C. House of Representatives*, II, 217–19.

27. Oct. 14, 1778, *Gadsden Writings*, 160.

NOTES TO CHAPTER ELEVEN

1. Daybook Entries, June–Sept. 1778, *Gadsden Writings*, 125; see also Gadsden to George Washington, May 13, 1787, *ibid*. 242.

2. Nevins, *American States*, 373; McCrady, *S. C. in the Revolution, 1775–1780*, 280–82; *S. C. and American General Gazette*, Dec. 10, 1778.

3. Adele Stanton Edwards, ed., *Journals of the Privy Council, 1783–1789* (Columbia, S. C., 1975), ix–x.

4. To Mrs. Charles Pinckney, Feb. 24, 1779, Gibbes, *Doc. Hist., 1776–1782*, 108.

5. For a brief evaluation of Lincoln, see Clifford K. Shipton, "Benjamin Lincoln: Old Reliable," in George Athan Billias, ed., *George Washington's Generals* (New York, 1964), 193–211.

6. Gadsden to Samuel Adams, Apr. 4, 1779, *Gadsden Writings*, 161–65; see also Miller, *Sea of Glory*, 528–29.

7. Moultrie, *Memoirs*, I, 433; William Johnson, comp., *Sketches of the Life and Correspondence of Nathanael Greene*, 2 vols. (Charleston, S. C., 1822), I, 271–72; McCrady, *S. C. in the Revolution, 1775–1780*, 358–67; Wallace, *History of S. C.*, II, 189–90.

8. Moultrie, *Memoirs*, I, 434.

9. July 6, 1779, *Gadsden Writings*, 165.

10. David Ramsay to William Henry Drayton, Sept. 1, 1779, in Gibbes, *Doc. Hist., 1776–1782*, 121; Gadsden to Samuel Adams, July 6, 1779, *Gadsden Writings*, 166; Ford, ed., *Journals of the Cont. Cong.*, XIII, 386–88. See also Aptheker, *American Negro Slave Revolts*, 22; Benjamin Quarles, *The Negro in the American Revolution* (Chapel Hill, N. C., 1961), 63–64, 198; Wallace, *History of S. C.*, II, 185–86; Wikramanayake, *A World in Shadow*, 150.

11. To Samuel Adams, July 6, 1779, *Gadsden Writings*, 166.

12. To William Henry Drayton, Sept. 1, 1779, in Gibbes, *Doc. Hist., 1776–1782*, 121–22.

13. Alden, *South in the Revolution*, 239; Higginbotham, *War of American Independence*, 355–57.

14. *Boston Gazette*, May 8, 1780, p. 1; quoted in Bruce Ingham Granger, *Political Satire in the American Revolution, 1763–1783* (Ithaca, N. Y., 1960), 187.

15. Lincoln's Report to Washington, Aug. 11, 1780, Washington Papers, LC; Moultrie, *Memoirs*, II, 105; Wallace, *History of S. C.*, II, 197–98.

16. To Henry Laurens, Apr. 17, 1780, Kendall Collection. See also McCrady, *S. C. in the Revolution, 1775–1780*, 465.

17. Johnson, *Traditions*, 247; Ramsay, *Revolution of S. C.*, II, 51.

18. One-paragraph letter of Christopher Gadsden, dated Apr. 16, 1780; *American Book-Prices Current* (New York, 1928), 700. The letter has not been found.

19. Representation of field officers to Lincoln, [April] 1780, in Charles Ammi Cutter, comp., *Catalogue of the Library of Jared Sparks, with a List of the Historical Manuscripts Collected by Him and Now Deposited in the Library of Harvard University*, 105 vols. (Cambridge, Mass., 1871), XII, 432–34.

20. Thomas Addis Emmet Collection, 7713, NYPL; Wallace, *History of S. C.*, II, 200; McCrady, *S. C. in the Revolution, 1775–1780*, 474–75.

21. Description by Lachlan McIntosh, quoted in [William Gilmore Simms], *South-Carolina in the Revolutionary War: Being a Reply to Certain Misrepresentations and Mistakes of Recent Writers, in Relation to the Course and Conduct of this State* (Charleston, S. C., 1853), 126–27; Ravenel, *Charleston*, 269, 273.

22. Simms, *S. C. in the Revolutionary War*, 146.

23. Proposals for the Surrender of Charles Town, May 8, 1780, *Gadsden Writings*, 176–78.

24. *Ibid.*, 167n.

25. Eliza Wilkinson to Miss M— —P— —, 1782, Caroline Gilman, ed., *Letters of Eliza Wilkinson* (New York, 1839), 14; Ravenel, *Charleston*, 273. The petition is in the Emmet Collection, 7625, NYPL.

26. Gadsden to Lincoln, May 11 and 12, 1780. *Gadsden Writings*, 169; Lincoln to Gadsden, May 12, 1780, Jared Sparks, ed., *Correspondence of the American Revolution*, 4 vols. (Boston, 1853), II, 120; Lincoln to George Washington, Aug. 11, 1780, Washington Papers, LC; Moultrie, *Memoirs*, II, 65–73.

27. Moultrie's account of the surrender is quoted in Simms, *S. C. in the Revolutionary War*, 150–62.

28. Alden, *South in the Revolution*, 241; Wallace, *History of S. C.*, II, 201–2.

29. Attorney General James Simpson to Lord George Germain, Aug. 30, 1780, PRO CO 5.178, LC trans.; see also William Knox to James Simpson, Nov. 9, 1780, *ibid.*; Wallace, *History of S. C.*, II, 225.

30. Quoted in McCrady, *S. C. in the Revolution, 1775–1780*, 719.

31. Moultrie, *Memoirs*, II, 114. For complete lists of the three groups of prisoners, see George Smith McCowen, Jr., *The British Occupation of Charleston, 1780–1782* (Columbia, S. C., 1972), 151–52.

32. Ramsay, *History of S. C.*, II, 254.

33. McCrady, *S. C. in the Revolution, 1775–1780*, 715–25 (the quotation is on 725); Bancroft, *History of the U. S.*, V, 393; Johnson, *Traditions*, 42, 195; Ramsay, *Revolution of S. C.*, II, 161–69, 458–59. For Cornwallis's account of the removal, see Benjamin Stevens, ed., *The Campaign in Virginia, 1781: . . . Six Rare Pamphlets on the Clinton-Cornwallis Controversy . . .*, 2 vols. (London, 1888), I, 267.

34. The dialogue is in Alexander Garden, *Anecdotes of the Revolutionary War in America* (Charleston, S. C., 1822), 169. Accounts of this encounter with more limited and slightly different versions of the dialogue may be found in Ramsay, *History of S. C.*, II, 254; Johnson, *Traditions*, 42; Porcher, *Gadsden*, 10.

35. Governor Patrick Tonyn to Committee of Prisoners, Nov. 18, 1780, S. C. Misc., Letters and Papers Relating to the History of S. C., 1780–1781, LC.

36. Edward McCrady, *The History of South Carolina in the Revolution, 1780–1783* (New York, 1902), 373–74.

37. Gadsden to George Washington, Aug. 10, 1781, *Gadsden Writings*, 170.

38. John Rutledge to the Delegates of S. C. in the Congress, Oct. 4, 1780, and Dec. 30, 1780, *Russell's Magazine*, I, 540; II, 270.

39. Ramsay, *History of S. C.*, II, 254.

40. Johnson, *Traditions*, 277–78; apparently the poem has not survived.

41. John Laurens to Henry Laurens, May 25, 1780, Bancroft Coll., S. C. and Misc. 131, p. 387, NYPL.

42. To George Washington, Dec. 28, 1780, Sparks, ed., *Correspondence of the American Revolution*, III, 188.

43. To the Delegates, Dec. 30, 1780, *Russell's Magazine*, II, 271.

44. McCrady, *S. C. in the Revolution, 1775–1780*, 728–29; Simpson to Germain, Dec. 31, 1780, PRO CO 178, LC trans.

45. John Rutledge to the Delegates, Sept. 20, 1780, *Russell's Magazine*, I, 538–40; see also John Rutledge to the President of the Congress, Aug. 18, 1780, S. C. Misc., 1780–1782, LC.

46. Pendleton to Madison, Oct. 23, 1780, Mass. Hist. Soc. *Proceedings* (2nd ser.), XIX, 117; Madison to Pendleton, Oct. 31, 1780, Burnett, *Letters*, V, 433–34. See also President of the Congress to Nathanael Greene, Sept. 24, 1780, *ibid.*, 388; Ford, ed., *Journals of the Cont. Cong.*, XVIII, 851, 964.

47. John Fiske, *The American Revolution*, 2 vols. (Boston and New York, 1891), II, 230; Garden, *Anecdotes*, 172; Ramsay, *Revolution of S. C.*, II, 168–69.

48. McCrady, *S. C. in the Revolution, 1780–1783*, 374–77; Ramsay, *Revolution of S. C.*, II, 298–301; Gadsden to George Washington, Aug. 10, 1781, *Gadsden Writings*, 169–71.

NOTES TO CHAPTER TWELVE

1. Aug. 10, 1781, *Gadsden Writings*, 170–71.

2. On the capture of Thomas and Philip, see Ramsay, *Revolution of S. C.*, II, 535n; Clark, ed., *State Records N. C.*, XVI, 762.

3. Gadsden, *et al.*, to Thomas McKean, President of the Congress, Aug. 25, 1781, *Gadsden Writings*, 171–73. See also Ford, ed., *Journals of the Cont. Cong.*, XXI, 914, 921; Johnson, *Traditions*, 43, 330–32; McCrady, *S. C. in the Revolution, 1780–1783*, 379; Ramsay, *History of S. C.*, II, 254; Wallace, *History of S. C.*, II, 227.

4. To Morton Wilkinson, Sept. 7, 1781, *Gadsden Writings*, 174–75.

5. Gadsden, *et al.*, to the Delegates of the State of South Carolina, Sept. 17, 1781, *ibid.*, 176–77.

6. Joseph Kershaw[?] to Gen. Harrington, Frederick Town, Md., Sept. 25, 1781, in Clark, ed., *State Records N. C.*, XV, 645.

7. Rutledge to the Delegates, Aug. 6, 1781, *Russell's Magazine*, III, 33–34; McCrady, *S. C. in the Revolution, 1780–1783*, 555–60, 562.

8. Quoted in Ramsay, *Revolution of S. C.*, II, 349. See also A. S. Salley, Jr., ed., *Journal of the House of Representatives of South Carolina, January 8, 1782–Feb. 26, 1782* (Columbia, S. C., 1916), 33–34; this very sketchy journal of the Jacksonborough Assembly does not record Gadsden's speech.

9. Aedanus Burke to Arthur Middleton, Jan. 30, 1782, *SCHGM* 26: 193.

10. David Ramsay to Benjamin Rush, Feb. 9, 1782, Burnett, *Letters*, VI, 307; McCrady, *S. C. in the Revolution, 1780–1783*, 572.

11. McCrady, *S. C. in the Revolution, 1780–1783*, 576–80.

12. Gadsden to Francis Marion, Nov. 17, 1782, *Gadsden Writings*, 194–97.

13. *Ibid.*, 196.

14. Edward Rutledge to Arthur Middleton, Dec. 12, 1781, Feb. 26, 1782, SCHGM 26: 208; 27: 9.

15. To Arthur Middleton, Feb. 26, 1782, SCHGM, 27: 7; see also McCrady, *S. C. in the Revolution, 1780–1783*, 587.

16. Oct. 16, 1782, *Gadsden Writings*, 179–83.

17. *First Census of the United States, 1790: South Carolina* (Washington, D. C., 1908), 38, 45, 51.

18. Gadsden to Morton Wilkinson, Sept. 7, 1781, *Gadsden Writings*, 175.

19. Oct. 29, Nov. 17, 1782, *ibid.*, 188, 194–96.

20. Oct. 29, Nov. 3, 1782, *ibid.*, 186–87, 189–90.

21. Nov. 5 and 17, 1782, *ibid.*, 191–92, 194.

22. Moultrie, *Memoirs*, II, 358–60; Ramsay, *History of S. C.*, II, 255; Ravenel, *Charleston*, 333–34; Wallace, *History of S. C.*, II, 320.

NOTES TO CHAPTER THIRTEEN

1. Theodora J. Thompson and Rosa S. Lumpkin, eds., *Journals of the House of Representatives, 1783–1784* (Columbia, S. C., 1977), 193–94, 206.

2. *Ibid.*, 70, 188, 327, 525, 540, 600, 632.

3. McCrady, *S. C. in the Revolution, 1780–1783*, 586–88; Wallace, *History of S. C.*, II, 331–33; see also Cassius [Aedanus Burke], *An Address to the Freeman of the State of South-Carolina* (Philadelphia, 1783).

4. Thompson and Lumpkin, eds., *Journals, 1783–1784*, 11, 13, 19, 39, 46, 218, 504, 543, 549, 706, 722; *The Statutes-at-Large of South Carolina*, ed. David J. McCord (Columbia, S. C., 1839), VI, 629–35; *Register of St. Philip's, 1754–1810*, 55, 260, 345; Gillon to Gadsden, Sept. 9, 1784, *Gazette of the State of S. C.*

5. *S. C. Gazette and General Advertiser*, July 15, 22, Aug. 12, 1783; Maier, "Charleston Mob," 190.

6. *S. C. Gazette and General Advertiser*, Sept. 20, 30, 1783; see also *S. C. Weekly Gazette*, Sept. 27, 1783; Edwards, ed., *Journals of the Privy Council, 1783–1789*, 81.

7. Feb. 10, 1784; Clark, ed., *State Records N. C.*, XVII, 129.

8. *S. C. Gazette and General Advertiser*, Apr. 29, 1784; see also U. B. Phillips, "The South Carolina Federalists," *Am. Hist. Rev.* 14 (Apr. 1909): 535–37.

9. Wallace, *History of S. C.*, II, 307–11.

10. *Gazette of the State of S. C.*, May 13, 1784.

11. *Gadsden Writings*, 206–28.

12. Berkeley Grimball, "Commodore Alexander Gillon of South Carolina, 1741–1794" (M.A. thesis, Duke Univ., 1951), 87, 89–90, 92, 95, 108; see also the sketch of Gillon in the *DAB*.

13. *Gazette of the State of S. C.*, July 22, 1784.

14. *Ibid.*, July 29, Aug. 19, Sept. 9, 1784; see also *Gadsden Writings*, 228–38.

15. Council Journal, Sept. 8, 1784, S. C. Archives.

16. Merrill Jensen, *The New Nation: A History of the United States during the Confederation, 1781–1789* (New York, 1950), 304–18; La Rochefoucauld Liancourt, *Travels through the United States of North America*, 2 vols. (London, 1799), I, 557, 572; Ramsay, *History of S. C.*, II, 219, 221, 222, 236–37; Wallace, *History of S. C.*, II, 327; Wallace, *Life of Laurens*, 428.

17. Francis and Cleland Kinloch to Gadsden, July 29, 1784, Book M 5, p. 284, and Cleland Kinloch to Gadsden, Jan. 10, 1801, Book D 7, p. 141, MCO.

18. Gadsden's own references to his slaves are in his will, *Gadsden Writings*, 311–14. See also Charleston County Will Book, 1800–1807, pp. 594ff.; General Index to Misc. Records and Bills of Sale to 1825, Book TT, 1781, p. 143, and Book ZZ, 1789–1792, p. 28; Inventories D, 1800–1810, pp. 366–67—all in S. C. Archives.

19. Jensen, *New Nation*, 215–16.

20. *Gazette of the State of S. C.*, Aug. 27, 1783; Apr. 29, Aug. 16, Sept. 13, 1784.

21. *S. C. Gazette*, Sept. 29, 1791; *City Gazette*, Nov. 22, 1791; *City Gazette and Daily Advertiser*, Oct. 10, 1795; Gadsden to Maj. Thomas Pinckney, Apr. 17, 1792, *Gadsden Writings*, 256. Gadsden's sporadic correspondence with businessmen in Philadelphia consists of his letters to LeRoy and Bayard, June 19, 1790; to Messrs. Vanderhorst and Gervais, Aug. 30, 1793; to Robert Burton, Mar. 28, Apr. 8, 1796; to George Simpson, May 4, 1801; to LeRoy, Bayard, and McEvers, Oct. 23, 1801, Jan. 7, 1802; to George Simpson, Oct. 19, 1803—all in *Gadsden Writings*, 252–53, 259, 260–62, 307–8, 309–10. The records in the MCO of the company's buying and selling land are extensive; they include Book Z 6, pp. 277, 326; Book R, p. 34; Book N 7, p. 106; Book L 6, pp. 418, 483, 529; Book M 6, p. 151; Book M 5, p. 284; Book D 7, p. 141. Advertisements in the local press of property which the company was handling include: *City Gazette and Daily Advertiser*, Mar. 24, Oct. 13, Dec. 11, 1793; Mar. 16, Nov. 1, 1796; *City Gazette*, Dec. 9, 1791.

22. Gadsden to Washington, May 13, 1787; Gadsden to John Adams, July 24, 1787; both in *Gadsden Writings*, 241–42, 243–44.

23. Oct. 29, 1787, *ibid.*, 245–47.

24. *Ibid.*, 248–50.

25. *Columbian Herald*, Apr. 17, 1788; A. S. Salley, Jr., ed., *Journal of the Convention of South Carolina which Ratified the Constitution of the United States, May 23, 1788* (Atlanta, Ga., 1928), 13, 15; House Journal, 1879, p. 6, and Index to Miscellaneous Records, 1776–25 May, 1846, Book A, p. 123, both in S. C. Archives; Merrill Jensen and Robert A. Becker, eds., *The Documentary History of the First Federal Elections 1788–1790*, 2 vols. to date (Madison, Wis., 1976–), I, 151, 202, 203, 211, 212.

26. House Journal, Jan. 30, 1783; Jan. 28, 31, Feb. 27, Mar. 6, 8, 10, 26, 1784; see pp. 73–74, 81, 231, 238, 257, 419; S. C. Archives.

27. *A Few Observations* (Charleston, Jan. 30, 1797), in *Gadsden Writings*, 279.

28. Gadsden to Thomas Morris, May 30, 1790, *Gadsden Writings*, 251; (Charleston) *City Gazette, or The Daily Advertiser*, June 1, 1790.

29. Gadsden to Thomas Morris, May 30, 1790, *Gadsden Writings*, 251-52; *City Gazette*, May 22, 1790; William A. Schaper, *Sectionalism and Representation in South Carolina* (New York, 1968 [1901]), 142-43; Wallace, *History of S. C.*, II, 348-51.

30. For a general characterization of the old-school Federalists and brief sketches of each one, see David Hackett Fischer, *The Revolution of American Conservatism: The Federalist Party in the Era of Jeffersonian Democracy* (New York, 1965), 1-28, 227-412. For a detailed and sensitive account of the South Carolina Federalists, see biography by George C. Rogers, Jr., of William Loughton Smith.

31. *City Gazette and Daily Advertiser*, Feb. 4, 1793, quoted in *Gadsden Writings*, 357; 15 Republicans to William Loughton Smith, 1794, Smith Letters, LC; Rogers, *Smith*, 276-77.

32. Gadsden's remark is in the *American Daily Advertiser* (Philadelphia), Aug. 24, 1795; cited in *Gadsden Writings*, 265, n. 3.

33. Henry Stephens Randall, *Life of Thomas Jefferson*, 3 vols (New York, 1858), II, 266; Rogers, *Smith*, 276-77; Wallace, *History of S. C.*, II, 354.

34. *A Few Observations*, in *Gadsden Writings*, 266-67.

35. *Ibid.*, 275-76.

36. *S. C. Gazette and Timothy's Daily Advertiser*, Apr. 23, 1798, *ibid.*, 280-81.

37. *City Gazette and Daily Advertiser*, May 7, 1798; Gadsden to Read, July 16, 1798, *Gadsden Writings*, 282-83.

38. Gadsden to Jacob Read, July 18, 1798, *Gadsden Writings*, 282.

39. *South Carolina State Gazette and Timothy's Daily Advertiser*, July 15, Aug. 29, Oct. 8, 1800, *ibid.*, 286-305.

40. On the election of 1800 in South Carolina, see Rogers, *Smith*, 348-52.

41. Gadsden to Adams, Mar. 11, 1801, *Gadsden Writings*, 305-07.

42. Adams to Gadsden, Apr. 16, 1801, Adams, ed., *Works of John Adams*, IX, 584; Gadsden to Adams, June 24, 1801, *Gadsden Writings*, 308-9.

43. Gadsden to Francis Marion, Nov. 17, 1782, Gadsden to John Adams, Mar. 11, 1801, *Gadsden Writings*, 186, 306; "Will of Wm. Bull Late Lieut. Gov. of S. C.," *SCHGM* 7: 150.

44. Gadsden to John Adams, Mar. 11, 1801, *Gadsden Writings*, 307.

45. M. I. Manigault to Mrs. Ralph Izard, Feb. 3 and Feb. 18, 1805, Ralph Izard Papers, South Caroliniana Library; see also "Notes on a letter of Christopher Gadsden to Daniel Horry, Feb. 24, 1804," Francis Marion Papers, III, 239, Bancroft Coll., NYPL.

46. Charleston County Will Book, 1800-1807, pp. 594ff.; Inventories D, 1800-1810, Charleston District, Equity Court, Report Book,

May 19, 1800–May 25, 1808, pp. 274, 305, 511–29, all in S. C. Archives. See also *Gadsden Writings*, 311–14. All of Christopher Gadsden's living grandsons were the sons of Philip. Christopher E. Gadsden became a bishop in the Episcopal church, James Gadsden was the United States minister to Mexico who negotiated the Gadsden Purchase in 1853, and John Gadsden became a United States district attorney.

47. Ramsay, *History of S. C.*, II, 255.

48. M. I. Manigault to Mrs. Ralph Izard, Aug. 27, 1805, Ralph Izard Papers; information in possession of Mrs. Van Smith, Summerville, S. C., 1932.

49. *City Gazette*, Aug. 30, 1805; (Charleston) *Courier*, Aug. 29, Sept. 11, 1805; William Read to Jacob Read, Sept. 2, 1805, S. C. Misc., NYPL. The ministers who conducted Gadsden's funeral were the Rev. Nathaniel Bowen and the Rev. Edward Jenkins. Many years after Gadsden's death, a new marker was placed upon the grave of his parents; upon it was inscribed the names of Thomas and Elizabeth Gadsden, and below that the words, "Their Son / Gen. Christopher Gadsden / Patriot / 1724–1805."

50. Ramsay, *History of S. C.*, II, 255.

Bibliographical Note

Only a fragment of materials have survived that can be used in writing a biography of Christopher Gadsden. The ravages of time, fire, and civil war probably account for most of the loss. Since Gadsden in his old age was so sensitive about his reputation as a troublemaker, he may have destroyed some letters himself. Most of the extant Gadsden materials are in the form of public letters he wrote for the newspapers, or committee reports in the journals of the legislative assemblies he served. A small selection of business correspondence is available, but personal letters that would reveal the details of Gadsden's private life are almost nonexistent. The "Gadsden Miscellany" formerly in the Presbyterian College Library at Clinton, South Carolina, is the only group of manuscripts that approaches being a collection of Gadsden Papers. Although the original documents have apparently been misplaced, they are available on microfilm in the South Caroliniana Library at Columbia, South Carolina. Other Gadsden items have had to be extracted from the papers of the leaders of the American Revolution. The majority of the Gadsden materials have been collected by Richard Walsh in *The Writings of Christopher Gadsden, 1746–1805* (Columbia, S. C., 1966), in which the editor gives clear and precise details about the locations of the originals. The authors of this biography have compared all of the manuscript and printed originals with those in the published volume but have chosen to cite the Walsh edition in the notes for the convenience of the reader.

Eighteen items not included in the published volume of writings have been discovered. In an advertisement published in the

South-Carolina Gazette, February 26, 1763, Gadsden confessed that he was the author of the Philopatrios letters and of an earlier advertisement signed "Auditor-Tantum." In the supplement to the *South-Carolina Gazette* for December 3, 1764, and the *Gazette* for December 24, 1764, Gadsden wrote two long letters, about 1,800 and 1,000 words, respectively, discussing the authority of the Royal Council with regard to money bills. Two letters in the Dartmouth Papers, Staffordshire County Record Office, England, have been edited by Robert M. Weir and published in the *South Carolina Historical Magazine* 75 (July 1974): 169–76.

Six items signed "Homespun Free-Man" or "H. F." in the *South-Carolina Gazette and Country Journal* are positively identified as Gadsden's in a letter from John Stuart to James Grant, February 20, 1766, in the James Grant Papers, Ballindalloch Castle, Scotland. The letters of "Homespun Free-Man" published on February 11, 25, and April 1, 1766, are long denunciations of the Stamp Act. A short letter published on March 18, 1766, includes a copy of a poem that Gadsden requested be printed. The items published on February 18 and March 18, 1766, are identical advertisements for a pamphlet on the history of Carolina through 1729 in which Gadsden intended to prove how the Stamp Act was unconstitutional. The evidence suggests that this pamphlet was never written.

The other uncollected writings of Gadsden include a one-page letter of Roger Smith and Gadsden to the General Committee of Merchants in Boston, October 13, 1768, published in the *New England Historical and Genealogical Register* 29 (July 1875): 246. Gadsden's description of a system of flag signals to warn the defenders of Charleston of the appearance of the enemy, dated March 9, 1776, is recorded in the diary of Major Barnard Elliott in the South Carolina Historical Society and published in William Bell Clark, ed., *Naval Documents of the American Revolution*, 8 vols. to date (Washington, D. C., 1969–), IV, 275, 277. In the *South Carolina and American General Gazette* for March 20, 1777, is a short letter in which Gadsden encloses and requests to have printed the extract of a letter of George Washington. A letter of about 500 words to John Rutledge, dated Fort Moultrie, June 7, 1777, is published in *American Autograph Journal* 4, no. 3 (June 1940): 330–32. A one-paragraph letter of Gadsden to an unknown addressee, dated Charles Town, April 16, 1780, is briefly sum-marized in *American Book-Prices Current* (New York, 1928), 700; the original has not been found. A letter to General William Henry Harrington, dated February 10, 1784, expressing op-timism about the future of the country and requesting assistance in settling a detail concerning the estate of his half-brother Thomas Gadsden is published in Walter Clark, ed., *The State Records of North Carolina*, 26 vols. (Goldsboro, N. C., 1886–1907), XVII, 129. "Notes on a letter of Christopher Gadsden to Daniel Horry, February 24, 1804," is in the Francis Marion Papers, III, 237, which is a portion of the George Bancroft Collection in the New York Public Library.

For other primary and secondary sources relative to Gadsden, Richard Walsh's bibliography for *The Writings of Christopher Gadsden* should be consulted. A useful guide for the study of South Carolina is Robert J. Turnbull, *Bibliography of South Carolina, 1563–1950*, 6 vols. (Charlottesville, Va., 1956–1960). The pamphlet and imprint literature for eighteenth-century South Carolina is extensive, and the Charleston Library Society is the richest repository. A helpful guide to this literature is Richard Parker Morgan, *Preliminary Bibliography of South Carolina, 1731–1800* (Clemson, S. C., n.d.). Unless otherwise indicated in the notes, copies of all pamphlets cited in this biography are available in the William R. Perkins Library, Duke University. An indis-pensable aid in the study of colonial and revolutionary South Carolina is Walter B. Edgar, N. Louise Bailey, and Elizabeth Ivey Cooper, eds., *Biographical Directory of the South Carolina House of Representatives*, 3 vols. to date (Columbia, S. C., 1974–). Wherever possible, the sketches of other South Carolinians of Gadsden's time have been drawn from this work. For sketches of other persons whose lives intersected with Gadsden's, the authors have relied upon the *Dictionary of American Biography*.

Index

Adams, Abigail, 145

Adams, John, 38, 49, 145, 163, 183, 241, 245; in Continental Congress, 122–24, 135, 138, 139, 140, 142; opinion of Gadsden, 126–27, 135, 140, 143, 144; as President, 244, 248, 249–50

Adams, Samuel, 54, 79; correspondence with Gadsden, 70–71, 113–14, 122, 192–93, 195–96; in Continental Congress, 122, 123, 126, 127, 135–36, 139

Adet, Pierre August, 248

Albany Congress, 142

Aldborough, 9, 10, 11

Alfred, 140, 142

Amercement, 218, 219, 220, 222, 226–28, 234

American Duties Act of 1764, 51, 53

Amherst, Jeffrey, 27

André, John, 187, 211–12

Anson, Captain George, 6, 15, 17

Ansonborough, 14, 15, 17, 69, 70, 72, 73, 101, 102, 237

Arbuthnot, Marriott, 196, 197

Arnold, Benedict, 143, 188, 211

Articles of Confederation, 169, 170, 225

Artillery Company, 23, 25, 26,

Artillery Company (*cont.*) 27, 29, 34–35, 53, 58, 68, 253. *See also* Military organizations

Artisans, 15, 53. *See also* Mechanics

Ashley Ferry, S. C., 12, 29, 30, 193

Backcountry, 22, 28, 39, 76, 111, 150; and Stamp Act, 65–67, 70; and nonimportation, 82–83, 91, 117, 130; Gadsden sympathizes with, 76, 88, 221; in state government, 129, 216, 244; and disestablishment, 153, 167–68

Balfour, Nisbit, 203, 204, 211, 212, 213

Barbados, 4, 10

Battle of Sullivan's Island, 159–61, 163, 178, 183, 184, 194, 222. *See also* Fort Moultrie *and* Sullivan's Island

Beaufort, S.C., 105–7

Bee, Thomas, 64, 112, 191, 197, 245

Beneventum Plantation, 237

Blackstone, William, 86

Bland, Richard, 123

Board of Trade, 38, 43, 47, 64

Boone, Thomas, 35–36, 39, 41, 43–44, 47, 48, 49, 55, 64, 103, 107, 119, 194

Christopher Gadsden and the American Revolution has been composed on the Mergenthaler Variable Input Phototypesetter in 10-point Baskerville with one and one-half point line spacing. Americana was selected for display and furnished from the VGC Photo Typositor. The book was designed by Judy Ruehmann, set into type by Computer Composition, Inc., printed offset by Thomson-Shore, Inc., and bound by John H. Dekker & Sons. The paper on which the book is printed bears the watermark of S. D. Warren and is designed for an effective life of at least three hundred years.

THE UNIVERSITY OF TENNESSEE PRESS /KNOXVILLE